THE
GOSPEL
— OF —
LUKE

A REFLECTIVE
COMMENTARY

DENIS McBRIDE

THE
GOSPEL
— OF —
LUKE

A REFLECTIVE
COMMENTARY

DOMINICAN PUBLICATIONS

This edition published (1991) by
Dominican Publications
42 Parnell Square
Dublin 1

Reprinted August 1994

This reprint October 2003

ISBN 0-907271-67-7

Cover design by David Cooke
Madonna and Child on cover by Patrick Pye

Printed in the Republic of Ireland by
ColourBooks Ltd. Baldoyle, Co Dublin

Scriptural quotations from the Revised Standard Version of the Bible
copyrighted 1946, 1952, © 1971, 1973.

First published in 1982 by Costello Publishing Co., Inc.
Northport. Long, Island, New York 11768

Imprimi potest Kevin Callaghan, C.Ss.R., Provincial Superior

Nihil obstat Reverend George A. Denzer. S.T.L.
Censor librorum
February 18, 1982
Imprimatur Most Reverend John R. McCann, D.D.
Bishop of Rockville Center
March 4, 1982

*For my mother and father,
in deep gratitude*

Preface

A WRITER writes for a variety of reasons, not least because he feels compelled to commit to paper what he believes in his heart. What he believes may be shared by a legion of others, but there is still the compulsion to tell the story through his own understanding of it. Although many had already written their versions of the story of Jesus, Luke was moved to put together his account of that story in the hope that it would touch others and bring them closer to his subject, Christ the Lord. Luke has clearly succeeded in his task: down the ages his Gospel account has moved many who welcomed as good news the message of Jesus which clearly favours the vulnerable of this world, the outcasts, those who find themselves outside the boundaries of religious and social approval. Any commentary must reflect the preferences of the original text, and I have tried to do that in this book.

I have attempted to combine scholarship with meditation in the hope that a reflective understanding will be born of the alliance; but the reader is the only judge of that. I would like to acknowledge my debt to many scholars who have helped me form some understanding of Luke's narrative: William Yeomans, S.J. for commissioning the work on behalf of the publisher, Harry Costello; Sr. Bernadette O'Donaghue whose patience and skill transformed an unreadable script into a coherent manuscript; my confrere, Joseph Doherty, C.SS.R., for casting a critical journalist's eye over the final version; Mrs. Veronica Crimmins for her dedicated liaison work with the publishers; my own Redemptorist community here at Hawkstone for their encouragement and support.

Hawkstone Hall,
Shrewsbury,
Shropshire.

Contents

THE GOSPEL OF LUKE
A Reflective Commentary

Introduction

The Purpose of the Gospel

IN THE PREFACE to his Gospel, Luke states clearly the purpose of his writing, "that you may know the truth concerning the things of which you have been informed" (1:4). Luke presupposes that Theophilus and those who read his Gospel can already claim some familiarity with the story of Jesus of Nazareth; Luke sees his own task as deepening that familiarity by presenting a historical framework to the truth of the Christian tradition. Particularly at a time when Christians influenced by Gnosticism were devaluing the importance of the historicity of the Gospel events, Luke presents the story of Jesus in terms of redemptive history which took place at a particular time and a particular place in the human story. Luke anchors his Gospel in the midst of history, and in so doing answers a profound human need. As Flender writes: "This side of Jesus' history is discernible only to faith. But that does not exclude the need for faith to be assured of the human side of that history".[1] Luke presents the human side of that history by presenting the human side of God.

Luke is writing his Gospel in the knowledge that Judaism has already rejected the person of Jesus and his message of salvation. The Messiah has come, and has not been acknowledged by his own people. In his Gospel, Luke focuses on the rejection of Jesus by the Jewish authorities, and presents Jesus' own awareness of this: "The Son of Man must suffer many things and be rejected by the elders and chief priests and scribes, and be killed, and on the third day, be raised" (9:22). The rejection of Jesus by the religious leaders of Judaism marks an important turning

1

point in redemptive history: the Gospel is given to the Gentiles. This radical change influenced much of Paul's theology and his own relationship with Judaism—which, in turn, could have affected Luke's theological outlook. For Luke, the new people, the new sons of Abraham, are those who accept the salvation offered by Jesus (19:9). And in writing his Gospel, Luke frequently reminds his reader that the salvation which Jesus first offered to Judaism is now offered to all peoples.

Authorship

The author of the third Gospel does not disclose his name, but early Christian testimony from the second century unanimously affirms the author to be Luke, a physician from Antioch in Syria, and a travelling companion of St. Paul. Luke was not a prominent member of the early Church and yet historical criticism has not contested that early tradition. The tradition is attested by:

Irenaeus c. 180 in *Adversus Haereses* (3, 1, 1; 3, 14, 1; 3, 15, 1). Arguing that orthodox Christians knew the authors of the four Gospels, Irenaeus affirmed that the author of the third Gospel was "Luke, a companion of Paul". That testimony was supported from Africa by Tertullian *(Adversus Marcionem* 4, 2), and from Egypt by Clement of Alexandria *(Stromateis* 1, 21). Origen, Eusebius and Jerome all repeated and upheld that tradition.

The Gospel Prologues c. 160–180 which have survived in 38 Latin manuscripts. Specifically, the anti-Marcionite Prologue to the third Gospel—the only one to have survived in Greek—attests the author to be Luke, "a Syrian from Antioch". It also states that Luke wrote Acts, that he was unmarried, and that "he fell asleep in Boetia at the age of eighty-four, full of the Holy Spirit".

The Muratorian Canon: a fragment referring back to the second-century list of New Testament books which were accepted by the church in Rome speaks of "the third book of the Gospels, according to Luke".

The internal evidence of the New Testament appears to agree with the above testimony. The first person in the two prefaces (1:3, Acts 1:1) seems to reappear in four passages in Acts in which the writer speaks of "we" (16:10-17; 20:5-16; 21:1-18; 27:1-28:16). These passages seem to be excerpts from the diary of Paul's travelling companion. The language and style of these passages are similar to the rest of the book, which has led most scholars to accept that the one author wrote the whole. Among those named as Paul's travelling companions, Paul mentions Luke (Col 4:14; 2 Tim 4:11; Philemon 24).

None of the above leads to the indisputable conclusion that Luke is the author of the third Gospel and of the Acts. However, in the absence of any serious scholarly proposal in favour of another person, it seems reasonable to accept the ancient tradition which connects both books with the name of Luke.

Date and Place of Composition

In the preface to his Gospel, Luke acknowledges that many people have preceded him in compiling narratives "of the things which have been accomplished among us" (1:1). It is generally accepted that Luke was familiar with Mark's account, which was probably written in the late 60's, and that Luke's Gospel was completed before that of John, 100-110.[2] Scholars are divided about the precise date of Luke's writing, and the dispute seems to centre on whether Luke wrote his Gospel before the destruction of Jerusalem in 70 or after that event.

In Acts, Luke does not record any event which took place after 62. If Luke was writing after 70, why did he not record the death of James in 62, the persecution of Nero which took place in Rome in 64 in which Peter and Paul are said to have perished, the Jewish rebellion of 66–70, and the destruction of Jerusalem in 70? Acts stops with Paul still under house arrest (28:30), and its apparently abrupt ending has led some scholars to argue that Luke's second volume was completed before Paul's death.

The dispute is focused on the interpretations of those passages in the Gospel which refer to the destruction of Jerusalem (19:43f; 21:20–24). In these unambiguous references to the destruction of Jerusalem and the temple, is Luke writing after the event? Some scholars argue that Luke's language shows details of what actually happened and which are recorded in the accounts of Josephus and Tacitus. Others argue that apart from the contention that prophecies can be recorded only after they are seen to have happened, Luke's description simply reflects the siege techniques of the day and is composed largely from Old Testament phraseology.

No date is without difficulties, but, as Ellis points out,[3] any date has to account for the current crises and concerns which are addressed in the pages of the Gospel. In that light, Manson's conclusion of "round about A.D. 70" seems adequate.

Nothing more definite can be said about the place of writing. The tradition from the anti-Marcionite Prologue names Achaea in Greece. We know from Luke's writing that he was addressing a largely Gentile Christian audience, unfamiliar with Palestine: thus he avoids phrases and matters peculiarly Jewish, and he avoids sayings and interpretations which could offend or be unintelligible to a Gentile readership. Southern Greece as the place of composition receives support from Irenaeus, Jerome and Gregory Nanzianzen.

Sources

In his prologue, Luke tells us of the "many" who have already written Gospels—accounts which are presumably available to him as sources for his own narrative. Along with these written sources, Luke has the oral tradition of eyewitnesses who were with Jesus during his earthly ministry and of the apostolic preachers. Finally, Luke mentions his own research. Thus prepared, Luke commits himself to the task of writing an orderly account.

Scholars are agreed that a version of Mark's Gospel was available to Luke at the time of writing, and many hold that this formed the foundation document of Luke's Gospel. Just over half of Mark's Gospel is found in Luke. Luke follows the Marcan order closely, although not slavishly: he omits a large section, 6:45–8:26, and inserts his own material, the largest section of which is the lengthy travel narrative, 9:51–18:14. Luke improves Mark's style, omits those Marcan sections which refer to Jesus' emotions and to the failings of the Twelve, as well as editing out of his version anything which he judges would be offensive or unhelpful to his Gentile readers.

There are about 230 verses which are common to Matthew and Luke but which are absent from Mark. Consisting mostly of teaching, these verses seem to come from a common source, which has been referred to traditionally as Q (from the first letter of the German *Quelle*, source). Although the common material is placed in different contexts in both Gospels, the argument still holds that Matthew and Luke had a common sayings source or sources. There is little agreement among scholars as to what precisely made up this hypothetical document,[4] and although there is no independent evidence to suggest the existence of such a document, it does serve as an intellectual shorthand to refer to the sources which were available to Matthew and Luke, and which each used in his own way.

About half of Luke's Gospel has no parallel in either

Mark or Matthew. This includes the infancy narrative, fourteen parables and some thirty narratives, miracle stories such as the bent woman (13:10-17) and the ten lepers (17:11-16), and sections of the passion and resurrection narrative such as the Good Thief, the Emmaus story, and the resurrection appearances near Jerusalem.[5] This source has been commonly referred to as L. It is interesting to note that Luke's favourite themes as well as his most distinctive words and phrases occur more frequently in the L passages than in those which he edits from Mark or Q. L would seem to be a collective name for the unnamed sources which Luke mentions in his prologue. Luke travelled extensively and would have had ample opportunity to collect oral and written sources for his writing, especially perhaps during his two-year stay in Caesarea while Paul was in prison (Acts 24:27).

There is an interesting parallel between Luke's special material and the Gospel of John. Both mention Samaria, and give prominence to Jerusalem and the Temple. There are several people mentioned only by Luke and John: Martha and Mary (John speaks of their brother, Lazarus, whom Jesus raises, while Luke uses this name in a parable), the second Judas among the twelve, and Annas, the high priest. Both state that Satan entered Judas, that it was the *right* ear of the slave which was cut off, that Pilate proclaimed Jesus' innocence three times, and that there were two angels at the tomb on the morning of the resurrection. It is unlikely that John used Luke as one of his sources, because the differences are as pronounced as the similarities. Caird's cautious conclusion seems right: "The unavoidable inference is that Luke and John were relying on two allied streams of oral tradition".[6]

Although it is clear that Luke used a number of written and oral sources for his narrative, it is equally clear that Luke was moved to write his own account, while exercising editorial freedom with the sources available to him. Luke's Gospel is not simply a clever rearrangement of other people's work; its plan and style and vision justify the title, "The Gospel according to Luke".

Structure

The structure of Luke's Gospel can be divided into the following sections:

Preface   1:1-4

1. *The Infancy Narrative   1:5-2:52*
Arranged with careful artistry, the Lucan infancy narrative has no parallel in Mark or Q. The language of the first two chapters is more Semitized than the Greek of the rest of the Gospel. It appears that among Luke's sources were the canticles and traditions of the Jewish churches in Judea which he adapted to his own purpose. Certainly, the atmosphere of the infancy narrative is more akin to the pentecostal prophetic spirit of the infant Church than the ministry of Jesus. This has led some scholars to argue that the narratives were composed after Acts.[7]

2. *The Preparation for the Public Ministry   3:1-4:13*
Luke's narrative style changes with his account of the preliminaries to the public ministry of Jesus, and the material is mainly derived from sources other than Mark. But, as with Mark and Q, Luke's formal beginning to the story of Jesus' ministry starts with the appearance of John the Baptist, whom Luke presents as the fulfilment of Old Testament prophecy. Luke concludes John's story before he begins the story of Jesus' first public appearance—thus John is imprisoned before the baptism of Jesus. The baptism and temptation of Jesus stand close together as the preface to the public ministry.

3. *The Ministry in Galilee   4:14-9:50*
Before he sets his face to the journey towards Jerusalem,

Jesus engages in a travelling ministry in Galilee during which he teaches and performs miracles, and then chooses disciples. In Mark the call to the disciples precedes Jesus' preaching and works of wonder; Luke reverses the order. Jesus' ministry of teaching and healing, which displays the nature of his mission, evokes a variety of responses from the people—including the criticism of the Pharisees and the curiosity of Herod Antipas. Luke follows Mark's pattern, but includes material from Q and from his distinctive sources.

4. *The Journey to Jerusalem   9:51-19:44*

The central division of Luke's Gospel is written in the form of a journey narrative from Galilee to Jerusalem. Concerned predominantly with the teachings of Jesus rather then with the journey itself, the material alternates between instructions given to the disciples and discussions with opponents. The journey to Jerusalem is not plotted along any map; it is a literary framework which Luke uses for his own purposes. Jesus, for example, is no nearer Jerusalem in 17:11 than he is in 9:51, and there is a vagueness about precise geography which discourages attempts to mark out a definite route—although Conzelmann has attempted to do precisely that.[8] Luke ceases to follow Mark at 9:50 and rejoins him at 18:15, where the chronological sequence is marked out in actual progress, via Jericho, to Jerusalem. Luke's central section corresponds in intention to Mark 10:1-52, where Jesus is on a teaching journey to Jerusalem, and although Luke does not use the Marcan source, he uses material from Q and material which is peculiar to himself.

5. *Jesus in Jerusalem   19:45-21:38*

Jesus has now reached journey's end in Jerusalem, and having already prophesied the destruction of the city, Jesus cleanses the temple in preparation for his own ministry there. Luke concentrates on the temple as the focal place of Jesus' final ministry, and describes the growing conflict between Jesus and the Jewish authorities. There will be no miracles in Jerusalem. The religious leaders oppose Jesus while the people listen to him daily in the temple. Luke alters Mark's setting (13:1) and omits 13:3 which has Jesus teaching the disciples on the Mount of Olives. For Luke the temple is the place for Jesus' public teaching in these final days, and the Mount of Olives is the place for rest and prayer at night. The material in this section is basically drawn from Mark and follows his pattern with a few alterations.

6. *The Passion, Resurrection and Ascension of Jesus 22:1-24:53*

The closing section of Luke's Gospel covers the Last Supper, the arrest and trial of Jesus, his death, the discovery of the empty tomb, and the appearance of the risen Lord to his disciples. This same pattern is followed by each of the Gospels, and it is easier to discover Luke's distinctive features than to judge how much he depends on Mark and Q. Luke's own material includes the morning trial before the Sanhedrin, Jesus before Herod, the good thief, and new appearance stories. Luke clearly depicts Jesus as the righteous one who willingly suffers a martyr's death in the conviction that it is the will of God, but whose story is finally marked by the glory which has been foretold in the Old Testament.

Theological Themes in the Gospel of Luke

The plan of Luke's overall writing traces the history of the divine plan from the coming of Jesus to his glorification in the ascension at Jerusalem (Gospel), and from the early Church in Jerusalem until the time when the universal scope of the Gospel is realised in the apostolic preaching in Rome, the centre of the known world (Acts). The central Easter event is seen to dominate the whole of the two volumes—even the infancy narratives, where the presence of the Holy Spirit moves people to proclaim with joy. The divine plan was foretold long ago, and there is an urgency and a necessity in its being unfolded. Thus the words of the risen Jesus sum up the plan of Luke's Gospel:

> Was it not necessary that the Christ should suffer these things and enter into his glory? And beginning with Moses and all the prophets, he interpreted to them in all the scriptures the things concerning himself (24:26–27).

This is not theological fatalism: it is the assertion that a divine purpose is working in the midst of human history, an assertion which is in clear opposition to seeing these events as a catalogue of the absurd. The divine activity is seen to be present from the opening scenes in the Gospel where the Holy Spirit is at work (1:15; 1:35), the Spirit which descends on Jesus at his baptism (3:22), and which leads him to face the enemy (4:1), and inspires him throughout his ministry (4:18). It is the gift of the same Spirit which Jesus promises the disciples to enable them in their turn to be witnesses to the plan of God (24:48–49).

The divine plan is clearly a universal one, and Luke's Gospel underlines the universality of God's salvation and the breadth of his concern. Luke uses the verb "to save" more than any other evangelist. Thus Marshall writes: "It is our thesis that the idea of salvation supplies the key to the theology of Luke".[9] From the beginning of the Gospel, the angels (2:14) and Simeon (2:32) witness to the good news that God's salvation is for all the people, and, unlike Mark and Matthew, Luke gives the full quotation from Isaiah which speaks of the coming day when "all flesh shall see the salvation of God" (3:6). The genealogy of Jesus does not limit Jesus' ancestry to Abraham but traces it back to Adam (3:38) which places Jesus in relationship to every man. The promise given to Abraham can be shared by all men, making them the children of Abraham (3:8). Luke's interest in God's abiding concern for all the people, not least the Jews themselves, is evident throughout the Gospel.

Jesus' particular concern for the outcast, the stranger, the poor, the sick, and sinners is prominent throughout Luke's

Gospel. Jesus consistently shows himself to be the friend of those in need, to those who find themselves out of place: "For the Son of Man has come to seek and to save the lost" (19:10). When Jesus outlines his mission for John's emissaries, among a list of miracles he includes "the poor have good news preached to them" (7:22). It is a sign that the messianic age has come when it is seen that God's prejudice for the vulnerable is at work in history. In the parable of the Good Samaritan, it is the outcast who proves to be the neighbour (10:37); it is the sinful woman who anoints the feet of Jesus (7:38); it is the outcast Zacchaeus who receives the salvation offered by Jesus (19:9); it is the penitent thief who is promised the eternal company of Jesus (23:43).

As in other oriental countries, women in the Palestine of Jesus' day were numbered among the lowly and despised. In none of the Gospels is the woman described with such support and sympathy as in the Gospel of Luke. Apart from Luke's portrayal of Mary as the true disciple who acts on the word of God, Luke introduces us to Elizabeth (1:39-58), Anna (2:36-38), the widow of Naim (7:11-17), the woman of the city (7:36-50), the Galilean women who accompanied Jesus' group (8:2-3), the two sisters, Martha and Mary (10:38-42), the women of Jerusalem (23:27-31), and the women who go to minister to the dead body of Jesus (23:55). Also, there are two parables proper to Luke in which women figure: the Lost Coin (15:8-10) and the Unjust Judge (18:1-8). In this litany, not one woman is presented as an opponent of Jesus: all are presented as figures who are touched by the word of God. And, most importantly of all, the first proclaimers of the good news of the resurrection are women (24:8).

The first two women who appear in Luke's Gospel, Elizabeth and Mary, are seen to be filled with the joy of the Holy Spirit which moves them to make prayers of praise. The connection between the Holy Spirit and prayer is clear in that it is the Spirit which inspires the joyful prayers of Zachary, Mary, Elizabeth and Simeon. And Jesus is at prayer when he receives the Spirit at the opening of his ministry (3:21-22).

Jesus' whole ministry is lived in a spirit of prayer, and Jesus can be seen at prayer before important moments in his own life: before his ministry (3:21); before the selection of the twelve (6:12); before Peter's confession of faith (9:18); before the transfiguration (9:28); before the teaching of the Lord's Prayer (11:1); before his arrest and passion (22:41); before his own death (23:34). In three parables, Luke underlines the importance of prayer: the friend at midnight (11:5-13), the unjust judge (18:1-8), and the pharisee and the publican (18:10-14). Luke's Gospel has given the Church four canticles of praise: the Benedictus, the Magnificat, the Gloria in Excelsis, and the Nunc Dimittis. And if these prayers are made in the Spirit, it is equally clear what the purpose of prayer is: to pray to the Father so that he will give "the Holy Spirit to those who ask him" (11:13).

The Holy Spirit which moves people to praise God is the Spirit of joy, and Luke has a generous vocabulary to express different characteristics of that joy.[10] In the beginning of the Gospel, the unborn prophet "leaped for joy" (1:44). In his own teaching Jesus proclaimed the good news that those who "weep now" will know the day when they "shall laugh" (6:21), and he enjoined his own disciples to "rejoice that your names are written in heaven" (10:20). Jesus himself "rejoiced in the Holy Spirit" (10:21) which led him into a prayer of thanksgiving to the Father. The people in their turn "rejoiced at all the glorious things" (11:17) Jesus did during his ministry.

Renunciation is the Gospel precondition of this joy (14:25-33), a joy which Luke often describes in terms of the banquet which captures the graciousness of God as the host who invites people to share in his joy (cf. the whole chapter 14). The three parables of chapter 15 all end on the note of joy: "Rejoice with me for I have found my sheep which was lost" (15:6); "Rejoice with me for I have found the coin which I had lost" (15:9); "let us eat and make merry; for this my son was dead, and is alive again" (15:24). Zacchaeus accepts Jesus' invitation to come down from his lonely perch and dine with him: so, "he made haste and came down, and received him joyfully" (19:6). The joy which Zaccheus experiences is in sharp contrast to those who remain unmoved by the invitation of Jesus. Throughout the Gospel, the graciousness and kindness of Jesus change people's attitudes and move them to praise God. Thus the Gospel of Luke comes to a close on the note of joy: the disciples have met the risen Lord and they can face the future—so they "returned to Jerusalem with great joy, and were continually in the temple blessing God" (24:53).

Notes

[1]H. Flender, *St. Luke: Theologian of Redemptive History*, trans. R. H. and I. Fuller (London, 1967) p. 66

[2]R. Brown agrees to 100-110 as the date for the final edition of John's Gospel and presents the hypothesis that "the *first* edition of John is to be dated to the same general period as Matthew and Luke" in *The Gospel According to John*, Vol. 1 (New York, 1966) p. LXXXIV

[3]E. Ellis, *The Gospel of Luke* (London, Oliphants, 1974) pp. 59-60

[4]J. Moffat lists 16 different reconstructions and then adds his own, *An Introduction to the Literature of the New Testament* (Edinburgh, 1927) p. 197 ff. B. H. Streeter adds another list, *The Four Gospels* (London, 1950) p. 291

[5]Cf. E. Ellis, *The Gospel of Luke, op. cit.*, for a table of comparison, pp. 24 ff.

[6]G. B. Caird, *Saint Luke* (Middlesex, 1963) p. 21

[7]Cf. R. Brown, *The Birth of the Messiah* (London, 1977) pp. 241-245

[8]H. Conzelmann, *The Theology of Saint Luke* (London, 1961) pp. 60 ff.

[9]H. Marshall, *Luke: Historian and Theologian* (Exeter, 1970) p. 92

[10]For a concise review of Luke's expressions for joy, cf. J. Navone, *Themes of Saint Luke* (Rome, 1970) pp. 71-75

Analysis of the Gospel

The Journey to Jerusalem   *9:51–19:44*

The Ministry in Jerusalem   *19:45–21:38*

The Passion, Resurrection and Ascension of Jesus   *22:1–24:53*

Chapter One

Luke 1:1-4   *The Introduction to the Story*

1 Inasmuch as many have undertaken to compile a narrative of the things which have been accomplished among us, ²just as they were delivered to us by those who from the beginning were eyewitnesses and ministers of the word, ³it seemed good to me also, having followed all things closely for some time past, to write an orderly account for you, most excellent Theophilus, ⁴that you may know the truth concerning the things of which you have been informed.

ALONE AMONG THE EVANGELISTS, Luke begins his Gospel with a brief preface written in classical Greek style. The preface makes a solemn opening to Luke's narrative, and reflects the traditional custom of secular writing. There is a striking parallel in Josephus, *Contra Apionem*, where the author introduces the first of two books:

> In my history of our *Antiquities*, most excellent Epaphroditus, I have made sufficiently clear... the extreme antiquity of our Jewish race.... Since, however, I observe that a considerable number of persons... discredit the statements of my history... I consider it my duty to devote a brief treatise... to instruct all who desire to know the truth concerning the antiquity of our race.... I shall now proceed to refute the rest of the authors who have attacked us (1:1–4).

Luke's preface follows the formal literary convention of the day and it serves to introduce his account to contemporary literature. The people to whom Luke addressed his Gospel were largely Gentile, and, no doubt, they would have felt at home with his introduction. It would serve to ease them into the unfamiliar territory of the Gospel; it would also underline the fact that the author was seeking to anchor his work in historical reality.

Luke is neither an apostle nor an eyewitness to the events which he relates in his Gospel, but he is inspired to tell the story which he has heard from trustworthy and authoritative sources, and to order the story in his own way. And, as shall be evident, that order is more logical than chronological. Luke does not tell the story from the point of view of the dispassionate observer, which would be a peculiar stance for an evangelist; rather, he tells the story from the point of view of one who is utterly committed to the universal significance of the story, and who seeks to share it "that you may know the truth".

The Gospel and the Acts are dedicated to Theophilus, a name which means "beloved by God". We know nothing of Theophilus except that he was probably a catechumen or interested patron who was concerned about the truth of Christianity. Luke's dedicating the work to him does not make his two volumes exclusive any more than a modern author who dedicates his work to a favoured person.

Luke's concern is not to write a piece of literature to display his literary talents. The purpose of his writing is a pastoral one—that Theophilus and all the beloved of God will come to know the truth and believe in the central figure of the Gospel, the person of Jesus of Nazareth. To do that, Luke tells the story of Jesus. Luke is a servant of the Word, and to tell his story he must use words, which he does with the care and sensitivity of a master storyteller. As W. H. Auden wrote:

"Words are for those with promises to keep".

Luke 1:5-25   The Annunciation of the Birth of John the Baptist

⁵In the days of Herod, king of Judea, there was a priest named Zechariah, of the division of Abijah; and he had a

wife of the daughters of Aaron, and her name was Elizabeth.
⁶And they were both righteous before God, walking in the
commandments and ordinances of the Lord blameless. ⁷But
they had no child, because Elizabeth was barren, and both
were advanced in years.

⁸Now while he was serving as priest before God when his
division was on duty, ⁹according to the custom of the
priesthood, it fell to him by lot to enter the temple of the
Lord and burn incense. ¹⁰And the whole multitude of the
people were praying outside at the hour of incense. ¹¹And
there appeared to him an angel of the Lord standing on the
right side of the altar of incense. ¹²And Zechariah was
troubled when he saw him, and fear fell upon him. ¹³But the
angel said to him, "Do not be afraid, Zechariah, for your
prayer is heard, and your wife Elizabeth will bear you a son,
and you shall call his name John.

¹⁴And you will have joy and gladness, and many will rejoice
at his birth; ¹⁵for he will be great before the Lord, and he
shall drink no wine nor strong drink, and he will be filled
with the Holy Spirit, even from his mother's womb. ¹⁶And
he will turn many of the sons of Israel to the Lord their God,
¹⁷and he will go before him in the spirit and power of Elijah,
to turn the hearts of the fathers to the children, and the
disobedient to the wisdom of the just, to make ready for the
Lord a people prepared."

¹⁸And Zechariah said to the angel, "How shall I know this?
For I am an old man, and my wife is advanced in years."
¹⁹And the angel answered him, "I am Gabriel, who stand in
the presence of God; and I was sent to speak to you, and to
bring you this good news. ²⁰And behold, you will be silent
and unable to speak until the day that these things come to
pass, because you did not believe my words, which will be
fulfilled in their time." ²¹And the people were waiting for
Zechariah, and they wondered at his delay in the temple.
²²And when he came out, he could not speak to them, and
they perceived that he had seen a vision in the temple; and he
made signs to them and remained dumb. ²³And when his
time of service was ended, he went to his home.

²⁴After these days his wife Elizabeth conceived, and for
five months she hid herself, saying, ²⁵"Thus the Lord has
done to me in the days when he looked on me, to take away
my reproach among men."

Luke opens his infancy narrative by placing the events

he is about to recount at a particular time and place in history—in the days of King Herod, who ruled over Palestine from 37 to 4 B.C. The first characters to be introduced in the Gospel story are an old married couple from the country (v. 39): a priest called Zechariah, a name which means "Yahweh remembers", and his wife, Elizabeth. Both belong to the tribe of Aaron, all the male members of which were priests. Before he mentions the childlessness of the couple, Luke states unambiguously that they are upright people; he describes them in terms used of the "anawim Yahweh", the faithful remnant of God, and this glowing description avoids the charge that barrenness was an affliction which God visited on sinful people (Lev 20:20). Both are advanced in years, which explains why the couple cannot have children *now*, but Luke adds the further note that Elizabeth was barren. The couple are doubly incapacitated, and there seems no human ground for hope.

The situation of the couple is not hopeless, however, given the history of the people of God. In the Old Testament, Sarah, Rebecca, Rachel, the mother of Samson, and Hanna were all barren; but their barrenness was no barrier to the promise and the plan of God. God's plan is not hindered by barren wombs and old age: paradoxically, these become grounds of new hope and possibility, and for the birth of famous men in the history of Israel. The birth of John is firmly set within that great tradition. There is a clear parallel between the announcement of the birth of Isaac (Gen 17): the announcement of the promise is made to an old man, who reacts to the presence of the supernatural with fear and awe. The annunciation is made to the husband; he is told that his wife will give birth to a male child, what name to call the child, and how the child will distinguish himself in his future life. Objections are made, but the visionary is given a sign to reassure him of the reality of the promise.

The setting for Luke's opening story is the temple, where he also brings his Gospel to a close (24:53). The priests, who officiated at the morning and evening sacrifice in the temple, were divided into twenty-four groups, each group serving one week every six months. There were so many priests in service—Jeremias estimates that there were 18,000 priests and levites in the Palestine of Jesus' day[1]— that it was a rare privilege for a priest to officiate, an honour which happened only once in his lifetime if he were fortunate. It is a very special day for Zechariah. He enters the sanctuary next to the Holy of Holies to offer incense, a symbol of the prayer of the people who are outside making their petitions to God. The angel appears to Zechariah who is fearful—a normal human reaction in the face of the supernatural. The angel counsels him not to be afraid, for his prayer has been heard—both his personal prayer and his priestly prayer, because his son will come as an answer to his parents' longings and an answer to Israel's hopes (v. 16).

The angel speaks of the joy and gladness which the birth of John will bring to many—not just to his parents—and outlines the future career of John. Even before he emerges from his mother's womb, John will be filled with the Holy Spirit which will help him to bring back many of the people of Israel to God. In the spirit of Elijah (cf. Mal 4:5, 6), John will lead a movement of conversion to God and prepare the people for the Lord.

After hearing this astounding announcement, Zechariah reacts cautiously, and, exactly as Abraham did before God (Gen 17:17), kindly reminds the supernatural visitor, in case he is unaware of mortal problems, about the practical limitations of old age. The angel counters this with, "I am Gabriel, who stand in the presence of God". Zechariah is concerned with human problems while the angel focuses on the power of God. Gabriel punishes Zechariah for his disbelief by making him dumb. Precisely when Zechariah has something to say he is punished by not being able to say it.

The people are waiting for Zechariah—the encounter with the angel has unavoidably delayed the old man. When the priest emerged from the sanctuary, he was required to give a blessing over the people (Num 6:24–26), but

Zechariah cannot speak. Luke says that the people saw
that he had experienced a vision—an acute perception, unless visions in the sanctuary were not rare occurrences.
After the time of his group's service in the temple,
Zechariah goes home.

Elizabeth does indeed conceive, as the promise foretold,
but she hides herself from the public gaze—perhaps because as an old lady she did not want to appear heavy in
public. Elizabeth seems to have regarded her barrenness as
a reproach, but now her long distress is over, for her body
tells her that new days are ahead and a new being is in the
making.

The old couple seem to have a comical look about them:
a pregnant old lady and a dumb old man, the makers of
history. But this is the opening scene of a Gospel in which
Luke will present the upside-down world of God, where
the humanly impossible becomes possible with God. So, a
barren old woman becomes heavy with the promise of
God, and she will give birth to that promise, who will prepare the way for the Promised One of God.

Luke 1:26-38   *The Annunciation of the Birth of Jesus*

²⁶In the sixth month the angel Gabriel was sent from God
to a city of Galilee named Nazareth, ²⁷to a virgin betrothed
to a man whose name was Joseph, of the house of David;
and the virgin's name was Mary. ²⁸And he came to her and
said, "Hail, O favored one, the Lord is with you!" ²⁹But she
was greatly troubled at the saying, and considered in her
mind what sort of greeting this might be. ³⁰And the angel
said to her, "Do not be afraid, Mary, for you have found
favor with God.³¹ And behold, you will conceive in your
womb and bear a son, and you shall call his name Jesus.
³²He will be great, and will be called the Son of the Most
High; and the Lord God will give to him the throne of his
father David, ³³and he will reign over the house of Jacob for
ever; and of his kingdom there will be no end." ³⁴And Mary
said to the angel, "How shall this be, since I have no husband?" ³⁵And the angel said to her, "The Holy Spirit will
come upon you, and the power of the Most High will over-

shadow you; therefore the child to be born will be called holy, the Son of God. [36]And behold, your kinswoman Elizabeth in her old age has also conceived a son; and this is the sixth month with her who was called barren. [37]For with God nothing will be impossible." [38]And Mary said, "Behold, I am the handmaid of the Lord; let it be to me according to your word." And the angel departed from her.

Luke's account of the annunciation of the birth of Jesus closely resembles the preceding narrative: both stories clearly stand in the literary tradition of biblical annunciations of birth in the Old Testament.[2] However, what distinguishes this annunciation story from all the other narratives is Mary's virginal conception and the unique greatness of the child. A virginal conception has no precedence in Jewish thought, and the arguments that Luke is influenced by Greek pagan legends remain powerfully unconvincing. Brown argues to the appropriateness of the virginal conception from a comparison of the two annunciation accounts in Luke: "In the JBap annunciation, when he introduces the two parents (1:7), Luke tells us of the human difficulty in their lives that prevents conception; and it is precisely that difficulty which is resumed in Zechariah's 'How' objection to the angel in 1:8. In the Jesus annunciation, when he introduces Mary (1:27), Luke mentions twice that she is a virgin; and it is that factor which is resumed in Mary's 'How' objection to the angel in 1:34: 'I have had no relations with a man.' If the age and barrenness of Zechariah and Elizabeth were divinely overcome in the conception of JBap, the human difficulty of the virginity of Mary must be overcome by divine power in the conception of Jesus."[3]

In the annunciation of Jesus' birth, Luke presents Jesus as superior to John: John will be the one who will prepare the people for the Lord; Jesus will be the one who will rule, and "of his kingdom there will be no end". Although through divine intervention, John was conceived in a human manner, and was filled with the Holy Spirit while still in the womb. That manner of divine intervention is clearly attested elsewhere in the Jewish Bible. The Holy Spirit is directly involved in the *conception* of Jesus, and comes upon Jesus' mother. Jesus is conceived in a way entirely appropriate to such a new creation—an unprecedented virginal conception through the power of the Holy Spirit—which points to his unique status as the Davidic Messiah and the Son of God.

Luke dates the annunciation of Jesus' birth in the sixth month of Elizabeth's pregnancy. The setting for the scene is the simple town of Nazareth, where there lives a virgin who is betrothed to a man called Joseph of the house of David. Luke will later trace the genealogy of Jesus through Joseph to David (3:23). The Jewish marriage consisted of two distinct stages: betrothal in the exchange of consent before witnesses, and then, usually after an interval of about a year, the groom would formally take the bride to his family home. Even though she remained for some time in her own family home after betrothal, the girl was legally considered to be a wife since the Jewish law regarded betrothal as a binding contract which could be broken only by divorce. Mary has gone through the first stage of the marriage and is betrothed to Joseph, but she has not yet moved in to live with him. She is still a virgin.

Gabriel, the messenger of God, addresses Mary respectfully as the favoured one of God. Mary is startled at the angel's saying, as Zechariah was startled at the angel's presence. Gabriel reassures Mary and tells her the purpose of his visit: she will bear a son and call him Jesus. Gabriel goes on to describe the future greatness of this child in a way which echoes Nathan's promise to David, which formed the basis for messianic expectation (2 Sam 7:9-16). As Zechariah countered the angel's proclamation by pointing to the difficulty of old age, Mary points to the fact that she is still a virgin. The R.S.V. translates v. 34b "because I have no husband"; but Luke has just told us the opposite in v. 27. The Semitic phrase tells us that Mary has had no previous sexual relations with any man: how then will she bear a son?

Mary's question gives Gabriel the opportunity to announce the extraordinary manner in which she will conceive—through the power of the Holy Spirit. Luke states that because of this conception (*dio kai*), the child will be called holy, the Son of God. Luke's theology does not include a pre-incarnational christology, and it seems from this verse that he sees the power of the Holy Spirit bringing the Son of God into existence. The recognition of Jesus as the Son of God will not be made so clearly again until after the resurrection. It is a recognition that people will have to come to because of Jesus' death and resurrection, rather than one which is easily made in Jesus' earthly ministry.

The angel gives Mary a sign. Elizabeth's pregnancy is not yet public knowledge for she has hidden herself, but Gabriel now tells Mary that her relative, who was both old and barren, is now six months pregnant. When God asked Abraham why Sarah laughed at the promise of her pregnancy, God put the question: "Can anything said by God be impossible?" (Gen 18:14). That question is now clearly answered by God's messenger, "For with God nothing is impossible."

Mary's response is unparalleled in the other annunciation narratives: she is the one who when hearing the word of God gladly allows that word to form her life. Later, her son will say during his public ministry: "My mother and my brethren are those who hear the word of God and keep it" (8:19-21). Mary is now presented as the perfect disciple who is a hearer of the word (rema) and a doer of the word. With that response, the angel takes his leave. Thus, Mary becomes the literal embodiment of the promise of God. Like Elizabeth, she conceives the promise, she becomes pregnant with the promise, and she will give birth to the promise. And the promise will be called "holy, the Son of God"

Luke 1:39-56   *The Visitation*

³⁹In those days Mary arose and went with haste into the hill country, to a city of Judah, ⁴⁰and she entered the house of Zechariah and greeted Elizabeth. ⁴¹And when Elizabeth

heard the greeting of Mary, the babe leaped in her womb; and Elizabeth was filled with the Holy Spirit [42]and she exclaimed with a loud cry, "Blessed are you among women', and blessed is the fruit of your womb! [43]And why is this granted me, that the mother of my Lord should come to me? [44]For behold, when the voice of your greeting came to my ears, the babe in my womb leaped for joy. [45]And blessed is she who believed that there would be a fulfilment of what was spoken to her from the Lord." [46]And Mary said, "My soul magnifies the Lord, [47]and my spirit rejoices in God my Savior, [48]for he has regarded the low estate of his handmaiden. For behold, henceforth all generations will call me blessed; [49]for he who is mighty has done great things for me, and holy is his name. [50]And his mercy is on those who fear him from generation to generation. [51]He has shown strength with his arm, he has scattered the proud in the imagination of their hearts, [52]he has put down the mighty from their thrones, and exalted those of low degree; [53]he has filled the hungry with good things, and the rich he has sent empty away. [54]He has helped his servant Israel, in remembrance of his mercy, [55]as he spoke to our fathers, to Abraham and to his posterity for ever." [56]And Mary remained with her about three months, and returned to her home.

In the course of his infancy narrative, Luke presents the reader with three substantial canticles of praise, the Magnificat, the Benedictus, and the Nunc Dimittis, which he attributes to Mary, Zechariah, and Simeon, respectively. Luke portrays the three speakers as representative figures of the anawim, the faithful remnant of Israel who put their complete trust and hope in God. The three canticles which they speak are equally representative of the hopes and longings of the anawim. Most scholars would agree that none of the speakers actually composed the canticles ascribed to them. It would appear that Luke has taken old compositions of Hebrew poetry which proclaimed the saving action of God, and applied their general sentiments to the specific occasion of the speakers in his Gospel. In composition and in outlook, the canticles are Jewish rather than Christian, and closely parallel the psalms and hymns written in the first and second century B.C. The parallels are clear in 1 Maccabees—which has led Winter to argue that the Magnificat and the Benedictus were originally Maccabean psalms.⁴ Whatever their specific origin, it would seem that Luke did not compose them.

Luke's account of Mary's visitation to Elizabeth brings together the two mothers who have been promised birth through divine intervention. Mary hurries to the home of her relative, Elizabeth, whom she greets. At the sound of her greeting, the babe in Elizabeth's womb leaps for joy. Mary has already received a revelation from Gabriel of what God has done for her relative; now Elizabeth, because of the movement of another messenger, is inspired to recognize what God has done for Mary. Luke has already stated how John would be filled with the Holy Spirit even from his mother's womb (v. 15) and how he would prepare people for the Lord (v. 17); now Luke shows how the unborn prophet recognizes the greatness of the unborn Lord, and moves his mother to recognize the presence of her Lord in Mary. Much later, John will be uncertain whether Jesus really is the promised one (7:19); but now is the moment for womb-shaking rejoicing, appropriate to the beginning of the messianic era.

Filled with the Holy Spirit, Elizabeth expresses her joy in a canticle praising Mary. She acclaims Mary as blessed (*eulogemenos*): strictly speaking, Elizabeth is not conferring a blessing on Mary, but joyfully acknowledging that Mary is already blessed by God: "Blessed are you (by God) among women". The double blessing recognizes that Mary is blessed precisely because the fruit of her womb is blessed. Elizabeth goes on to indicate her own unworthiness that the mother of "my Lord" should visit her, and explains that she knew Mary was indeed the mother of the Lord because of the movement of her unborn child in response to the greeting of Mary. Elizabeth's canticle comes to a close in a final beatitude in which she rejoices in Mary's faithful obedience in believing that the word of God would find fulfilment in her, an obedience which stands in sharp contrast to the disbelief of Elizabeth's own husband when he heard the "good news".

In her canticle, Elizabeth praised Mary as mother of the Lord; now, Mary responds by praising God in a hymn of gladness. The Magnificat is an echo of the canticle of Hannah who voiced her prayer in thanksgiving for the Lord's turning her barrenness into pregnancy (1 Sam 2:1-10). Some scholars attribute the Magnificat to Elizabeth, arguing that it is more appropriate coming from a woman who has been raised from barrenness; but the manuscript evidence clearly favours Mary as the speaker. Further, since "low estate" does not necessarily refer to barrenness but can be a description of the state of the anawim, and since v. 48, which many scholars would see as a Lucan addition, speaks of "handmaid"—a word which Mary uses to describe herself in the annunciation scene (v. 38)—the ascription to Mary would seem to make more sense.

The Magnificat is a prayer made from the position of the downtrodden and the poor of God who praise God for his might, his mercy and his continued concern. The prayer reflects both what God has done for the individual and for the community, which gives the speaker reason to praise God for his attributes of holiness, mercy, strength, care, and remembrance of promises. It praises God who is not just a giver of promises but a keeper of promises. It is the prayer of the poor of God who rejoice that littleness has been blessed. In that sense, it is the hymn of a Cinderella people: the proud are toppled from their precious pedestals; the mighty find themselves unemployed; the little people are unimportant no more; the hungry are attended to at last; the rich are solemnly awarded nothing. The Magnificat celebrates the wisdom of reversal and praises the revolution of God—what he has achieved in establishing a kingdom where the forgotten and the lowly are held precious in the sight of God.

If the Magnificat praises God for his concern and testifies to his continuing fidelity, it is equally clear about God's attitude to those who are involved in oppression: they are "scattered", "put down", "sent empty away". No sympathy is given to those who live well because someone somewhere dies of neglect—a theme which Luke will develop throughout the pages of his Gospel. The God of Israel is the God who saves (v. 47) and who is actively involved in liberating his people from the powers which oppress them. The prayer speaks of a God who has unambiguous positions on religious, social and economic matters: in that sense, the Magnificat is a revolutionary hymn of praise.

After the conclusion of Mary's canticle, Luke states that Mary stays with Elizabeth another three months. The time of pregnancy was regarded as ten lunar months, so Luke has Mary depart for home before the birth of John the Baptist. The visitation over, the scene is now clear for the two births of John and Jesus, each of which will be recounted in separate birth narratives.

Luke 1:57-80   The Birth of John

⁵⁷Now the time came for Elizabeth to be delivered, and she gave birth to a son. ⁵⁸And her neighbors and kinsfolk heard that the Lord had shown great mercy to her, and they rejoiced with her. ⁵⁹And on the eighth day they came to circumcise the child; and they would have named him Zechariah after his father, ⁶⁰but his mother said, "Not so; he shall be called John." ⁶¹And they said to her, "None of your kindred is called by this name." ⁶²And they made signs to his father, inquiring what he would have him called. ⁶³And he asked for a writing tablet, and wrote, "His name is John." And they all marveled. ⁶⁴And immediately his mouth was opened and his tongue loosed, and he spoke, blessing God. ⁶⁵And fear came on all their neighbors. And all these things were talked about through all the hill country of Judea; ⁶⁶and all who heard them laid them up in their hearts, saying, "What then will this child be?" For the hand of the Lord was with him.

⁶⁷And his father Zechariah was filled with the Holy Spirit, and prophesied saying,

⁶⁸"Blessed be the Lord God of Israel, for he has visited and redeemed his people, ⁶⁹and has raised up a horn of salvation for us in the house of his servant David, ⁷⁰as he spoke by the mouth of his holy prophets from of old, ⁷¹that we should be saved from our enemies, and from the hand of all who hate

us; ⁷²to perform the mercy promised to our fathers, and to remember his holy covenant, ⁷³the oath which he swore to our father Abraham, ⁷⁴to grant us that we, being delivered from the hand of our enemies, might serve him without fear, ⁷⁵in holiness and righteousness before him all the days of our life. ⁷⁶And you, child, will be called the prophet of the Most High; for you will go before the Lord to prepare his ways, ⁷⁷to give knowledge of salvation to his people in the forgiveness of their sins, ⁷⁸through the tender mercy of our God, when the day shall dawn upon us from on high ⁷⁹to give light to those who sit in darkness and in the shadow of death, to guide our feet into the way of peace."
⁸⁰And the child grew and became strong in spirit, and he was in the wilderness till the day of his manifestation to Israel.

As the messenger of God had foretold, Elizabeth gives birth to a son. The neighbours and relatives discover the good news after the birth has taken place, and they come to rejoice with Elizabeth that the Lord has looked so kindly on her. The occasion for the gathering is the family ceremony of circumcision, which normally took place eight days after the birth (Gen 17:12), and the naming of the child, which usually happened immediately after birth. There was a tradition in priestly circles to name the child after the grandfather; however, the expectation in this gathering is to call the new child after his father. Elizabeth intervenes to say that the child will be called John, a name which means "Yahweh's gracious gift". The child's name speaks of his origin and vocation: he comes as a gift from God, and his life will be a gift to God's people.

Clearly, Elizabeth is departing from traditional practice for the neighbours remind her that none of her relatives is so called. Since there is no precedent for the name in the family, the gathering appeals to Zechariah by making signs —it appears that he is deaf as well as dumb. Zechariah calls for a writing tablet, which he no doubt kept handy over the recent months, and confirms what his wife has said: since Zechariah was deaf and could not hear what his wife said, the surprise is probably at the unexpected confirmation of the unusual choice. It is possible that Zechariah had used the writing tablet to communicate the name to Elizabeth, but it appears that Luke is telling us that both parents acted, without collusion, under the inspiration of God.

Gabriel had imposed silence on Zechariah "until the day that these things come to pass" (v. 20); the promised things have now come to pass and Zechariah's mouth is opened and his tongue is freed. The awe of the neighbours increases an octave when Zechariah speaks again: they are fearful—a traditional Lucan response to a supernatural event. The unusual events which accompanied the circumcision and naming of John drive those who witnessed them to carry the tale to others. So, the story of these marvellous events is spread around the hill country, and those who hear the story cherish it and ask themselves about the future role of this child. It is only after Luke ushers the neighbours off the literary scene that he inserts the canticle of Zechariah.

When Zechariah finds his voice again, he does not use it to take issue with God or his messenger for the imposed silence which he has had to endure. Zechariah speaks words of blessing and praise and prophecy. The silence is forgotten: words are for blessing and thanking God for the visitation he has made to his people. The neighbours may speculate about the future of the child, but Zechariah knows what lies in the child's future story, and he will echo that revelation in the canticle.

Some scholars argue to a clear division in the structure of the Benedictus: vv. 68-75 in the form of a *beraka* or blessing which praises God for his faithfulness in redeeming his people, and vv. 76-79 in the form of a *genethliakon* or birthday hymn made in honour of the new child. Certainly, vv. 68-75 are general in tone and repeat the traditional formula of a hymn of praise in first addressing praise to God and then enlisting reasons for that praise—as well as expressing the mentality of the anawim as previously set forth in the Magnificat; but given that Luke has adopted a general hymn of praise—as he did with the Magnificat—vv. 76–77 can be seen as Luke's addition for the purpose of specifying the future role of John the Baptist in the context of the coming Messiah. These lines answer the neighbour's question about the future of the child. Verses 78–79 are general in tone and can be seen as part of the original hymn. This way of looking at the structure of the canticle sees it as a composite whole, with Luke's insertion in vv. 76–77.

The canticle begins by speaking of the promised redemption of Israel as an accomplished fact because the Lord God has entered history to raise up "the horn of his anointed", the Davidic Messiah. This is the fulfilment of the promise of God spoken from long ago through the words of the prophets. This stress on salvation as an accomplished event gives weight to Brown's thesis that the Benedictus was originally composed by Jewish Christians: "The hymn composed by Jewish Christians remains the most plausible explanation. Such a group would have shared with their pre-Christian Jewish forebears the martial language of the messianic psalms and even of the Qumran War Scroll (IQM), but their language would not have been cast in a past accomplished tense rather than the future."[5]

The hymn moves back in history to the time beyond David when God made his promise to Abraham (Gen 22:16–18). It recalls the covenant and its purpose: that the people would be delivered from the hands of their enemies, so that they could serve God without fear of those enemies in a spirit of holiness and justice for the remainder of their lives.

Zechariah directly addresses his son and prophesies his future accomplishments within the saving plan of God—an echo of the words of Gabriel (16–17). The description of John recalls the words of Is 40:3 and the Elijah figure of Mal 4:5—the prophet whose mission it is to go before the Lord and prepare his ways. Knowledge of salvation is through the forgiveness of sins—a specifically Christian concept which Luke develops throughout the Gospel and which has its clearest expression after the resurrection

(24:47). In conclusion, the canticle summarises the main ideas already expressed and gives its final focus to the figure of the Messiah, who is described as the rising light, *anatole*, an old description for the Messiah (Zech 3:8). The Messiah will guide the people in the way of peace. And peace will be his first address to his disciples after the resurrection (24:36).

Finally, in a brief note testifying to the physical and spiritual growth of John, Luke rounds off this section before moving on to the story of the birth of Jesus. John makes his preparation for his public ministry in the wilderness, the traditional testing ground for the people of God and the prophets. When Luke returns to the story of John, he will continue it where he left it—in the desert (3:2).

Notes

[1]Cf. J. Jeremais, *Jerusalem in the Time of Jesus* (London, 1969) pp. 198-204

[2]For a comparison of the biblical annunciation stories, see the tables in R. Brown, *The Birth of the Messiah, op. cit.*, pp. 156; 248; 297

[3]R. Brown, *ibid.*, p. 301

[4]P. Winter, "Magnificat and Benedictus—Maccabean Psalms?", *Bulletin of the John Rylands Library* 37 (1954) pp. 328-347

[5]R. Brown, *The Birth of the Messiah, op. cit.*, p. 378

Chapter Two

Luke 2: 1-7   ***The Birth of Jesus***

> 2 In those days a decree went out from Caesar Augustus that all the world should be enrolled. ²This was the first enrollment, when Quirinius was governor of Syria. ³And all went to be enrolled, each to his own city. ⁴And Joseph also went up from Galilee, from the city of Nazareth, to Judea, to the city of David, which is called Bethlehem, because he was of the house and lineage of David, ⁵to be enrolled with Mary, his betrothed, who was with child. ⁶And while they were there, the time came for her to be delivered. ⁷And she gave birth to her first-born son and wrapped him in swaddling cloths, and laid him in a manger, because there was no place for them in the inn.

THE DRAMA OF DIVINE PARADOX CONTINUES: barren Elizabeth has given birth to the prophet of the new age; dumb Zechariah has spoken poetry; now it is time for the virgin to bring forth the promised one of God. Luke has engaged all three in the early story of Jesus, and now he brings Caesar Augustus on to the stage, a man who is unwittingly responsible for the journey of Mary and Joseph to the city of David, the seat of the promise. Augustus, who was acknowledged as the saviour of the world because of the peace he established during his reign, now unknowingly helps in the birth of the real saviour of the world.

Scholars have unresolved questions about the historical accuracy of the events surrounding Luke's birth narrative: there is no historical record of a universal census at the time specified by Luke; the Roman custom of taxation was based on the individual's place of residence, not his place of ancestry; Quirinius was governor of Syria during the years A.D. 6-9, some ten years after the birth of Jesus.[1] Ingenious attempts have been made to resolve the historical difficulties, but the important question which can be answered concerns Luke's intention, which is clear: the census places the birth of Jesus within the frame of world history; it also situates the birth in Joseph's ancestral city, Bethlehem, the place prophesied for the beginning of the Messiah.

Luke gives more attention to the interpretation of Jesus' birth by the angels and the shepherd's visitation than he does to the birth itself. His account of the birth of Jesus is simple and brief: while the couple are in Bethlehem, Mary's time comes; she delivers her firstborn, warms him in swaddling cloths and lays him in a manger because there is no room in the lodgings. Luke does not say where the birth took place, only where Mary laid the child. The manger was a feeding trough for animals (cf. Is 1:3). Tradition dating back to Justin has the birth in a shepherd's cave; other traditions speak of the birth place as the courtyard of the inn, where the animals would be tied up, and which would act as a natural overflow from the inn. Mary swaddles the child: swaddling cloths were baby-wraps for keeping the child snug and warm. As the rich and mighty Solomon reflected on his own birth:

> I was nursed with care in swaddling cloths. For no king has had a different beginning of existence; there is for all mankind one entrance into life, and a common departure. (Wis 7: 4-6)

So, the story of Jesus' beginning is told.

There is an eternal enchantment about the simplicity of Luke's nativity scene. Innocence emerges with a howl in the winter of an expectant world. There is the fairy-tale beginning of simple origins with the promise of a reversal of fortune. There is comedy and mystery in the promised one of God in the form of a tiny, vulnerable creature in swaddling cloths. There is tragedy in the knowledge of what will become of the child; but, for the moment,

tragedy is a stranger. This is the night of perpetual dawn,
when, as Marcellus says in *Hamlet,* the cock crows the
whole night through:

> Some say that ever 'gainst that season comes
> Wherein our Saviour's birth is celebrated,
> The bird of dawning singeth all night long;
> And then, they say, no spirit dare stir abroad;
> The nights are wholesome; then no planets strike,
> No fairy takes, nor witch hath power to charm,
> So hallow'd and so gracious is that time.
>
> (1,i,158-164)

The Christian tradition celebrates the hallowed and
gracious time at Christmas. The Christmas celebration is
not about a cosmic utterance or a bolt from heaven; it is
about a particular child come into the world at a particular
time: Luke's whole account stresses this particularity.
Amidst the whole alphabet of seasonal distractions, Luke's
basic message stands firm: Jesus, the promised one of
God, has entered history.

Luke 2: 8-20   *Proclamation to Shepherds*

⁸And in that region there were shepherds out in the field,
keeping watch over their flock by night. ⁹And an angel of
the Lord appeared to them, and the glory of the Lord
shone around them, and they were filled with fear. ¹⁰And
the angel said to them, "Be not afraid; for behold, I bring
you good news of a great joy which will come to all the
people; ¹¹for to you is born this day in the city of David a
Savior, who is Christ the Lord. ¹²And this will be a sign for
you: you will find a babe wrapped in swaddling cloths and
lying in a manger." ¹³And suddenly there was with the
angel a multitude of the heavenly host praising God and
saying,
¹⁴"Glory to God in the highest, and on earth peace among
men with whom he is pleased!"
¹⁵When the angels went away from them into heaven,
the shepherds said to one another, "Let us go over to

Bethlehem and see this thing that has happened, which the Lord has made known to us." [16]And they went with haste, and found Mary and Joseph, and the babe lying in a manger. [17]And when they saw it they made known the saying which had been told them concerning this child; [18]and all who heard it wondered at what the shepherds told them. [19]But Mary kept all these things, pondering them in her heart. [20]And the shepherds returned, glorifying and praising God for all they had heard and seen, as it had been told them.

Luke's account of the proclamation and interpretation of Jesus' birth clearly parallels his account of the events surrounding the birth and naming of John, and scholars have been happy to examine both sequences as a diptych. However, I think there are interesting parallel moments between the story of Jesus' birth and the story of his resurrection, where Luke stresses the significance of both events.

Proclamation of Birth *2: 8-20*	*Proclamation of Resurrection* *24: 1-11*
a) appearance of angel	a) appearance of angels
b) to shepherds (unable to be legal witnesses)	b) to women (unable to be legal witnesses)
c) reaction of fear	c) reaction of fear
d) "do not be afraid"	
e) angel's *interpretation* of event	e) ("linen cloths lying there", John 20: 5 "he is not here, but is risen")
f) *sign:* "wrapped in swaddling cloths" "lying in a manger"	f) angels' *interpretation* of event
g) witness: "made known saying which had been told them"	g) witness: "told this to the apostles"
h) reaction of hearers: astonishment	h) reaction of hearers: disbelief

The end of the nativity scene finishes with the shepherds as they "returned, glorifying and praising God"; the conclusion of the resurrection narrative is made as the disciples "returned to Jerusalem with great joy and were continually in the temple praising God".

The shepherds who are keeping the night company while they watch their sheep are the first to hear the message of joy that the long-awaited Messiah has been born in Bethlehem. The little people are the first people to hear the news. The men who inhabited the fringes of civilization were regarded as an unhappy mixture of gypsy and roaming thief because of their undeveloped capacity to distinguish between "mine" and "thine". Because of the roving nature of their job they could not honour the demands of the ceremonial law, and so were regarded as religious outcasts; because they were regarded as untrustworthy, they were disqualified from appearing as legal witnesses. In spite of all that, they are elected to be the first witnesses of the people to the birth of the Christ.

The popular, romantic image of the shepherd does not include the harshness of the wilderness, the smell of the unwashed, the loneliness and danger of the job, the sheer difference of a life which communed more with sheep than with men. The shepherd may have had a place of importance in the folk-lore of the Israelite people, but he had no place of importance in their society at the time of Jesus.[2] Even if the shepherds were caring for flocks marked for temple sacrifice—since it was understood that any animal found between Jerusalem and Bethlehem was destined to be a sacrificial victim[3]—the shepherds engaged in this work still shared the outsider image. But it is appropriate that Luke's account stresses the shepherds as the first visitors to Jesus. When the babe in the manger grows up, he will seek out those who are despised as outcasts by orthodox society and religion. The shepherds are an indication of Jesus' own preference for the outcast, which Luke will show clearly throughout the Gospel.

So, it is to the shepherds that an angel appears to announce the good news. The shepherds show their fear in the presence of the supernatural, but the angel reassures

them (1: 13, 30) and tells them the good news. The angel
identifies the new baby with three titles: Saviour, Christ and
Lord—titles which Jesus' own followers will understand
after the resurrection. The angel gives the shepherds a sign:
the first, "wrapped in swaddling cloths", is not unusual; the
second, "lying in a manger", is an unusual sign and will give
them an idea where to look. As if to confirm the angel's
message, the shepherds are treated to a heavenly host which
hymns a canticle, Gloria in excelsis Deo. They proclaim glory
to God in heaven and peace on earth to those whom God has
favoured (cf. 19: 38). After their short canticle, the angels
bow out of the scene.

The shepherds decide to follow the instructions of the
angel, and, like Mary (1: 39), they make haste to their appointed destination. The prophet Isaiah had written of his vision:

The ox knows its owner,
       and the ass its master's crib;
  but Israel does not know,
       my people does not understand. (1:3)

But now, the poor of Israel come to the manger and join
Isaiah's sleepy twosome in the ox and the ass in recognizing
the tiny occupant. The shepherds tell their story to Mary and
Joseph, and unnamed others.

Finally, Luke recounts the reactions of the unnamed
hearers, of Mary, and of the shepherds. The response of
the hearers is to wonder at the story of the shepherds. The
shepherds themselves return to their flocks, glorifying and
praising God: there is no hint that they carry the message
to others. Mary is portrayed as the one who *kept* all these
things so that she could come to understand their complex
meaning. When Jesus begins his public ministry, there is
no indication that anyone remembers supernatural events
surrounding his birth, there is no hint that anyone has
knowledge of his real identity. The believers who surrounded his birth seem to have long departed, without
leaving a memory of early marvels. It is Mary who has to
work at interpreting these events—she is the only adult of

the infancy narrative who will play any role in the later
Gospel. And Mary has to work at understanding who her
son really is. She, like the disciples, will keep events in her
heart until the day comes when she can make sense of them
(Acts 1: 14)

Luke 2: 21-40   *The Presentation of Jesus*

²¹And at the end of eight days, when he was circumcised,
he was called Jesus, the name given by the angel before he
was conceived in the womb.

²²And when the time came for their purification according
to the law of Moses, they brought him up to Jerusalem to
present him to the Lord²³ (as it is written in the law of the
Lord, "Every male that opens the womb shall be called holy
to the Lord") ²⁴and to offer a sacrifice according to what is
said in the law of the Lord, "a pair of turtledoves, or two
young pigeons."²⁵Now there was a man in Jerusalem, whose
name was Simeon, and this man was righteous and devout,
looking for the consolation of Israel, and the Holy Spirit was
upon him. ²⁶And it had been revealed to him by the Holy
Spirit that he should not see death before he had seen the
Lord's Christ. ²⁷And inspired by the Spirit he came into the
temple; and when the parents brought in the child Jesus, to
do for him according to the custom of the law, ²⁸he took him
up in his arms and blessed God and said,

²⁹"Lord, now lettest thou thy servant depart in peace, according to thy word; ³⁰for mine eyes have seen thy salvation
³¹which thou hast prepared in the presence of all peoples; ³²a
light for revelation to the Gentiles, and for glory to thy people Israel."

³³And his father and his mother marveled at what was said
about him; ³⁴and Simeon blessed them and said to Mary his
mother, "Behold, this child is set for the fall and rising of
many in Israel, and for a sign that is spoken against ³⁵(and a
sword will pierce through your own soul also), that thoughts
out of many hearts may be revealed."

³⁶And there was a prophetess, Anna, the daughter of
Phanuel, of the tribe of Asher; she was of a great age, having
lived with her husband seven years from her virginity, ³⁷and
as a widow till she was eighty-four. She did not depart from
the temple, worshiping with fasting and prayer night and

day. ³⁸And coming up at that very hour she gave thanks to God, and spoke of him to all who were looking for the redemption of Jerusalem.

³⁹And when they had performed everything according to the law of the Lord, they returned into Galilee, to their own city, Nazareth. ⁴⁰And the child grew and became strong, filled with wisdom; and the favor of God was upon him.

In accordance with the Jewish law, Jesus is circumcised on the eighth day and, like John, is also named on that day. Luke devotes only one verse to the scene and stresses the significance of the naming. In the circumcision, Jesus is subject to the requirements of the Law; in the naming, Jesus is subject to the will of God who communicated the name through Gabriel's command (1: 31).

In the presentation and purification, Luke moves the scene from Bethlehem to the temple in Jerusalem. Luke's condensed account conflates two ceremonies, the purification of the mother and the presentation of the child. In the Mosaic Law, a woman was regarded as ritually unclean for forty days after the birth of a male child. At the end of that time, she was required to present herself for the rite of purification to a priest; she was to make her offering to the priest at the door of the sanctuary (Lev 12: 6 ff). Although Luke speaks of "their" purification, the law required only the mother's (Lev 12: 1). Mary is obedient to the law and makes the offering of the poor, two turtle-doves or two pigeons.

Alongside this account, Luke has the presentation of Jesus. Like the purification, this too was a requirement of the law. The Mosaic Law held that the first-born male, whether human or animal, belonged to God (Ex 13: 2); however, after the tribe of Levi dedicated themselves to that purpose, parents of the first-born were released from the original demand of the law by an act of redemption, in which they paid a ransom to a priest for the child (Num 18: 16). In Luke's account, there is no mention of a ransom—probably because like Samuel, Jesus is being consecrated to the service of the Lord.

The presentation of Jesus is an echo of an older scene when Elkanah and Hannah took their child, Samuel, to the sanctuary in Shiloh to offer him in the service of the Lord; there, they were met by an aged priest, Eli, who blessed the parents of the child (1 Sam 1: 24-28). Luke has already introduced us to an old couple, Elizabeth and Zechariah, and to the shepherds, representing the poor of Israel. Now it is the time for an old twosome in Simeon and Anna to play their part in the story of the Christ child. The presentation and the purification serve as a backdrop against which Simeon and Anna, who are described in the terms of the anawim who have faithfully awaited the consolation of Israel, can make their presence and purpose known.

The Holy Spirit has already revealed to Simeon a consoling promise that he would not meet death until he had seen the Messiah. After years of waiting on that promise, Simeon is guided by the Spirit to enter the temple; there he meets the three new arrivals and takes the child Jesus in his arms. He blesses God, and hymns the poetry of the Nunc Dimittis.

As with the Magnificat and the Benedictus, the Nunc Dimittis is a mosaic of Old Testament thoughts which are recalled and set in the new context of their fulfilment in the messianic era. As Israel was ready to die after he had looked on the face of his lost son, Joseph (Gen 46: 30), so Simeon is now prepared to die because he has seen the fulfilment of the Lord's promise in Jesus. There is no reason for Simeon to keep death at bay—the very thing which gave his life purpose has now happened, so he can make his departure in peace in the knowledge that his own death will be affected by the life and death of this child.

In this canticle, Zechariah had blessed the Lord "for he has visited and redeemed his people" (1: 68). Now, the canticle of Simeon widens the sphere of Jesus's influence to include not only the people of Israel, but the Gentile peoples. Luke recounts that Mary and Joseph are astonished at what Simeon says. This might appear surprising since Mary has already been told of the stature of the child in the annunciation, and both she and Joseph have been told of the proclamation of the angels by the shepherds. Why then the surprise? This has led some scholars to argue that the annunciation, the nativity, and the presentation are separate traditions, none of which supposes the existence of the other. But it is possible to see the surprise of Mary and Joseph as a Lucan device to underline something of supreme importance: a stranger has just told Mary and Joseph something which has not been revealed to anyone before, and which is not contained in any of the previous scenes: the significance of Jesus for the Gentile world.

In the second part of his oracle, Simeon turns to address Mary, and, as with the other canticles, Luke enters a more specific note to the sequence. Simeon foretells the negative aspects of the ministry of Jesus, how the child is destined to cause division—something which Jesus will speak of in his own ministry(12: 51-53). Simeon speaks to Mary to tell her that a sword will pierce her own soul. As the mother of this child, Mary will have to pay a price, and the soul is the ultimate place where all prices are paid. The image of the sword piercing the soul continues the thought of the previous verse: the sword will divide Mary's soul. Mary is the mother of Jesus, but she will have to learn to be his disciple (8:21). As Mary nurtures the child and sees him grow up, she will have to learn to let her son go in the knowledge that he is destined for the many—something which is brought out in the next scene. Mary will also have to learn to accept her son as her Lord. And all this is going to be heart-rending and painful.

After these difficult words, the mood changes with the prophetess Anna coming on the scene. It is unclear whether she is eighty-four, or whether she has been a widow for that time. She is described as a faithful one, one who never leaves the temple: this is hardly meaning that she was permanently encamped there; it is probably meant in the same spirit as the oft-heard, "She's never out of the church". Anna, like Simeon, is one of the poor and faithful remnant of God who has awaited the messianic era. She is the one who gives thanks, and she is the final witness of the infancy narrative to testify to the salvific importance of Jesus. From now on in the Gospel, Jesus will have to work towards being accepted as he will have to work towards growing in understanding who he is himself.

So the threesome return to "their own city, Nazareth", which prepares us for Jesus' later emergence as the prophet from Nazareth. As with John the Baptist (1: 80), the birth story of Jesus comes to a close emphasizing how he grows up physically and spiritually. Before Jesus begins his public ministry, there is much heart-searching and heart-sharing to do. And, according to Simeon, the same is true of his mother.

Luke 2: 41-52   *Jesus among the Teachers*

⁴¹Now his parents went to Jerusalem every year at the feast of the Passover. ⁴²And when he was twelve years old, they went up according to custom; ⁴³and when the feast was ended, as they were returning, the boy Jesus stayed behind in Jerusalem. His parents did not know it, ⁴⁴but supposing him to be in the company they went a day's journey, and they sought him among their kinsfolk and acquaintances; ⁴⁵and when they did not find him, they returned to Jerusalem, seeking him. ⁴⁶After three days they found him in the temple, sitting among the teachers, listening to them and asking them questions; ⁴⁷and all who heard him were amazed at his understanding and his answers. ⁴⁸And when they saw him they were astonished; and his mother said to him, "Son, why have you treated us so? Behold, your father and I have been looking for you anxiously." ⁴⁹And he said to them, "How is it that you sought me? Did you not know that I must be in my Father's house?" ⁵⁰And they did not understand the saying which he spoke to them. ⁵¹And he went down with them and came to Nazareth, and was obedient to them; and his mother kept all these things in her heart.
⁵²And Jesus increased in wisdom and in stature, and in favor with God and man.

Luke's Gospel opens with Zechariah serving in the temple and it closes with the disciples blessing God in the temple. Interestingly, Luke is the only evangelist to recount an incident from the hidden life of Jesus—incidents which abound in the apocryphal Gospels—and that takes place in the temple of Jerusalem. Strictly speaking, this section does not belong to the infancy narrative, since Jesus is no longer a child. The portrayal of Jesus as the one who must be involved in his Father's service rather than at the service of his natural family is an anticipation of Jesus' later ministry when Jesus often reflects on how he must (*dei*) fulfill the mission given him by his Father (4: 43; 9: 22; 13: 32; 17: 25).

The scene opens with the journey from Nazareth up to Jerusalem, a journey which will later form for Luke the narrative context of Jesus' public ministry from 9: 51-19: 44. Traditionally, all Jews tried to attend the feast of the Passover in Jerusalem at least once in their lives. Like many Palestinian Jews, Mary and Joseph go every year, and they bring Jesus with them in his twelfth year. In later customs, the Jewish boy was introduced to adulthood when he was twelve years old—he became *bar mitzvah,* a son of the law. He was then expected to assume the adult obligations which the law imposed. In going to Jerusalem, it is possible that Jesus was celebrating an earlier form of this rite of passage: he was no longer a child; he had begun the process of being a man.

The story tells us that Jesus stayed in Jerusalem, unknown to Mary and Joseph who had started travelling back to Nazareth. It was the custom at that time for whole villages to travel together to and from the feasts in Jerusalem. They would travel by caravan, the men and the women keeping their separate companies, until they would camp together at night. It was not until the end of the first day's travelling that Mary and Joseph realised their loss: probably, Luke's setting allows for a day's search, and another day's journey back to Jerusalem.

After three days they find Jesus with the teachers in the temple. Interestingly, Luke describes Jesus sitting among "the teachers"—who will be described in the public ministry as "scribes" and "lawyers" with the suggestion that they did not accept Jesus. Jesus is not playing the precocious theologian, but is "listening to them and asking questions". All who hear Jesus' answers are astonished at his insight and understanding. Previously, Luke has spoken of astonishment at what others have said of Jesus; now people are astonished at Jesus himself.

The astonishment is shared by Mary and Joseph, in spite of the angel's pronouncement at the annunciation, the shepherd's story of the angels' proclamation, and the prophecy of Simeon—which has led some scholars to see this story as a pre-Lucan narrative. The astonishment of Mary and Joseph would be understandable if this was the first inkling they had of the true identity of their son. Also, Mary's rebuke would be easier to read without the previous revelation about Jesus. Mary's question focuses on herself and Joseph, while Jesus' reply focuses on his Father. His first priority, his "I must", is to be where his Father wants him, and to do as his Father commands him.

Luke says that they did not understand Jesus' saying, a reaction to Jesus' word which will happen throughout his later ministry. It is clear from Luke's Gospel that no one understood the divine sonship of Jesus until after the resurrection. That understanding comes only when Jesus has completed his mission and when the Spirit of understanding is sent (Acts 1: 14). If the wisdom and work of Jesus in this scene anticipate that of his public ministry, so the reaction of Mary and Joseph anticipates the later reaction of the disciples. However, Luke adds the same note that Mary "kept all these things in her heart", the same response which she made when the shepherds told her of what the angels proclaimed in their message (2: 19).

The threesome make their return journey to Nazareth, where Jesus is obedient to Joseph and Mary. Thus Jesus leads a normal family life until the time comes for the beginning of his public ministry. Jesus will increase in wisdom and stature; but what for him is a long process of preparing for public life, is for Mary the process of preparing to let her son go and preparing to accept him as her Lord. But she keeps the words and events in her heart, which is the reaction of the true disciple. When Jesus makes his appearances after the resurrection, he will disclose the significance of the words and events which referred to himself (24: 25-27, 45-46). Meanwhile, they must be kept in the heart.

Notes

[1]Cf. G. Ogg, "The Quirinius Question Today" in *Expository Times* 79, 1967-68, pp. 231-236

[2]Cf. R. T. Murphy, *The Bible Today* 15, Dec. 1964, pp. 986-991

[3]Mishnah, *Shelakim* 7: 4

Chapter Three

Luke 3: 1-6   *The Beginning of John's Ministry*

3 In the fifteenth year of the reign of Tiberius Caesar, Pontius Pilate being governor of Judea, and Herod being tetrarch of Galilee, and his brother Philip tetrarch of the region of Ituraea and Trachonitis, and Lysanias tetrarch of Abilene, ²in the high-priesthood of Annas and Caiaphas, the word of God came to John the son of Zechariah in the wilderness; ³and he went into all the region about the Jordan, preaching a baptism of repentance for the forgiveness of sins. ⁴As it is written in the book of the words of Isaiah the prophet, "The voice of one crying in the wilderness: Prepare the way of the Lord, make his paths straight. ⁵Every valley shall be filled, and every mountain and hill shall be brought low, and the crooked shall be made straight, and the rough ways shall be made smooth; ⁶and all flesh shall see the salvation of God."

IN A SOLEMN BEGINNING to the public ministry of Jesus, Luke introduces the adult John the Baptist by firmly placing him on the stage of imperial and local history. John's emergence from the wilderness is formally dated by reference to the reign of Tiberias Caesar and to the lesser political and religious leaders of the local scene. Some scholars argue that this opening to the public ministry of Jesus forms the original beginning of the Gospel—the infancy narrative being a preface which was added later by Luke. However, as Cadbury points out, this form of beginning after the physical start of the book was a literary device which marked the real starting-point of the narrative, and has many parallels in ancient historical writing.[1] Augustus died on 19th August, A.D. 14, which probably makes Luke's dating of John's ministry A.D. 28/29.

Having set the scene, Luke describes how "the word of God came to John", a standard introduction to the prophetic call (Jer 1: 1; Joel 1: 1). Luke last mentioned John in 1: 80, where the young John was "in the wilderness till the day of his manifestation to Israel." That day has arrived, and the moment has come for John to leave the wilderness and disclose his mission and his message to the people of Israel. Unlike Matthew and Mark, Luke says nothing of John's appearance or dietary habits; the emphasis is on John's preaching which focuses on baptism of repentance for the forgiveness of sins. Nor does Luke emphasize John's ministry of baptizing: the stress is on John's role as a prophet and on his prophetic word which points to the significance of baptism.

There was a form of baptism which pre-existed John, a ceremony for initiating converts into Judaism. Gentiles who became proselyte Jews had to submit to a baptism which signified moral and ritual cleansing. The interesting note about John's baptism is that it placed Jews in the same category as Gentiles: John's preaching told the Jews to reaffirm their commitment to the covenant by repentance and baptism, which would lead to God's forgiveness. For Luke, repentance itself is a gift of God (Acts 5: 31), and that repentance is signified in the act of baptism by water, which foreshadowed the baptism of the Spirit in the new age.

In all four Gospels, John's mission is seen as a fulfilment of Old Testament prophecy. Each Gospel quotes Isaiah 40: 3, which speaks of the voice which calls people to prepare for the coming of the king, and applies it to John's role in preparing for the coming of the Messiah. Luke quotes the whole of Isaiah 40: 3-5, in which the imagery of preparation for the coming king is continued, and Isaiah's prophecy of the time when "all flesh shall see the salvation of God" is recalled. This last verse gives substance to one of the central themes of Luke's Gospel, the universality of salvation. Simeon has already recorded that note in his canticle (2: 80) and now the universal experience which he spoke of is near at hand.

The imagery of Isaiah which Luke uses speaks of mountains which have to be flattened, valleys which have to be filled in, crooked ways which have to be made straight, rough roads which have to be smoothed—all to ease the passage of the approaching king. The imagery is ageless. It speaks of heavy road-works ahead: tortuous bends to be straightened, traffic re-routed, and plenty of employment for everyone. The landscape which the Baptist is committed to putting right is not the landscape of Palestine, but the landscape of the human heart, with its own mountainous regions, deep valleys, scenic routes, shabby views, twisted turns, no-go areas, traffic jams, and peculiar highway code.

John's task is to attend to the underground kingdom of the human heart in preparing for the coming of the Messiah. And he does this in proclaiming a baptism of repentance. John's baptism is not a sign that all the preparation work has been accomplished; it is a sign that the preparation work has begun, that people are beginning to involve themselves in preparing for the coming one. It is a prophetic sign which carries with it the assurance that God is at work among the people. In his preaching, John invites all the people to change their ways, which means an interior change of heart. That change of heart will allow the coming Messiah to have Lordship over the unclaimed territory. And the promise is that if he is Lord there, journeys to the interior will be adventures of discovery to where God reigns, rather than excursions into a landscape of horror, into some shadowland of false frights, where the images and the reflections are unfocused and unreal, because the forgiveness of God has not been allowed entry.

Luke 3: 7-20   *The Call to Repentance*

7He said therefore to the multitudes that came out to be baptized by him, "You brood of vipers! Who warned you to flee from the wrath to come? 8Bear fruits that befit repentance, and do not begin to say to yourselves, 'We have

Abraham as our father'; for I tell you, God is able from these stones to raise up children to Abraham. ⁹Even now the axe is laid to the root of the trees; every tree therefore that does not bear good fruit is cut down and thrown into the fire."

¹⁰And the multitudes asked him, "What then shall we do?" ¹¹And he answered them, "He who has two coats, let him share with him who has none; and he who has food, let him do likewise." ¹²Tax collectors also came to be baptized, and said to him, "Teacher, what shall we do?" ¹³And he said to them, "Collect no more than is appointed you." ¹⁴Soldiers also asked him, "And we, what shall we do?" And he said to them, "Rob no one by violence or by false accusation, and be content with your wages."

¹⁵As the people were in expectation, and all men questioned in their hearts concerning John, whether perhaps he were the Christ, ¹⁶John answered them all, "I baptize you with water; but he who is mightier than I is coming, the thong of whose sandals I am not worthy to untie; he will baptize you with the Holy Spirit and with fire. ¹⁷His winnowing fork is in his hand, to clear his threshing floor, and to gather the wheat into his granary, but the chaff he will burn with unquenchable fire."

¹⁸So, with many exhortations, he preached good news to the people. ¹⁹But Herod the tetrarch, who had been reproved by him for Herodias, his brother's wife, and for all the evil things that Herod had done, ²⁰added this to them all, that he shut up John in prison.

Being a member of a select group has its own problems. One of the problems of belonging to the chosen people is that one can think it is a right rather than a privilege, a prerogative rather than a responsibility, something that gives one an edge on everyone else. One can begin to expect preferential treatment, for no other reason than the fact that one belongs to the right crowd. So, there is the name-dropping game in the hope that attention will be paid, that preference will be given, and that regular expectations can be forgotten. Hotel managers and head waiters may acknowledge that kind of activity; John the Baptist dealt it a death-blow. John makes it very clear that no one can enter the kingdom of God simply because he happens to live at the right address.

John anticipated the argument of his hearers that they

could be saved because they had Abraham as their father. John asserts that nobody can be saved simply because he has the right theological pedigree: that is to live on borrowed goodness and on borrowed fidelity. People are not saved because they share a certain ancestry in Abraham: that is not enough. Trees are reckoned as good not by their roots but by their fruits: so with the people of God: good roots are not enough, there have to be fruits which people can see. Roots speak of the past, fruits speak of the present; and John is interested in the present before God. It is because of the present, not the past, that conversion is needed. And John makes a play on the words *abnayya* (stones) and *banayya* (children) to make the point that God is able to raise children from the very stones.

John is committed to the belief that conversion and repentance are not a simple matter of a ritual, where the individual undergoes a baptismal splash, as if that were a kind of coming-out party which signifies that the individual has "arrived" in society or in the community. The baptism of John is not a sign that one has arrived; it is a sign that one has begun, that one has started the life-long task of committing oneself to God. When the people ask John: "What then shall we do?" John does not tell them in the spirit of Lady Bracknell to acquire at least one acceptable parent before the day is quite over: the people are in no need of ancestors, but they are in need of a change of heart.

And the change of heart is not a vague gesture; it is evident in an ethic of life. The tax-collectors of the time purchased the right to collect various minor taxes, a system which invited abuse, and one which rendered the tax-collectors ritually unclean. John does not tell them to go on unemployment; he tells them to amend their ways. Likewise the soldiers, probably in this instance those who protected the tax-collectors, are enjoined by John to behave with honesty and to be content with the wages they receive, without getting involved with the tax-collectors in lucrative arithmetic.

People reacted to John's preaching by wondering whether he was the promised Messiah; but Luke makes it clear that John himself was not competing with Jesus for the title of Messiah. There was a tradition among John's disciples that he was the Messiah, but Luke portrays John as one who was not a party to that belief. In fact, Luke closes the passage with the anticipated imprisonment of John: John fades out before Jesus appears on the scene. But before John bows out of the scene, Luke presents him as one who is conscious of the greatness of Jesus, and aware of the difference between his own baptism and the baptism of Jesus. John is not mean-spirited; when Christ comes, it is time for him to go.

And so, the herald of the Messiah is imprisoned, and his ministry comes to a close. John made enemies, principally because of the values and beliefs which he lived and preached. John was not imprisoned for someone else's beliefs, but for his own. When prophets publicly profess their values, that prophetic activity can make others nervous to the point where they ensure the imprisonment of the voice which threatens their way of life; but, at least John has the consolation of his own preaching that he is imprisoned because of what he stands for. And, for John, that is salvation indeed.

Luke 3: 21-38   *The Baptism and Genealogy of Christ*

[21]Now when all the people were baptized, and when Jesus also had been baptized and was praying, the heaven was opened, [22]and the Holy Spirit descended upon him in bodily form, as a dove, and a voice came from heaven, "Thou art my beloved Son; with thee I am well pleased."

[23]Jesus, when he began his ministry, was about thirty years of age, being the son (as was supposed) of Joseph, the son of Heli, [24]the son of Matthat, the son of Levi, the son of Melchi, the son of Jannai, the son of Joseph, [25]the son of Mattathias, the son of Amos, the son of Nahum, the son of Esli, the son of Naggai, [26]the son of Maath, the son of Mattathias, the son of Semein, the son of Josech, the son of

Joda, [27]the son of Joanan, the son of Rhesa, the son of
Zerubbabel, the son of Shealtiel, the son of Neri, [28]the son of
Melchi, the son of Addi, the son of Cosam, the son of
Elmadam, the son of Er, [29]the son of Joshua, the son of
Eliezer, the son of Jorim, the son of Matthat, the son of
Levi, [30]the son of Simeon, the son of Judah, the son of
Joseph, the son of Jonam, the son of Eliakim, [31]the son of
Melea, the son of Menna, the son of Mattatha, the son of
Nathan, the son of David, [32]the son of Jesse, the son of Obed,
the son of Boaz, the son of Sala, the son of Nahshon, [33]the
son of Amminadab, the son of Admin, the son of Arni, the
son of Hezron, the son of Perez, the son of Judah, [34]the son
of Jacob, the son of Isaac, the son of Abraham, the son of
Terah, the son of Nahor, [35]the son of Serug, the son of Reu,
the son of Peleg, the son of Eber, the son of Shelah, [36]the son
of Cainan, the son of Arphaxad, the son of Shem, the son of
Noah, the son of Lamech, [37]the son of Methuselah, the son
of Cainan, [38] the son of Enos, the son of Seth, the son of
Adam, the son of God.

Understandably, we might be surprised to see Jesus join
the queue of people to be baptized. Why did he do it? He
had no need to repent; he had no need to proclaim his
belief in his Father with whom he could claim some familiarity; he had no sins to be forgiven. And yet if the baptism
was not the kind of empty ritual which Jesus disparaged in
his own preaching, we can presume that there must have
been a purpose to it. Luke mentions the baptism of Jesus
only in a participial clause, a literary shyness which is sur-
passed only by the outright silence of John's Gospel which
does not mention the baptism of Jesus at all. In view of a
tradition which regarded John the Baptist as the Messiah,
perhaps Luke was reluctant to dwell on Jesus' baptism by
John the Baptist. Luke goes a step further and has the Baptist in prison before Jesus' baptism takes place—so John
does not appear in Luke's baptismal scene.

The baptism of Jesus comes at the opening of his public
mission, when Jesus begins the task for which he came into
the world. Jesus' baptism was his initiation into his new life
of public ministry. That baptism is described in the language
of entrances—an initiation, a gateway, an introduction, a

beginning, a splash, a start—is important for the understanding of the event. Jesus was *beginning* a new life; he was
at the stage of crisis—not in our sense of catastrophe, but in
the Greek sense of *krisis,* an important turning-point. And a
turning-point is the beginning of a new way.

The baptism of Jesus signals his beginning, his birth into
a public life that would lead eventually to his death. His
baptism was a public profession that he was now becoming
involved in the most important part of his life: his mission
to all the people. It was Jesus' gateway, not his port of arrival; it was his official starting-point. Jesus would later
speak of his death in terms of baptism when he would say,
"I have a baptism to be baptised with". (Luke 15: 20)
Jesus' public life on earth was bounded by his baptism in
the Jordan and his baptism on the cross.

Jesus was baptized in the waters of the Jordan. Water,
which is a symbol of baptism, has within it its own ambiguity, an ambiguity which can speak of death and life,
not just the life and death of Jesus, but the experiences of
ambiguity which the baptized go through when they
become committed to a life lived in a certain community.
The symbol speaks of a variation on the theme of crucifixion and resurrection. Water can be a symbol of life and
death; answer to a thirst, reason for a chill; it is shallow, it
is deep; you can paddle your feet in it, you can be up to
your neck in it; you can dive into its embrace, you can fail
to escape its clutches; it is the dream of the mirage, it is the
dread of the nightmare; it is black, and blue and red, it is
colourless; it can be solidified but not diluted. The rich
symbolism speaks of a variety of experiences which Jesus
was *letting himself in for* with his admission in baptism.

After his baptism, while he is at prayer, Jesus is formally
recognized by his Father, and is anointed in his task by the
Holy Spirit. At the opening of his public life, Jesus receives
the assurance that his Father is pleased with him, and he
receives the investiture. All is now ready for the mission.
Luke tells us that Jesus was thirty years old when he began
his ministry.

Luke then gives us the genealogy of Jesus through Joseph: scholars have asked whether this throws doubt on the virginity of Mary, but the acceptable practice of giving a genealogy was through the father, and since Joseph was the legal father, this would have been the normal practice. Interestingly, the genealogy is given from Jesus to Adam, rather than the reverse, from Adam to Jesus, or from Abraham to Jesus. In his baptism, Jesus had just been recognized as "my beloved Son", and now Adam is recognized as "the son of God". Adam, man, is the concrete summary of the universality of human evil; Jesus is the concrete summary of the universality of salvation. Jesus does not depend on Adam for his significance; rather, Adam depends on Jesus for his significance. Jesus gives Adam a retroactive importance—hence Luke's genealogy makes sense, not just to make the point that Christ's salvation is for all, not just the sons of Abraham; but, that it is only in Christ that Adam can receive the honourable title of "the son of God".

So, Jesus is now prepared for his public life, a life which will have its effects not only in the future, but as far back as Adam. In his baptism, Jesus now begins to get involved in a whole litany of human experiences, which would tax his humanity to the full. Nobody knows whether Jesus knew exactly what he was letting himself in for with his baptism; but then, very few people do at the start of any commitment in life. And there is a mercy in that.

Notes

¹H. Cadbury, *The Making of Luke-Acts,* (London, S.P.C.K. 1958) pp. 204-207

Chapter Four

Luke 4: 1-13   The Temptation in the Desert

4 And Jesus, full of the Holy Spirit, returned from the Jordan, and was led by the Spirit ²for forty days in the wilderness, tempted by the devil. And he ate nothing in those days; and when they were ended, he was hungry. ³The devil said to him, "If you are the Son of God, command this stone to become bread." ⁴And Jesus answered him, "It is written, 'Man shall not live by bread alone.'" ⁵And the devil took him up, and showed him all the kingdoms of the world in a moment of time, ⁶and said to him, "To you I will give all this authority and their glory; for it has been delivered to me, and I give it to whom I will. ⁷If you, then, will worship me, it shall all be yours." ⁸And Jesus answered him, "It is written, 'You shall worship the Lord your God, and him only shall you serve.'"
⁹And he took him to Jerusalem, and set him on the pinnacle of the temple, and said to him, "If you are the Son of God, throw yourself down from here; ¹⁰for it is written, 'He will give his angels charge of you, to guard you,' ¹¹and 'On their hands they will bear you up, lest you strike your foot against a stone.'" ¹²And Jesus answered him, "It is said, 'You shall not tempt the Lord your God.'" ¹³And when the devil had ended every temptation, he departed from him until an opportune time.

AFTER HIS PUBLIC BAPTISM, Jesus is led by the Spirit into the desert. Traditionally, the desert was seen as the land which was not blessed by God; it was the place where the jackals roamed, and the demons wandered; it was the land where there was no security, no sure exit: a land totally innocent of comfort and consolation. The desert was a place of trial, a place where the heart of man was quickly revealed to himself. The desert still is the place where man can be utterly alone, where he has nowhere to hide, where there

are no shadowlands to comfort him. It is the place where
even the sun becomes an enemy, where it is too hot in the
day and too cold in the night. It is the void. It is the place
where Jesus comes face to face with his enemy. It is the
place where Jesus comes face to face with himself.

When Malcolm Muggeridge was preparing to film a re-
enaction of the temptations in the desert, he wondered
how to portray the presence of the devil on the screen.
"Finally, it was decided that the devil's presence should be
conveyed only by a long dark shadow falling across the
sand, and lengthening as the colloquy with Jesus proceeded. It may even have been Jesus' own shadow; dialogues
with the devil have a way of turning out to be solilo-
quies."[1] Whether Jesus had a close encounter with the per-
sonification of evil, or a conversation with the questioning
side of himself is not the issue here; the issue which Luke
concentrates on is Jesus' relationship with his Father, and
how that relationship of trust is put to the test.

Jesus has been fasting during the forty days, and he is
hungry. Jesus' hunger is important to the scene. As man,
Jesus is experiencing a human hunger, and it is precisely at
a time when Jesus is suffering because of his humanity that
the devil probes his relationship with his Father. After his
baptism, Jesus heard a voice which recognized him as the
beloved son of the Father; now he hears a voice which
questions that relationship: "If you are the Son of
God. . ." One of the voices recognizes his unique vocation; the other voice questions it. One voice confirms Jesus
in his identity; the other voice questions Jesus' self-iden-
tity. Jesus has to decide which voice to heed; which belongs
to his Father, which belongs to the evil one. In the course
of the three temptations, he makes the decision that the
voice which questions his identity as the Son of God is the
voice of evil. And when he is on the cross, he will hear the
echo of that voice: "If you are the Son of God, come down
from the cross" (Mt 27:40).

In the first temptation, the devil is afraid that Jesus will
accept human hunger, a hunger that is not proper to God,

but to man. The devil does not want Jesus to take his mission from his Father seriously, and accept the poverty of the human lot. Paradoxically, what the devil fears is not the power of God, but the powerlessness of God become man. The devil's temptation is a repeat of the oldest temptation in the world: to play at being God. Only God in his power can extricate himself miraculously from hunger by turning a stone into bread. The devil tempts Jesus to cheat on his humanity, to allay his hunger by using divine power. The devil tempts Jesus to alter his Incarnation and not accept the impositions of the human condition. But Jesus says no to the temptation, and affirms his acceptance of the mission he has received from his Father.

In the second temptation, the devil offers Jesus the glory of the kingdoms of the world, if he will worship the devil rather than the Father. Again, Jesus' relationship with his Father is put to the test. The devil tries to seduce Jesus with the offer of immediate power, with a short-cut to success. Jesus refuses to take short-cuts, and elects to win hearts and kingdoms through his life and love and values, rather than exercise borrowed power from the hands of evil.

Jesus answers the two temptations, not with his own word but with a quotation from scripture; in the third temptation, the devil tries his hand at scriptural quotation himself, and invites Jesus to put the word of God to the test by doing a swan dive from the pinnacle of the Temple. Jesus is tempted to test God in a feat of gaudy exhibitionism, by playing a theological stunt man. But Jesus refuses to test God; he refuses to employ the bizarre and the fantastic, the histrionics of the superman; he refuses, as he would later refuse Herod, to play court entertainer. He trusts the word of his Father. He accepts his incarnational role as man, because he knows that it is in accepting humanity that he will eventually save it. And that humanity has first to be accepted in his own flesh.

In *The Brothers Karamazov,* Dostoevsky gives a psychological interpretation of the three temptations of Christ in his story of the Grand Inquisitor. Christ returns to the earth during the time of the Spanish Inquisition, only to be captured by the Grand Inquisitor. The Inquisitor argues with his prisoner that he left man a terrible heritage of freedom in refusing the offers of the devil in the desert. The cardinal explains to Christ that he must be burned as a heretic because he cannot have the prisoner coming into the world again with empty hands offering people freedom. The Inquisitor argues that Christ has greatly burdened people with freedom, and that it has taken the Church centuries to persuade people to strike a bargain: the Church will give them peace of mind, if they will give the Church their freedom. With freedom there is pain and suffering, and the Inquisitor has freed men from the pain of freedom, and given them peace in servitude. But the Inquisitor does not burn Christ; he lets him go out into the dark alleys of the town, no doubt assured that no one will want his Gospel of the pain of freedom.

Of course, the Inquisitor's offer is seductive; but it is no bargain, it is servitude. No one has the right to take away the pain that comes with freedom: to take away that, is to take away life. And the devil tried to take away Jesus' freedom, he tried to take away Jesus' pain as he was experiencing hunger, he tried to offer Jesus immediate power in exchange for the pain he would experience in trying to win men's hearts. Jesus said no to the devil, and yes to his humanity. He accepted the pain that comes with human freedom, the pain that comes in working out and working through his own identity as the Son of God.

At the opening of his public life, Jesus' experience in the desert was an experience of profound trial. It was also a period of clarification, a period in which he worked out what he was opposed to. It always helps to know who your enemy is; it always helps to have a seminar with him in the desert: at least, you know what you are up against. The experience for Jesus was an opportunity to clarify his own position, even though it might not have been articulated in all its depths. Enemies have a particular way of helping you to clear your head of fuzziness and clarify your own standpoint: you might even be grateful to them. At least, when the voice of your enemy sounds again, you will catch your breath: it doesn't do to be out of breath when you face your enemy.

Luke 4: 14-30   Rejection in Nazareth

[14]And Jesus returned in the power of the Spirit into Galilee, and a report concerning him went out through all the surrounding country. [15]And he taught in their synagogues, being glorified by all.

[16]And he came to Nazareth, where he had been brought up; and he went to the synagogue, as his custom was, on the sabbath day. And he stood up to read; [17]and there was given to him the book of the prophet Isaiah. He opened the book and found the place where it was written,

[18]"The Spirit of the Lord is upon me, because he has annointed me to preach good news to the poor. He has sent me to proclaim release to the captives and recovering of sight to the blind, to set at liberty those who are oppressed, [19]to proclaim the acceptable year of the Lord."

[20]And he closed the book, and gave it back to the attendant, and sat down; and the eyes of all in the synagogue were fixed on him. [21]And he began to say to them, "Today this scripture has been fulfilled in your hearing." [22]And all spoke well of him, and wondered at the gracious words which proceeded out of his mouth; and they said, "Is not this Joseph's son?"

[23]And he said to them, "Doubtless you will quote to me this proverb, 'Physician, heal yourself; what we have heard you did at Capernaum, do here also in your own country.'"

[24]And he said, "Truly, I say to you, no prophet is acceptable in his own country.[5] But in truth, I tell you, there were many widows in Israel in the days of Elijah, when the heaven was shut up three years and six months, when there came a great famine over all the land; [26]and Elijah was sent to none of them but only to Zarephath, in the land of Sidon, to a woman who was a widow. [27]And there were many lepers in Israel in the time of the prophet Elisha; and none of them was cleansed, but only Naaman the Syrian." [28]When they heard this, all in the synagogue were filled with wrath. [29]And they rose up and put him out of the city, and led him to the brow of the hill on which their city was built that they might throw him down headlong. [30]But passing through the midst of them he went away.

At the outset of his ministry, Jesus experiences the rejection of his own townspeople of Nazareth. Luke tells us that the reports about Jesus' work in Galilee were favourable, but the message seems somewhat confused when it comes to Nazareth. Luke summarises Jesus' ministry in Nazareth by condensing into a single event a series of incidents which would have taken place over a period of time. We are introduced to a variety of reactions which people undergo when they are confronted with Jesus: enthusiasm and doubt, admiration and annoyance, wonder and small-mindedness. The mixed reaction is an accurate index of what is to come, and rejection is going to make predictable appearances in Jesus' calendar of experiences. In this first public event which Luke writes about, Jesus is almost executed. Luke seems to be telling us that Jesus' ministry almost did not get off the ground: the prophet was nearly put to death before he had time to prophesy.

The first of Jesus' sermons which Luke commits to writing forecasts Jesus' preferences: for the poor, for the captives, for the blind, for the oppressed. At the opening of his public ministry, Jesus is presented as the one who has clear, personal preferences for certain groups of people, groups of people who can place their hope in him, because in him the acceptable time of favour has come for all the forgotten people.

Some people are awed by his gracious words and concern, while others are more concerned about his pedigree and his address. The neighbours of Jesus were no different from any neighbours; Jesus, for all his mission to mankind, still had to handle local suspicion, gossip, behind-the-curtain omniscience, experts in character demolition, locals who could never believe that anything or anyone special could emerge without *their* spotting it first. Prophets are accepted provided that they come from backwoods somewhere else: there is nothing quite so unpromising as the local backwoods. Jesus does not seem to show any surprise at the response; he seems to anticipate it. But, it still has an affect on him. Mark underlines the affect in his Gospel when he writes of Nazareth: "he was not able to perform miracles there" (Mk 6: 5).

Jesus accepts that a prophet is not accepted in his own country. He is not free from local prejudice, he is not free from the normal, haphazard way that people look at other people and at events. People get tangled in his roots: they cannot see the tree for the roots. People complain that Jesus does not perform wonders locally while at the same time letting it be known that they do not believe in him anyway. Jesus tells the people that his mission is one which is addressed to all the peoples. But the locals become angry when Jesus does not share their small-mindedness, their meanness of vision; when he suggests that he is outside of their pettiness, and that he will have no part in it. Jesus makes it clear that he is not going to live down to their expectations of him.

Like many groups, the group from Nazareth wanted Jesus to be different in the same way that they were different. They wanted Jesus to share the same diseased outlook as themselves: as someone said, "sanity is a matter of having the same diseases as everyone else". But Jesus makes it clear that he is different, that he does not share their clannish idea of salvation, their mean image of God, their suspicious view of each other; that there is more to God than their expectations. Jesus may share their nervousness about local boys making good, but then that is because he has a reason to be nervous about the cost of making good.

When your local audience suddenly becomes a mob, then you have a reason to be nervous. Jesus' audience were at such a loss for words that they did what many mobs did before them: they tried the final solution: beat your opponent to death. But Jesus makes himself scarce so that he can continue to honour his speaking engagements for the morrow. Early on in his life, Jesus makes it his business to know when to run; to know when to escape. Jesus is not a programmed computer looking for an executioner: he is shy of threatening mobs who are intent on his death, and does not stay around when the company clearly wants to kill him. So, he lives to speak and pray another day.

Luke 4: 31-44   A Sabbath in Capernaum

³¹ And he went down to Capernaum, a city of Galilee. And he was teaching them on the sabbath; ³²and they were astonished at his teaching, for his word was with authority. ³³And in the synagogue there was a man who had the spirit of an unclean demon; and he cried out with a loud voice, ³⁴"Ah! What have you to do with us, Jesus of Nazareth? Have you come to destroy us? I know who you are, the Holy One of God." ³⁵But Jesus rebuked him, saying, "Be silent, and come out of him!" And when the demon had thrown him down in the midst, he came out of him, having done him no harm. ³⁶And they were all amazed and said to one another, "What is this word? For with authority and power he commands the unclean spirits, and they come out." ³⁷And reports of him went out into every place in the surrounding region.

³⁸ And he arose and left the synagogue, and entered Simon's house. Now Simon's mother-in-law was ill with a high fever, and they besought him for her. ³⁹And he stood over her and rebuked the fever, and it left her; and immediately she rose and served them.

⁴⁰ Now when the sun was setting, all those who had any that were sick with various diseases brought them to him; and he laid his hands on every one of them and healed them. ⁴¹And demons also came out of many, crying, "You are the Son of God!" But he rebuked them, and would not allow them to speak, because they knew that he was the Christ.

⁴² And when it was day he departed and went to a lonely place. And the people sought him and came to him, and would have kept him from leaving them; ⁴³but he said to them, "I must preach the good news of the kingdom of God to the other cities also; for I was sent for this purpose." ⁴⁴And he was preaching in the synagogues of Judea.

In contrast to the rejection which he experienced in his own town of Nazareth, Jesus now receives a favourable reception in Capernaum. Situated on the northern shore of the lake of Galilee, Capernaum was a busy trading town and the centre for the fishing industry of the region. It was a good place for a prophet to begin his ministry: there were plenty of people travelling to and from Capernaum who would carry the story of this prophet from Nazareth. Stories would be traded with the same energy as the goods, and no doubt the stories suffered the same mixed fate as the goods: over-priced, undervalued, mishandled, repackaged, exaggerated according to the credulity of the hearer, exchanged according to the capacity of the market. The story of Jesus was never free from the fluctuations of the market-place; and Jesus' own incarnation involved handling not only what people would do to his body, but what people would do to his name. And in the process of this sabbath day, Jesus' name will be recognized and acknowledged not by the people of Capernaum, but by the demons.

Luke gives us the first insight into Jesus' healing ministry: two individual cures which take place on the sabbath, and the curing of the sick and the infirm which takes place at sunset. The first recorded cure of Jesus is by way of a frontal attack on the kingdom of Satan, the kingdom which he has come to destroy. Unlike the devil's voice in the desert which tempted Jesus with the taunt: "If you are the Son of God. . ." (4: 3), the demon reveals his knowledge of who Jesus is. The enemy is in no doubt about the true identity of Jesus. If knowledge of someone's name gave one power over that person, perhaps this was a contest of power. The power of Satan and the power of Christ claim knowledge of the other. But there is no power-sharing; Jesus shows his supreme authority over the kingdom of darkness. Jesus speaks with authority which is immediately effective: where before there had been only torment, now there is peace. And the people are astonished. Luke mentions that they wondered; he does not tell us whether they believed.

Luke then takes us away from the crowds to the cottage of Peter's mother-in-law. Again, the focus is on the authoritative word of Jesus which releases the woman from her fever. When she is healed, Peter's mother-in-law rises and ministers to those present. This incident, which could have been witnessed only by a few, and would have been a memory cherished by Peter, presents us with Jesus as one who is not simply concerned with crowds or with the spectacular; he is moved to pay attention to the world of the particular, to the world of private agony and private hurt.

With the next scene, we are back outside again. The time is sunset, and those who observed the sabbath strictly would feel free now to bring the sick and the infirm to Jesus. Again, it is the demons who recognize Jesus, but Jesus does not want their fearful, reluctant recognition; he wants the free recognition of faith. That demons can accurately recognize and acknowledge Jesus is a warning that acknowledgement is not enough: the devils do as much. The people of Capernaum were moved to wonder at the marvellous works of Jesus; they were moved to seek him out. But later, Jesus is to condemn Capernaum as one of the towns which acknowledged the wonders, but where people were not disposed to believe in him (10: 15). If acknowledgement is not enough, neither is wonder; Jesus desires the faith of the people, a faith that is evident in the way they live their lives.

So, Jesus seeks solitude in a lonely place. The healer needs private space, and time to be by himself, away from the constant demands of the crowd. Throughout his ministry, Jesus escapes from the crowd to be alone, and to pray to his Father. His need for solitude, and his prayer to the Father are signs of his humanity: gods, by definition, do not seek solitude, nor do they need to pray. But the crowd seeks him out and petitions him to stay with them. They want to possess him and own him, they want Jesus to perform his miracles for them alone. Jesus declines the invitation to be a one-town wonder-worker, and tells the people that the kingdom of God is for others beyond the reach of Galilee. His is not a regional calling; it is a universal one. Jesus makes it clear at the outset of his ministry that he will not be cloistered or tabernacled for the exclusive benefit of any one community. So, he must tread other paths, where the natives will not be so keen to keep him in their midst; and he will learn that there is a particular price for the universal gospel which he preaches. And the price is himself.

Notes

[1]M. Muggeridge, *Jesus,* (New York: Harper and Row, 1975), p. 51

Chapter Five

Luke 5: 1-11   The Call of Simon Peter

5 While the people pressed upon him to hear the word of God, he was standing by the lake of Gennesaret. ²And he saw two boats by the lake; but the fisherman had gone out of them and were washing their nets. ³Getting into one of the boats, which was Simon's, he asked him to put out a little from the land. And he sat down and taught the people from the boat. ⁴And when he had ceased speaking, he said to Simon, "Put out into the deep and let down your nets for a catch." ⁵And Simon answered, "Master, we toiled all night and took nothing! But at your word I will let down the nets." ⁶And when they had done this, they enclosed a great shoal of fish; and as their nets were breaking, ⁷they beckoned to their partners in the other boat to come and help them. And they came and filled both the boats, so that they began to sink. ⁸But when Simon Peter saw it, he fell down at Jesus' knees, saying, "Depart from me, for I am a sinful man, O Lord." ⁹For he was astonished, and all that were with him, at the catch of fish which they had taken; ¹⁰and so also were James and John, sons of Zebedee, who were partners with Simon. And Jesus said to Simon, "Do not be afraid; henceforth you will be catching men." ¹¹And when they had brought their boats to land, they left everything and followed him.

THE EAGER FOLLOWERS OF JESUS crowd him out of their company so that he takes refuge on a boat, courtesy of Simon. Jesus addresses the crowd, but we are not told what he says. The crowd fades out of the scene, and the spotlight moves to Simon Peter. Simon is instructed to put out into the deep to catch fish. Simon feels obliged to make the practical observation that they worked at that all night only to come up with zero, but he defers to the authoritative word of Jesus. Simon addresses Jesus as Master, *Epistata,* a title which Luke employs only when he is

70

speaking of a disciple who submits in obedience to the power of Jesus.

So, they go out again into the deep and they do not come up with zero; the nets are bursting, and they have to commandeer the help of their companions to bring in the catch. Simon's reaction to Jesus is interesting. In contrast to the people of Capernaum who wanted Jesus to stay in their midst and work wonders for them, Simon does not invite Jesus to stay around and boost the fishing trade: he asks Jesus to go away, to keep the company of sinful men no more. Simon's instinct is not to manipulate the power of Jesus for his own advantage; rather, his instinct is to create distance between sinfulness and holiness, between wrongdoing and goodness.

Happily, Jesus does not take Simon's advice; he does not accept the outlook that the governing rubric between sinner and Master should be distance. For the sinner to argue that God should keep his distance might not be so much a posture of humility as a ploy to keep the challenge of goodness at bay. Goodness is less of a challenge when it lodges in someone else's house. Jesus does not accept the argument that a person's inadequacy and unworthiness are barriers to keep God out; rather, it is for sinners that Christ has come in the first place. Sinfulness is not a barrier to keep God out; it expresses a real need for God to come in. Simon Peter is the first person in the Gospel to openly acknowledge his sinfulness; he is also the first disciple to be called.

So, the good news is that Jesus does not get nervous at Simon Peter's admission of sinfulness. Simon thought that Jesus should steer clear of the likes of him, but the truth is that if sinfulness were a diriment impediment for being in Jesus' company, then Jesus would be very lonely indeed. Simon Peter focuses on his past performance as a sinner, he focuses on the shadowland of his own weaknesses; Jesus, in contrast, focuses on Peter's future as a disciple and leader, on his ability to become a fisher of men.

The image of God which Jesus presents in this exchange

is the image of a God who can handle sinners, who does not mark sinners as high security-risks to be avoided like a plague; rather, he is a God who gives people a new start. Jesus takes Simon away from prostration and breast-beating and preoccupation with sinfulness to give Peter an image of himself as a leader of men who will bring people into the presence of God. Jesus underlines Simon Peter's worth; he does not join Simon's conspiracy to knock Peter to such an extent that neither is capable of doing anything. Simon acknowledges his sinfulness: that is enough: God can handle the rest. Jesus moves the conversation on; he moves Peter on; he gives Peter a generous image of a discipleship which does not entail powerless immobility, but a discipleship which invites Simon Peter to imagine himself and God more generously. So, Peter stops feeling all at sea, and begins a ministry in which he is the fisher of men, in which he is challenged to draw out the worth in other people that Jesus drew out from him.

Luke 5: 12-16   *Jesus and the Untouchable*

> ¹² While he was in one of the cities, there came a man full of leprosy; and when he saw Jesus, he fell on his face and besought him, "Lord, if you will, you can make me clean." ¹³And he stretched out his hand, and touched him, saying, "I will; be clean." And immediately the leprosy left him. ¹⁴And he charged him to tell no one; but "go and show yourself to the priest, and make an offering for your cleansing, as Moses commanded, for a proof to the people." ¹⁵But so much the more the report went abroad concerning him; and great multitudes gathered to hear and to be healed of their infirmities. ¹⁶But he withdrew to the wilderness and prayed.

Jesus' reputation as a healer has spread, and now people seek him out to minister to them. A leper comes to Jesus to ask him to heal the uncleanness of leprosy. The leper was regarded as an outcast; his uncleanness put him beyond the boundaries of social and cultic acceptance. Leprosy itself covered a wide variety of infectious skin diseases, and the treatment for the leper is prescribed in Leviticus 13-14. The leper is to wear torn clothes and leave his hair unkempt; he has to cry "Unclean" when he approaches anyone. He is to live alone in a dwelling which is at a safe distance from the rest of the community. In effect, the leper experienced total isolation from the rest of humanity; he dwelt in the kingdom of the lost and the forgotten, and his psychological isolation must have been at least as numbing as his physical ailment.

When Simon Peter was confronted with the power of Christ, he argued that there should be a distance between sinfulness and goodness; the tradition of the Torah argued that there should be a distance between cleanness and uncleanness. But as Jesus ignored Simon's argument, so he ignores the tradition of the law, and he bridges the gap between cleanness and uncleanness. One of the titles which he has received is Saviour, *Sōtēr,* and the chief task of the Saviour is to save, *sōzō,* which also means to heal, to make whole. Jesus' healing ministry is a sign of the messianic age (Luke 7: 22); it is a sign that the Saviour is at work in the midst of men.

The leper puts the matter delicately, pointing out to Jesus that he can cure him if he wants to. The leper focuses on his own uncleanness, on that which keeps him away from the life and worship of the community. And Jesus' reaction is a generous one: he does not harangue the leper; he does not tell him that sickness is from God and should be accepted: Jesus gives an unambiguous yes in answer to the leper's plea for healing. Jesus' human concern is clear; even though he was breaking the law by coming into contact with uncleanness, an act which would, according to the law, defile him too, Jesus reaches out and touches the leper. Jesus is not afraid that he will catch the contagious disease; he is concerned that the leper will catch his contagious healing and be cured. The power of healing is more contagious than the power of disease.

Jesus then observes the Mosaic Law, which shows his continued concern for the future acceptance of the leper into the community. In the Israelite tradition, there was such a close connection between sin and sickness, that the priest was regarded as the medical officer who judged sickness, and who gave people a clean bill of health. So, the healing of the leper must be attested by the priest so that the priest can officially proclaim the leper clean, and offer sacrifice. Jesus honours this tradition, so that the leper can make his formal re-entry into the community.

So, Jesus again seeks the solitude of the wilderness to pray to his Father. He has just cured the leper, the one from whom people turned away in disgust. Jesus would soon have the experience of the leper; he would soon validate the prophecy of Isaiah, when, as Suffering Servant, he himself would be the one afflicted with a marred appearance, without comeliness and without beauty, the one from whom men would hide their faces because they esteemed him not. Christ would know the experience of isolation and dejection of the outcast. But, for the moment, the crowd do not hide from him; they seek him out. And as the people seek after Jesus, he seeks after his Father, so that he can be immersed in the power which makes healing and the future possible.

Luke 5: 17-26   Forgiveness and Healing

[17] On one of those days, as he was teaching, there were Pharisees and teachers of the law sitting by, who had come from every village of Galilee and Judea and from Jerusalem; and the power of the Lord was with him to heal. [18]And behold, men were bringing on a bed a man who was paralyzed, and they sought to bring him in and lay him before Jesus; [19]but finding no way to bring him in, because of the crowd, they went up on the roof and let him down with his bed through the tiles into the midst before Jesus. [20]And when he saw their faith he said, "Man, your sins are forgiven you." [21]And the scribes and the Pharisees began to question, saying, "Who is this that speaks blasphemies? Who can forgive sins but God only?" [22]When Jesus perceived their questionings, he answered them, "Why do you question in your

hearts? [23]Which is easier, to say, 'Your sins are forgive you', or to say, 'Rise and walk'? [24]But that you may know that the Son of man has authority on earth to forgive sins"—he said to the man who was paralyzed—"I say to you, rise, take up your bed and go home." [25]And immediately he rose before them, and took up that on which he lay, and went home, glorifying God. [26]And amazement seized them all, and they glorifed God and were filled with awe, saying, "We have seen strange things today."

When confronted with the goodness of Jesus, Simon Peter had asked Jesus to keep his distance; when the leper came to Jesus, the law required Jesus to keep his distance in case of defilement; now the Pharisees appear in the Gospel for the first time, the ones whose name means "separated ones", the experts in the art of distancing themselves from other people. Jesus has already shown that he has not come close to man in order to be distant from him, that he has not come to separate himself from the sinner or the outcast; so, it is only to be expected that he will be taken to task by the separated ones, by those who focus all their energy in external behaviour in order to stay clean and within the bounds of the law.

Luke underlines the presence of the Pharisees and the teachers of the law, and he has legions of them come in from the surrounding areas. The opposition is heightening. They are a hostile audience, a factor which could adversely affect any teacher; but Luke tells us that the power of the Lord was with Jesus, a power which could overcome opposition and antipathy.

The paralytic makes his unusual entrance onto the scene, courtesy of his friends. The paralytic is a man of utter helplessness who depends entirely on his friends to bring him before Jesus, and he is not disappointed in his friends' ingenuity and faith. Interestingly, Jesus performs the miracle because of the faith of the paralytic's *friends;* their faith is sufficient. Jesus first forgives. It was an old rabbinic teaching that no healing could take place unless the sins of the person were forgiven. Jesus' forgiveness is evidence of his concern to heal the whole man, to offer spiritual healing as well as physical healing. Jesus offers the inner healing of the forgiveness of sins, and suggests that that is more difficult than physical healing, which is demonstrative proof of power.

The Pharisees are quick to charge Jesus with blasphemy, arguing that only God can forgive sins, a charge that will be recalled at Jesus' trial. Jesus shows them that he has power as the Son of Man to forgive sins, and gives them the sign of the physical healing. The physical healing of the paralytic is not merely to make a point: Jesus does not use the pain of people as convenient debating points; throughout the Gospel, he is moved by people who are bound in sin or bound in pain to release them from the bondage. Jesus knew that miracles do not bring belief; they sustain an already existing belief. Miracles did not persuade the Pharisees; miracles made them uncomfortable. They did not understand the miracles because they did not believe in Christ. Blake put the point well when he wrote: "Truth can never be told so as to be understood, and not be believed."

Jesus makes it clear in this teaching that forgiveness and healing are not realities which are true only because they are postponed to the after-life; they are here in the present as signs of God's saving activity. We are invited to live not *as if* forgiveness and healing were present among us, but *because* they are present here and now. Again, the image of God which Jesus is communicating is the image of a generous God who wants people to relate to him *now* in terms of healing and forgiveness. Jesus speaks to the people of a God who is moved by human pain and human alienation to do something: forgiveness is a response to sin, healing is a response to sickness: those are not mean responses, or reluctant gestures, but the munificent gifts of a loving God. And that is good news.

Luke 5: 27-32   *Feasting with Outsiders*

[27]After this he went out, and saw a tax collector, named Levi, sitting at the tax office; and he said to him, "Follow

me." ²⁸And he left everything, and rose and followed him.
   ²⁹And Levi made him a great feast in his house; and there
was a large company of tax collectors and others sitting at
table with them. ³⁰And the Pharisees and their scribes murmured against his disciples, saying, "Why do you eat and
drink with tax collectors and sinners?" ³¹And Jesus
answered them, "Those who are well have no need of a physician, but those who are sick; ³²I have not come to call the
righteous, but sinners to repentance."

Jesus continues to make it clear that he has come to
minister to the outsiders, the tax-collectors, sinners, all
those who find themselves beyond the boundary of social
or religious approval. Regarded with undisguised disdain
by their employers and their countrymen, the tax-
collectors were seen as collaborators with the occupying
power, ritually unclean because they mixed with Gentiles,
and totally untrustworthy because of their occupation.
Barred from the synagogue, they were professional outsiders, classed alongside murderers and prostitutes. It is all
the more surprising that the prophet from Nazareth not
only speaks with them, but calls one of them, Levi, to be
his disciple. Jesus' action is at total variance with the accepted practice of the day.
   The Pharisees are at the other end of the social scale
from the tax-collectors: they are the insiders, who live safe
within the precincts of the law. The Pharisees would not
even let their garments touch a tax-collector for fear of
defilement, much less volunteer to have a meal with them.
The Pharisees are therefore shocked when Jesus shares the
most social of all events, the meal, with the tax-collectors.
In their own concern to avoid defilement, the Pharisees
were not worried about the sick, but about themselves in
case they would be infected. So, the Pharisees treated the
tax-collectors and that ilk as people in a large isolation
ward, separated from the rest of healthy Jewry; an isolation ward, which no doctor would visit lest he would catch
the disease.
   The image which Jesus will often use of the kingdom of
God is the image of a banquet, not the image of the isola-

tion ward. Jesus often uses the image of the banquet, an absolutely divine party where all the broken, and the sick and the wounded would come to be fed, as a lively image of God's kingdom. All the people who attend have to do is admit that they are hungry, that they need nourishment. Jesus in his turn accepts the invitation to Levi's banquet; he does not get nervous at the business of the host; he does not check out the guest list before he commits himself; he accepts graciously, and meets Levi's friends. Levi, in his turn, accepts the invitation of Jesus to attend the banquet of the Lord.

Jesus speaks of himself in the image of the physician who has come to heal the sick. Sin is seen in terms of a sickness which can be cured. Jesus makes the point that the physician's primary concern is not whether he will catch the patient's illness, but whether the patient will catch the cure. Jesus says ironically that he has not come to call the righteous: the righteous are incapable of being called because they refuse the diagnosis that they are sick. And as Nerissa said in *The Merchant of Venice,* "they are sick that surfeit with too much as they that starve with nothing." Ultimately, it is the righteous who inhabit the isolation ward and lock out the help of the healer. And they call their isolation ward 'reality'.

Luke 5: 33-39   *Reason to Rejoice*

[33]And they said to him, "The disciples of John fast often and offer prayers, and so do the disciples of the Pharisees, but yours eat and drink." [34]And Jesus said to them, "Can you make wedding guests fast while the bridegroom is with them? [35]The days will come, when the bridegroom is taken away from them, and then they will fast in those days." [36]He told them a parable also: "No one tears a piece from a new garment and puts it upon an old garment; if he does, he will tear the new, and the piece from the new will not match the old. [37]And no one puts new wine into the old wineskins; if he does, the new wine will burst the skins and it will be spilled, and the skins will be destroyed. [38]But new wine must be put

into fresh wineskins. ³⁹And no one after drinking old wine desires new; for he says, 'The old is good.'"

Some people's response to parties and banquets is a cocktail of glumness and meanness, with a dash of jealousy thrown in for good measure. Some people get nervous when they see other people enjoying themselves; they look at their watches and wonder when it is all going to end; they wait until dreariness and dullness again possess the atmosphere; they wonder why everyone cannot be as dull and normal as they are. The disciples of the Pharisees wondered a peculiar wonder: why Jesus' disciples were enjoying themselves in their master's company, why they were not fasting as good disciples should. After all, the Pharisees fasted twice a week. Why did Jesus' disciples not share the same difference?

Jesus responds to this mean talk with the image of a wedding feast. In Palestine, the wedding celebrations lasted a week, and the guests were exempted from observing any fasts during the time of celebration. At a wedding, fasting would not only be an odd attitude, it would be rude to the hosts and the other guests. Fasting would exclude one from table-fellowship, from sharing completely in the joy and festivity of the occasion. Jesus argued that the time of his presence could be compared to a wedding feast, and he had no intention of having his disciples kill the party atmosphere by organizing fasts. A reign of joy, not a reign of penance, is the description of the messianic age.

With the coming of Christ, the old way has passed away: now is the time for new wine, for new vitality, for new rejoicing. The new wine needs new skins in which to ferment; the new kingdom needs a new atmosphere in which to grow—and the image which Jesus uses to describe that atmosphere is the image of the wedding feast. And that is a time when even old enemies learn that they have something to be joyful about together; when the in-laws can discover each other as unhorned beings; when the focus of attention is on union, not division; when kill-joys are asked to make a quiet exit and come back when they are disposed to share in the celebrations.

Is that a dream? Is is the haunted image of Caliban?

> The isle is full of noises
> Sounds, and sweet airs, that give delight, and hurt not.
> Sometimes a thousand twangling instruments
> Will hum about mine ears; and sometimes voices.
> That, if I then had wak'd after long sleep,
> Will make me sleep again; and then, in dreaming.
> The clouds methought would open and show riches
> Ready to drop upon me, that, when I wak'd,
> I cried to dream again.
>
> (The Tempest, III, ii, 132-139)

When the dream is true, one should rejoice in the truth, in the wedding feast. After all, the time will come for the nightmare, when the bridegroom will be hauled away to keep his appointment with the executioners. But, the moment is not yet. Rejoicing is the order of the day. Sadness is to be put aside with the old patches. The feast is still on.

Chapter Six

Luke 6: 1-11   Conflict on the Sabbath

6 On a sabbath, while he was going through the grain-fields, his disciples plucked and ate some ears of grain, rubbing them in their hands. ²But some of the Pharisees said, "Why are you doing what is not lawful to do on the sabbath?" ³And Jesus answered, "Have you not read what David did when he was hungry, he and those who were with him: ⁴how he entered the house of God, and took and ate the bread of the Presence, which it is not lawful for any but the priests to eat, and also gave it to those with him?" ⁵And he said to them, "The Son of man is lord of the sabbath."

⁶On another sabbath, when he entered the synagogue and taught, a man was there whose right hand was withered. ⁷And the scribes and the Pharisees watched him, to see whether he would heal on the sabbath, so that they might find an accusation against him. ⁸But he knew their thoughts, and he said to the man who had the withered hand, "Come and stand here," And he rose and stood there. ⁹And Jesus said to them, "I ask you, is it lawful on the sabbath to do good or to do harm, to save life or to destroy it?" ¹⁰And he looked around on them all, and said to him, "Stretch out your hand." And he did so, and his hand was restored. ¹¹But they were filled with fury and discussed with one another what they might do to Jesus.

IN JUDAISM, the sabbath of solemn rest was regarded as a day when all Jews would abstain from any kind of work. It was a day which was hallowed by God, a day of rest during which people could regain their strength, and call to mind the greatness and fidelity of God. The purpose of the sabbath observance was positive: it was a release to benefit the people, not a device to trap them if they made the wrong move. But the danger was that the purpose of the sabbath was lost under the weight of rigid prohibitions which the interpreters put on it. Among the thirty-nine types of prohibited work were reaping, threshing and preparing food, all of which the disciples transgressed on their way through the cornfields. Visiting the sick, clapping of hands, healing unless it was to save life, also made up the peculiar list of prohibitions.

The Pharisees appear on the scene to object to what the disciples are doing, and Jesus takes up their cause himself. He quotes the incident where David and his followers ate bread which was reserved for the priests: when David's need was in conflict with the letter of the law, the need was upheld rather than the law (1 Sam 21: 1 ff.). And there is a greater than David here. Christ focuses the attention on human need rather than observance of the interpretations of the law; and when people remember the law, but forget what the law is for, then they abuse the whole purpose of the law, which is for the good of the people. No regulation should override the fundamental purpose of the law, and when the law becomes the master to be served slavishly, rather than a servant to be employed wisely, then it negates itself. It becomes a god which demands sacrifice, and the sacrifice is usually human.

Jesus further clarifies his position when he takes the initiative and heals the man with the withered hand on the sabbath. Again the law is subservient to the real need of an individual. Jesus puts the case clearly when he asks whether the sabbath, which honours the work of God, is a day for saving life or destroying it. And the implication is that to refuse to save life is to destroy it. The argument is that when confronted with pain, we cannot take refuge in the thicket of the law to prove our innocence: if we do, it will be our so-called innocence which will constitute the crime. The law can never liberate anyone from the responsibility of human concern—not even for a day. Christ does not wait to heal the man on the morrow; he gives the man rest from his suffering on the day of rest. There is no forbidden time where helping is concerned. The only time for helping is now: tomorrow is always too late. And if the law justifies the wait, then the law itself is sick and in need of healing.

Jesus knew well that the law could be used as a weapon as well as a shield, and that when it is used as a weapon it is nearly always the poor and the broken and the hurt who are the casualties and the targets. And Jesus knew that the Pharisees were using the law as a weapon against him. While Jesus was concerned with healing the sick man, an action which was forbidden by the law, the Pharisees were busy plotting against Jesus. It is a strange law which outlaws healing and countenances plotting. It is a strange mind which cannot see the sadness of a tortuous position which prevents one man from healing, while allowing others to plot the healer's demise. In that case, there is no defence counsel which can protect that law: the law has condemned itself. And it is Jesus, not the law, who heals the man with the withered hand. The case against Jesus is dismissed, but the case against the law continues to be heard.

Luke 6: 12-19   *Choosing the Twelve*

¹²In these days he went out to the mountain to pray; and all night he continued in prayer to God. ¹³And when it was day, he called his disciples, and chose from them twelve, whom he named apostles; ¹⁴Simon, whom he named Peter, and Andrew his brother, and James and John, and Philip, and Bartholomew, ¹⁵and Matthew, and Thomas, and James the son of Alphaeus, and Simon who was called the Zealot, ¹⁶and Judas the son of James, and Judas Iscariot, who became a traitor.

¹⁷And he came down with them and stood on a level place, with a great crowd of his disciples and a great multitude of people from all Judea and Jerusalem and the seacoast of Tyre and Sidon, who came to hear him and to be healed of their diseases; ¹⁸and those who were troubled with unclean spirits were cured. ¹⁹And all the crowd sought to touch him, for power came forth from him and healed them all.

After Jesus' baptism, and before he was anointed by the Holy Spirit, Luke records that Jesus prayed. Before he began his public life, before he did any public speaking at all, Jesus prayed to his Father. Now, before Jesus chooses his twelve followers he again goes into seclusion and prays. The choosing of the twelve is a turning-point in Christ's life, it is the beginning of his own community who will involve themselves in the same work as himself. So, Jesus does an all-night vigil far away from the crowds. He goes up a mountain to be alone with his Father, to pray about his decision which will affect the whole future of his church.

Only when the night has gone, does Jesus choose twelve men from the group of his disciples. Disciple means 'pupil' and Jesus had an unknown number of them. But out of their general number, he selects twelve as apostles. Jesus himself is the first *apostolos*, the one who is sent. Jesus is sent on a mission by his Father, and now, in his turn, he chooses those who are to be sent, who are to be authorized to act in his name, who are to represent him and what he stands for to the world. And as the old Israel was formed of twelve tribes, the new Israel will be led by twelve apostles who "will sit on thrones judging the twelve tribes of Israel" (Luke 22: 30).

The twelve men whom Jesus chooses are spectacularly unspectacular choices to help him spread his kingdom, and his selection speaks of his wisdom of the contrary. Luke supplies us with no potted biographies, no character profiles, no journalistic insights into their background: just a list of names, a few of whom we shall meet again, most of whom will remain all but nameless. But we know that they did not emerge from the ranks of the powerful and the influential; they were men who had no easy access to power, no ready platform for influencing the minds of their own people. They were men who would have to work through their own prayer, their tentative discernments, their cluttered outlooks, their favourite memories and stories, their various disagreements, their lopsided resolve, their special talents, to spread the good news of the kingdom. Jesus never denied them that process; it was the only way his kingdom could be established. It was all part of the incarnation: the risk of becoming flesh.

After his prayerful choice, Jesus comes down with them and stands "on a level place". The choice has been made and the work starts on the level, with everyone's feet firmly on the ground. No rarefied atmosphere, no apostolic seclusion, no educational enclosure on the mountain top: the geography of the ground floor, where the crowds crowd, where the action is, and where the main business is to be done. And the very first action the apostles witness is Christ using his power to heal, to deliver people from bondage, to free them from their mobile prisons. And the challenge remains for any apostle who is still to be found on the level ground.

Luke 6: 20-26   Sermon on the Level

> [20]And he lifted up his eyes on his disciples, and said: "Blessed are you poor, for yours is the kingdom of God.
>
> [21]"Blessed are you that hunger now, for you shall be satisfied.
>
> "Blessed are you that weep now, for you shall laugh.
>
> [22]"Blessed are you when men hate you, and when they exclude you and revile you, and cast out your name as evil, on accont of the Son of man! [23]Rejoice in that day, and leap for joy, for behold, your reward is great in heaven; for so their fathers did to the prophets.
>
> [24]"But woe to you that are rich, for you have received your consolation.
>
> [25]"Woe to you that are full now, for you shall hunger.
>
> "Woe to you that laugh now, for you shall mourn and weep.
>
> [26]"Woe to you, when all men speak well of you, for so their fathers did to the false prophets.

Like Moses who descended the mountain to deliver God's word to the people (Ex 32: 15), Jesus comes down the mountain where he chose his apostles to speak his word. He has ministered to the people on level ground so that the sick can be brought to him. Now, in the presence

of the crowds, he addresses his disciples. He speaks the
four beatitudes and the four woes. He directs his words to
his disciples: "Blessed are you". Each beatitude is balanced
with a woe:

Blessed are you	*Woe to you*
who are poor	who are rich
who are hungry	who are full
who weep	who laugh
who are reviled	who are lauded

The sermon has clear parallels with Matthew's more
elaborate presentation in the Sermon on the Mount which
takes up three chapters, 5-7.[1] In the sermon, Jesus tells the
poor and the hungry, the mournful and the reviled, that
the kingdom of God is for such as they. In the old
economy, it was the *anawim Yahweh,* the quiet of the land,
the afflicted ones, who inherited the promise of the Lord.
And so the tradition continues. The poor and the hungry,
the hurt and the afflicted, these are the ones who have the
first invitations to come into the kingdom of God. Jesus
later speaks of the kingdom in terms of a magnificent banquet, where the guest list is composed of a human pano-
rama of rejects. The banquet is for the forgotten people,
the ones who are the most precious in the eyes of God.
    In the upside-down kingdom of Jesus, which has more
affinity with the world of the fairy tale than the world of
conventional wisdom, it is the eldest son, the one who is
the summary of self-assurance, the one who has everything
going for him, the one who inherits the earth's goods, who
is rich and highly regarded, who ends up with empty
hands. It is the youngest son, the one who is a summary of
weakness, the one with the least going for him, who does
not automatically inherit the world's goods, the one who
has to rely on the most unlikely sources for help, who eventually inherits the kingdom. In the Gospel and in the fairy
tale, it is the reject, the forgotten one, the despised one,

who eventually finds rest, like the poor Lazarus, in the bosom of Abraham to live happily ever after. It is what Tolkien called *eucatastrophe,* which does not deny sorrow, but denies sorrow to have the last word.

In that sermon, Jesus does not give a blanket support to poverty, hunger, weeping and hurt: these are not lovely states to be acquired, and only a masochist or a tortuous theologian would argue otherwise. As Archbishop Helder Camara said: saints may be found in slums, but one cannot retain slums in order to make them the breeding ground of saints. Destitute poverty is not a condition to be achieved; it is a condition to be avoided; but, it still remains true that Jesus' preference for the poor had a social basis. And the one thing that Jesus does need is space to work in: an acknowledgement that our needs are always beyond our capacities, that our needs can only be ultimately answered by God alone.

The best commentary on the sermon is Jesus' own life. Jesus did not live his life *as if* he were blessed by God; he lived in the knowledge that his life was indeed blessed by God. And he experienced poverty: the poverty of standing alone against the crowds, the poverty of human circumstance, the poverty of total reliance on his own Father. He experienced hunger, not just the hunger that has to be answered by bread, but the hunger that has to be answered by doing what you know to be right. He experienced mourning at the death of his friend and in his profound experience of abandonment by his Father and his disciples. He was no stranger to being held up as a clown for the amusement of all; he knew the experience of rejection and betrayal, coming very close at hand. But all this was experienced in the name of his mission: it was not "adopted" as some precious theological posture; it was the *outcome* of a specific life lived in the knowledge and in the enthusiasm of God.

The beatitudes are not prescriptions for getting poor or hungry or mournful or afflicted. They are addressed to those who are already involved in committing themselves to Christ, and they give instances of what happens when the kingdom of God arrives in this broken world. They speak of a variety of experiences that people go through as a *result* of getting involved with God's way of doing things, with the promise that God can handle the poverty, the hunger, the tears, the rejection. And the promise is that God handles all these things, lifting his disciples out of them—and that is good news indeed. God is not committed to keeping his disciples at the level of getting stung—if that were true the beatitudes would read: "Blessed are you who weep now, for you shall weep even more." But the promise is of uplift, not of putdown.

The vision of God presented in the beatitudes is the vision of a generous God. He is a God who is aware of the tragedy, but who eventually reverses the tragedy into comedy. "Blessed are you who mourn" is the tragedy; "for you shall laugh" is the comedy. And it is the comedy which is the promise, not the tragedy.

Luke 6: 27-38   *Love and Mercy*

[27]"But I say to you that hear, Love your enemies, do good to those who hate you, [28]bless those who curse you, pray for those who abuse you. [29]To him who strikes you on the cheek, offer the other also; and from him who takes away your coat do not withhold even your shirt. [30]Give to every one who begs from you; and of him who takes away your goods do not ask them again. [31]And as you wish that men would do to you, do so to them.

[32]"If you love those who love you, what credit is that to you? For even sinners love those who love them. [33]And if you do good to those who do good to you, what credit is that to you? For even sinners do the same. [34]And if you lend to those from whom you hope to receive, what credit is that to you? Even sinners lend to sinners, to receive as much again. [35]But love your enemies, and do good, and lend, expecting nothing in return; and your reward will be great, and you will be sons of the Most High; for he is kind to the ungrateful and the selfish. [36]Be merciful, even as your Father is merciful.

[37]"Judge not, and you will not be judged; condemn not,

and you will not be condemned; forgive, and you will be forgiven; [38]give, and it will be given to you; good measure, pressed down, shaken together, running over, will be put into your lap. For the measure you give will be the measure you get back.''

Jesus now gives his vision of human action, a vision which is characterized by its magnanimity, and is contrasted with the minimalistic outlook of accepted wisdom. As vision, it is unqualified by any exception or mitigating circumstances; it is awesome in its appeal for generosity of spirit. Jesus' vision of human behaviour seems at such variance with the view that most people have of human behaviour that many people regard it as humanly unachievable, and, therefore, ignore it. The vision is unachievable from a purely human point of view; the ethic is divine, and it requires divine help. It invites people to be as generous in their attitude to others as God is to them. But if people have a mean attitude to God, then it is no surprise when they discover they have a mean attitude to everyone else.

Jesus gives the disciples the basic imperative of the kingdom: they are enjoined to love their enemies and do good to those who hate them; and they will have plenty of opportunity to try that in the near future. They are asked to step further than the demands that people make on them. And we wonder whether it is all impossible, until we hear the echo of Thomas More's words which he spoke to the judges who condemned him:

I verily trust and shall therefore right heartily pray, that though your lordships have now here on earth been judges to my condemnation, we may hereafter in heaven merrily all meet together, to our everlasting salvation.

That is the most exquisite exegesis of the text on forgiving and praying for one's enemies. When the condemned man can pray for his judges, then nothing in this world can harm him.

The image of God which Luke presents us with in this passage is the image of a God who is kind to the ungrateful and the selfish, a God who does not cap human meanness with divine meanness. And Jesus in his own life had to work hard at honouring his ethic: not hoarding insults, returning forgiveness for wrongdoing, answering the mounting demands that people make of him. And that process was not a bloodless or a painless affair: it cost Jesus everything; he had to live up to the generosity of spirit which he required in others. He offered love first, even though he knew that the return would never measure up to what was offered; he never bargained love for love; he never became involved in stock-taking returns. His life argued that love is the only real social contact without which no other contract can stand at all.

And Jesus expects that those who have received his gifts will share them. Love is given because somebody somewhere is dying for the lack of a kind word; mercy is given because somebody somewhere is cloistered in his own wrong-doing; blessings are given because somebody somewhere is bound by his own curses. These are gifts which create worth in another person; they build temples in swampland; they introduce people to the forgotten geography of paradise. Blake put the point well when he wrote in *The Clod and the Pebble:*

> Love seeketh not Itself to please
> nor for itself hath any care,
> But for another gives its ease,
> And builds a Heaven in Hell's despair.

Luke 6: 39-49   *On Discipleship*

[39]He also told them a parable: "Can a blind man lead a blind man? Will they not both fall into a pit? [40]A disciple is not above his teacher, but every one when he is fully taught will be like his teacher. [41]Why do you see the speck that is in your brother's eye, but do not notice the log that is in your

own eye? [42]Or how can you say to your brother, 'Brother, let me take out the speck that is in your eye,' when you yourself do not see the log that is in your own eye? You hypocrite, first take the log out of your own eye, and then you will see clearly to take out the speck that is in your brother's eye.

[43]"For no good tree bears bad fruit, nor again does a bad tree bear good fruit; [44]for each tree is known by its own fruit. For figs are not gathered from thorns, nor are grapes picked from a bramble bush. [45]The good man out of the good treasure of his heart produces good, and the evil man out of his evil treasure produces evil; for out of the abundance of the heart his mouth speaks.

[46]"Why do you call me 'Lord, Lord,' and not do what I tell you? [47]Every one who comes to me and hears my words and does them, I will show you what he is like: [48]he is like a man building a house, who dug deep, and laid the foundation upon rock; and when a flood arose, the stream broke against that house, and could not shake it, because it had been well built. [49]But he who hears and does not do them is like a man who built a house on the ground without a foundation; against which the stream broke, and immediately it fell, and the ruin of that house was great."

In this passage, Luke presents us with a list of Jesus' sayings on discipleship. If the disciple is to be a good teacher, he must first of all be a good learner: he must firstly listen and attend to the word of his teacher. And in days when there were no books easily available for reference, all the knowledge came through the teacher. A disciple would choose his teacher carefully, because his future as a teacher would be dependent on his own choice of teacher. Jesus stresses that it is not only important for the disciple to know the way: he must do the way, he must enact the truth of his own teaching, otherwise his integrity as a teacher is in question. The disciple must experience his own conversion first, he must undergo an inward change before he exacts the same process of others. If the disciple is ignorant of *doing* good, then he is no longer worthy of the title.

Jesus places the argument of good discipleship and bad discipleship with the results that they bear. The good disciple bears good fruit, and his goodness will be evident in his ministry to others. This is a clear sign for those who are being ministered to: if the disciple's ministry does not bear fruit in their lives, if they do not experience the power and the effectiveness of his prayer and work, then the disciple's authenticity is up for question. In Jesus' own ministry, people were evidently better for having contact with him: people were healed, they were delivered from a variety of bondage, they experienced forgiveness, they experienced release from past burdens; and all these experiences were not imaginary, they were real and effective. So, with the true disciple: people do not have to guess at his authenticity, the test is in the fruit it bears.

Jesus tells his hearers the parable of the two houses. As any builder knows, a house is as strong as the foundation on which it is built. You can have a beautiful modern house which has won all the architectural prizes this side of eternity, but one which has a weak foundation. And when the rains come and beat on the house, when the waters rise, the building's beauty will not save it: it will collapse. You can have another house which is an architectural monstrosity, but which can withstand any onslaught because it is built on firm rock. The same is true of discipleship: it is as strong as the foundation on which it is built.

The disciple who only hears the word of God and does nothing about what he hears invites disaster: his discipleship will collapse when heavy weather comes. The disciple who hears the word of God and does it is able to handle the heavy weather that comes his way. And, of course, the rains will come, and the winds of fortune and misfortune will blow, and uninvited storms will inevitably come. Every disciple has to face the winter of his discipleship, and whether his discipleship lasts until the spring depends on his close relationship with God. The spring always has its revenge on the winter in the cycle of the seasons, but the winter still comes, and sometimes it is very long indeed.

Notes

[1]For a detailed study of comparison, cf. W. D. Davies, *The Setting of the Sermon on the Mount,* (Cambridge, 1964).

Chapter Seven

Luke 7: 1-10   *The Faithful Centurion*

7 After he had ended all his sayings in the hearing of the people he entered Capernaum. ²Now a centurion had a slave who was dear to him, who was sick and at the point of death. ³When he heard of Jesus, he sent to him elders of the Jews, asking him to come and heal his slave. ⁴And when they came to Jesus, they besought him earnestly, saying, "He is worthy to have you do this for him, ⁵for he loves our nation, and he built us our synagogue." ⁶And Jesus went with them. When he was not far from the house, the centurion sent friends to him, saying to him, "Lord, do not trouble yourself, for I am not worthy to have you come under my roof; ⁷therefore I did not presume to come to you. But say the word, and let my servant be healed. ⁸For I am a man set under authority, with soldiers under me: and I say to one, 'Go,' and he goes; and to another, 'Come,' and he comes; and to my slave, 'Do this,' and he does it." ⁹When Jesus heard this he marveled at him, and turned and said to the multitude that followed him, "I tell you, not even in Israel have I found such faith." ¹⁰And when those who had been sent returned to the house, they found the slave well.

LUKE ADDRESSED HIS GOSPEL TO THE GENTILES, to those who were not Jews. Although Jesus had very little contact with Gentiles, Luke records the incident between Jesus and the Gentile centurion during which Jesus lavishes praise on a man who is held up as model of faith. The time for preaching to the Gentiles has not yet come (21: 24), but Luke's story has an interesting parallel in the first Gentile convert who is also a centurion (Acts 10). Jesus compares the faith of the Gentile to the faith of the rest of Israel, and the Gentile emerges the better for the comparison. Jesus' reaction to the faith of the centurion is a very human one: he "marvels" that such profound faith in his person can be found in a man who would have been regarded by the strict Jews as beyond the boundary of God's mercy. Yet again, it is the outsider whom Jesus chooses as a model for the faith of his kingdom.

The reason for the mediated encounter between the centurion and Jesus is that the centurion's slave is sick. That the centurion bothered so much about the health of his slave is no small matter; that he should risk going public on his concern by placing his trust in the healing ministry of the itinerant prophet from Nazareth shows the character of the man. The centurion's concern is not with his reputation as a public figure, it is for the sick slave who is unable to leave the house to see Jesus himself. And the centurion involves elders of the Jews in his mission: like another public official, he could have gone to Jesus alone under the cover of darkness, so that if nothing happened, if the whole affair was a theological flop, no one would know and he could emerge with his reputation intact. But the expectancy of the centurion is high: he believes that Jesus will heal his slave.

Again, when Jesus is confronted with sickness, his reaction is to heal it, not to deliver a sermon on the value of accepting sickness as a trial from God. Although the servant is healed, the focus of the attention is on the faith of the centurion. In fact, the slave is healed *because* of the faith of the centurion: like the paralytic, the vicarious faith of friends is enough for a healing. Luke does not say that Jesus and the centurion actually met: as the centurion is impressed by the power of Christ's word to heal over distance, so Jesus is impressed by the faith of the centurion he has never met. The centurion's faith, like the healing of Jesus, is carried through the power of the word.

Throughout his ministry, Jesus is impressed by the faith of people to such an extent that he grants their wishes to benefit a third party. The slave did not have to believe in the power of Jesus to be healed: that was not a requirement for the cure. For Jesus, it is sufficient that there is faith in the community—that faith can help and uplift others. The faith of one man can help the community. In the Old

Testament, God was impressed by the faith of Abraham to save other people. So, in the New Testament, Jesus is impressed by the faith of one man to exercise his power in favour of someone else. It helps if every community has at least one man of faith.

Luke 7: 11-17   *The Son of the Widow of Nain*

[11]Soon afterward he went to a city called Nain, and his disciples and a great crowd went with him. [12]As he drew near to the gate of the city, behold, a man who had died was being carried out, the only son of his mother, and she was a widow; and a large crowd from the city was with her. [13]And when the Lord saw her, he had compassion on her and said to her, "Do not weep." [14]And he came and touched the bier, and the bearers stood still. And he said, "Young man, I say to you, arise." [15]And the dead man sat up, and began to speak. And he gave him to his mother. [16]Fear seized them all; and they glorified God, saying, "A great prophet has arisen among us!" and "God has visited his people!" [17]And this report concerning him spread through the whole of Judea and all the surrounding country.

Two crowds converge. One is following Jesus, the other is following the dead body of a young man. One is following life, the other is following death. Two figures form the focus of attention: Jesus of Nazareth and a widowed mother, who has lost her only son. There is no pleading, there is no cry for a miracle, there is no soliciting for wonders. The simple story is that Jesus is moved with compassion for the widow, he suffers with her, he tells her not to weep; and he soon gives her reason not to weep. He touches the bier, and again his compassion overcomes the ritual uncleanness that would come from contact with the dead. With his authoritative word, he commands the dead man to rise. The dead man sits up and begins to speak. Jesus reclaims him for the land of the living, and he gives the son back to his mother. And the mother need weep no more.

Luke gives us a simple story which speaks volumes of the

compassion of Jesus. Jesus is not portrayed as the un-moved mover: when people are afflicted, he is moved—not in a powerless way, where he is helpless to do anything, but in a way where he is able to transform the suffering into joy, the death into life. The miracle which Jesus performs is not conditional on the faith of anyone: the issue which is at the heart of this miracle is the compassion of Jesus. Jesus does not ask for faith as a prior sign; he does not wait for a plea to come from the lips of the widowed mother: Jesus moves first, because he is first moved. He does not perform the miracle as an argumentative ploy to attest to his supreme authority; he does not perform the miracle as a pedagog-ical tool to make a point: he is moved by the sight of afflic-tion before him, and that is enough in itself.

This is the first time that Luke uses the title *Kyrios,* Lord, to describe Jesus. And the time is appropriate. When Jesus shows himself as master of life and death, as Lord of the living and the dead, he is given the title *Kyrios.* And Jesus is shown as the Lord of life in the present tense, not as someone who has to wait until some future time before he can exercise his power to that effect. Jesus is in-volved in reclaiming the dead now as a part of his own life's work; he is making the point that he is the resurrec-tion and the life *now.* The time of his Lordship is always now.

Luke presents us with a very touching image of Jesus in this passage. Jesus is the one who takes the initiative, who speaks first, who notices suffering and desolation, and who does not bypass them on the road. Jesus is not afraid of getting his hands dirty, of being regarded as unclean, in his movement of compassion. When he meets suffering at the crossroads, he does not take the route of least resis-tance and flee from the face of pain. He transforms it by his touch and by his word. He brings happiness to life. And he asks people to live in the knowledge that he is capable of that *now.* And that is enough to make anyone sit up and take notice.

Luke 7: 18-28   *Answer and Tribute to John*

¹⁸The disciples of John told him of all these things. ¹⁹And
John, calling to him two of his disciples, sent them to the
Lord, saying, "Are you he who is to come, or shall we look
for another?" ²⁰And when the men had come to him, they
said, "John the Baptist has sent us to you, saying, 'Are you
he who is to come, or shall we look for another?'" ²¹In that
hour he cured many of diseases and plagues and evil spirits,
and on many that were blind he bestowed sight. ²²And he
answered them, "Go and tell John what you have seen and
heard: the blind receive their sight, the lame walk, lepers are
cleansed, and the deaf hear, the dead are raised up, the poor
have good news preached to them. ²³And blessed is he who
takes no offense at me."

²⁴When the messengers of John had gone, he began to
speak to the crowds concerning John: "What did you go out
into the wilderness to behold? A reed shaken by the wind?
²⁵What then did you go out to see? A man clothed in soft
clothing? Behold, those who are gorgeously appareled and
live in luxury are in kings' courts. ²⁶What then did you go out
to see? A prophet? Yes, I tell you, and more than a prophet.
²⁷This is he of whom it is written,
  'Behold, I send my messenger
    before thy face,
  who shall prepare thy way before
    thee.'
²⁸I tell you, among those born of women none is greater than
John; yet he who is least in the kingdom of God is greater
than he."

Luke has already told us that John the Baptist is the
prisoner of Herod Antipas. John now sends his disciples to
enquire of Jesus if he really is the one "who is to come" or
whether he has to wait longer for the fulfilment of the promise. Luke does not record any meeting between Jesus and
John, and he suggests that John's view of Jesus is ambiguous and uncertain, whereas Jesus' view of John is
clearly supportive. John is still questioning, and no doubt
he would not have retained his own separate group if he
had been persuaded that Jesus was indeed the Coming One.

Perhaps John, like many of Jesus' other close relatives, was confused about the role Jesus was playing, particularly the people he seemed to be around. Jesus kept the company of the kind of people that John roundly condemned.

Jesus interprets his messianic mission in the prophetic terms of the Servant of the Lord (Is 29: 18; 35: 5; 42: 6; 61: 1), and he invites John's disciples to speak of what they have seen and heard. Jesus asks them to witness to their own experience: what they have seen with their own eyes, and heard with their own ears is sufficient witness to the point. Jesus then lists six signs: five of which are miracles of healing, one of which is the preaching to the poor. It may appear strange that preaching to the poor is listed among other miracles; but then, in reflection, perhaps it is the greatest miracle and sign of all: that the poor from whom people can apparently benefit the least are the ones who receive attention in the kingdom of God. And the signs listed are not past signs; they are present signs that the kingdom of God is present in the world today.

Jesus' closing remark, "Blessed is he who takes no offence at me", is a delicate plea for understanding. There is the prayer that John in his confusion, in his attempt to understand the signs of the times, will not stumble and break faith. That, at the very least, he will not take offence at what Jesus is doing. Jesus goes on the testify to the importance of John to the crowds. He underlines the immense importance of John, and the work he has achieved. But John's work is still put in perspective: it was the work of the messenger who announces the arrival of the other, and now that the Other has arrived, the work of the messenger is finished. Jesus puts the point forcefully when he says that even with all John's importance, those who enter the kingdom are more important than he who prepares for its coming.

Jesus places the attention on the present task: entering the kingdom which he has come to establish. And that is true for John the Baptist as well. John, like everyone else, needs the faith to see that Jesus is the promised one of God. John too has moments when he wonders whether

Jesus is the one for whom he was preparing. He too has to struggle with his own doubts, with his own half-formed ideas of what the Coming One would look like, act like, be like. And Jesus does not react with impatience to John's disciples: he invites them to pay attention to the heart of their own experience of God.

Luke 7: 29-35   Rejection of Jesus and John

[29](When they heard this all the people and the tax collectors justified God, having been baptized with the baptism of John; [30]but the Pharisees and the lawyers rejected the purpose of God for themselves, not having been baptized by him.)
[31]"To what then shall I compare the men of this generation, and what are they like? [32]They are like children sitting in the market place and calling to one another, 'We piped to you, and you did not dance; we wailed, and you did not weep.' [33]For John the Baptist has come eating no bread and drinking no wine; and you say, 'He has a demon.' [34]The Son of man has come eating and drinking; and you say, 'Behold, a glutton and a drunkard, a friend of tax collectors and sinners!' [35]Yet wisdom is justified by all her children."

The Pharisees and the lawyers refused the baptism of John, and their rejection of the Baptist anticipates their rejection of Jesus. Both John and Jesus invited their hearers to change their attitudes and their way of life with the coming of the messianic age. And as both are rejected by the religious authorities of the day, so both are accepted by the outcasts of the day. In this passage from Luke, one can almost hear Jesus sigh with weariness at the perversity of his listeners whom he compares to children who play games in the market place. He is tired of the sheer contrariness of people who relate to prophets with the sophistication of children playing games. Neither John nor Jesus is playing games; they both had a message of profound importance which required an adult response, not a childish yelp of dissatisfaction.

As Jesus said: John the Baptist came from a tradition of

asceticism; he lived a hard life in the desert which was above reproach, yet the people said that John was possessed for cutting himself off from the rest of society. Then Jesus comes, mixing in with all sorts of people, being with them at wedding feasts and funerals, speaking of the kingdom of God as a divine banquet where the food and wine flow freely, and yet the people accuse him of being a drunkard. When he ate with the establishment he was a snob; when he ate with sinners and outcasts, he was a reject. John's unsociability was devilish; Jesus' sociability was frivolous. Either way, it appeared as if Jesus and John had to lose.

But Jesus is tired of the game, for that was all it was. His own ministry and that of John complement each other, yet each is criticised for not doing what the other is doing. So, no matter what approach they take, it has to be the wrong one. Jesus replies that wisdom is shown right by her children. The ultimate verdict does not lie with the childish critics, but in the goodness which is brought to birth through the ministries of John and Jesus. The people might criticize John for his isolation, but he moved the hearts of many people and brought them into the presence of God in a way that no other prophet before him had. The people might criticize Jesus for moving easily in the company of the great and the small, but no one in their history had manifested the face of God as Jesus had done.

The fruits of the work of Jesus and John speak for themselves in those who responded to their message. Jesus and John both knew well that they could never be acceptable to a certain matinee gallery who always wanted a different drama from the one which was currently playing, who always wanted a different message from the one they were presently hearing. But neither Jesus nor John plays to that gallery: the drama which they are involved in does not change according to the whims and momentary fancies of a fitful audience. Their drama is real; it is the drama of God. And that is no game of make-believe: it is the real thing.

Luke 7: 36-50   *The Graciousness of Jesus*

³⁶One of the Pharisees asked him to eat with him, and he went into the Pharisee's house, and sat at table. ³⁷And behold, a woman of the city, who was a sinner, when she learned that he was sitting at table in the Pharisee's house, brought an alabaster flask of ointment, ³⁸and standing behind him at his feet, weeping, she began to wet his feet with her tears, and wiped them with the hair of her head, and kissed his feet, and anointed them with the ointment. ³⁹Now when the Pharisee who had invited him saw it, he said to himself, "If this man were a prophet, he would have known who and what sort of woman this is who is touching him, for she is a sinner." ⁴⁰And Jesus answering said to him, "Simon, I have something to say to you." And he answered, "What is it, Teacher?" ⁴¹"A certain creditor had two debtors; one owed five hundred denarii, and the other fifty. ⁴²When they could not pay, he forgave them both. Now which of them will love him more?" ⁴³Simon answered, "The one, I suppose, to whom he forgave more." And he said to him, "You have judged rightly." ⁴⁴Then turning toward the woman he said to Simon, "Do you see this woman? I entered your house, you gave me no water for my feet, but she has wet my feet with her tears and wiped them with her hair. ⁴⁵You gave me no kiss, but from the time I came in she has not ceased to kiss my feet. ⁴⁶You did not anoint my head with oil, but she has anointed my feet with ointment. ⁴⁷Therefore I tell you, her sins, which are many, are forgiven, for she loved much; but he who is forgiven little, loves little." ⁴⁸And he said to her, "Your sins are forgiven." ⁴⁹Then those who were at table with him began to say among themselves, "Who is this, who even forgives sins?" ⁵⁰And he said to the woman, "Your faith has saved you; go in peace."

In one of the most descriptive stories in the Gospel, Luke presents a striking contrast between a man and a woman, the host and an uninvited guest, and their different attitudes to Jesus. Simon the Pharisee is one of the separated ones, a member of the religious sect which is proud of the distance it keeps from sin and sinners. Simon plays host to Jesus, and addresses him with respect. Simon is sufficiently intrigued by what Jesus has said and done to invite him to table, something that is a risk since Jesus has already earned himself the reputation of a blasphemer. At a meal attended by such a public figure as Jesus, it would be no surprise that the occasion should attract onlookers, eager to listen to what was said: that was an accepted practice of the day. A dinner like Simon's would have been good theatre for the legion of the curious, and good teaching for the various groups of disciples. However, it is probable that Simon did not reckon on the woman who was a sinner, probably a prostitute, stealing the attention.

It is certain that Simon did not expect to be compared to his discredit with the lady of the night. That Jesus should hint to Simon that he could take lessons in hospitality from a prostitute was probably not on Simon's menu. Simon has offered Jesus the minimal acts of courtesy in receiving a guest; he has been polite according to the book, but he has not expended any energy in showing Jesus that he is especially welcome. In contrast to Simon, the woman comes prepared to anoint Jesus, and is so overcome by the emotion of the moment that the tears flow freely, and she kisses his feet, dries them with her hair, and anoints them with oil. Simon has been self-consciously exact in his manners; the woman has been unselfconsciously generous in her manner.

The scene is not without its own humour, and Jesus handles the whole scene very graciously. He does not get nervous at the woman's hair tickling his toes; he does not give the impression that he is tolerating what is going on; he does not get embarrassed and make a quick exit. Jesus' presence communicates itself very strongly in this scene; he is master of the situation, and he supports the woman when he speaks. He makes it clear that he prefers the woman's more demonstrative welcome to Simon's officially proper one, that he prefers the woman's extravagance to Simon's propriety.

In contrast to Jesus, Simon is not taken by the woman. He obviously knows her reputation, and the fact that she lets her hair down in public is a sign that she is not oversensitive about public morals. Only loose women loosened their hair. Loose hair was normally taken as a public signal that the woman was willing to negotiate a certain transaction. And Simon wonders whether Jesus can see all this. Simon's view of the woman stops at recognizing her sinfulness: his view is locked into that recognition. Simon only has a view of the woman as a sinner; Jesus has a vision of the woman as a saint. Jesus can see the woman's possibility in his own vision of love and forgiveness. And Jesus' vision of love and forgiveness transforms the view of sinfulness which he sees. Simon's view puts a full stop after sinfulness, and that is a definition of hell. Jesus' vision focuses on possibility in his love, and that is a definition of heaven.

Jesus' forgiveness releases the woman to love, his forgiveness changes her past into something which has been accepted by God. So, her past is no longer a matter for regret, it is a matter for rejoicing because it has been accepted and transformed by God. Forgiveness alters the past; it heals it; it makes the past into past perfect, something which is completely over with, and no longer haunts the present tense. Now, the woman is free to travel in the way of the Lord, because his forgiveness has unburdened her. She can travel in the knowledge that she is forgiven and loved.

Chapter Eight

Luke 8: 1-15   The Seed that Struggles to Grow

8 Soon afterward he went on through cities and villages, preaching and bringing the good news of the kingdom of God. And the twelve were with him, ²and also some women who had been healed of evil spirits and infirmities: Mary, called Magdalene, from whom seven demons had gone out, ³and Joanna, the wife of Chuza, Herod's steward, and Susanna, and many others, who provided for them out of their means.

⁴And when a great crowd came together and people from town after town came to him, he said in a parable: ⁵"A sower went out to sow his seed; and as he sowed, some fell along the path, and was trodden under foot, and the birds of the air devoured it. ⁶And some fell on the rock; and as it grew up, it withered away, because it had no moisture. ⁷And some fell among thorns; and the thorns grew with it and choked it. ⁸And some fell into good soil and grew, and yielded a hundredfold." As he said this, he called out, "He who has ears to hear, let him hear."

⁹And when his disciples asked him what this parable meant, ¹⁰he said, "To you it has been given to know the secrets of the kingdom of God; but for others they are in parables, so that seeing they may not see, and hearing they may not understand. ¹¹Now the parable is this: The seed is the word of God. ¹²The ones along the path are those who have heard; then the devil comes and takes away the word from their hearts, that they may not believe and be saved. ¹³And the ones on the rock are those who, when they hear the word, receive it with joy; but these have no root, they believe for a while and in time of temptation fall away. ¹⁴And as for what fell among the thorns, they are those who hear, but as they go on their way they are choked by the cares and riches and pleasures of life, and their fruit does not mature. ¹⁵And as for that in the good soil, they are those who, hearing the word, hold it fast in an honest and good heart, and bring forth fruit with patience.

JESUS NOW BEGINS HIS WANDERING JOURNEY through
the towns and villages of Decapolis, bringing the message
of his kingdom to those he meets on the road. His twelve
chosen ones accompany him, and also some women who
have experienced healing and are sufficiently well-off to
pay for the expense of the road. Jesus has already experienced discouragement and hostility; he has felt the
mounting opposition, particularly from the scribes and
Pharisees. He has been thrown out of the synagogues, and
he now takes to the open road in his missionary journey to
preach the message of his kingdom. In his own preaching,
Jesus has experienced his word falling on many kinds of
ground, but in spite of the hardness and the poor showing,
he assures his disciples that planting the word of God in the
hearts of men is a worthwhile task. And a good harvest will
come from it all.

Jesus now concentrates on preaching the kingdom of
God (Mk 1: 14; Mt 4: 17). He tells his model parable of the
kingdom, the sower who went out to sow. It is not a
"nice" story in the sense that people can listen to it and go
away unchallenged, unchanged, and unthreatened by what
they hear; this parable, like Jesus' other parables, is the
kind of story which invited and challenged people to make
a decision about their life, but it is also the kind of story
that eventually led him to his crucifixion. The stories which
Jesus told were powerful enough to lead men to organise
his execution. Jesus' stories issued an adult challenge to
people: to recognize the truth that was in the story, to
recognize the truth in their own lives, and take decisive action. Jesus began the process of the inbreaking of the
kingdom of God by breaking people into his stories, stories
which people were invited not only to listen to, but to find
themselves part of.

Luke gives us the parable of the sower, and also an
allegorical explanation. Some scholars think that the explanation was written in by the early Church: that is possible, but the tradition of the Hebrew *mashal* which Jesus
worked in also included allegory. Jesus was not necessarily

shy of allegory; he was certainly not shy of explaining his points in further detail to his disciples. Jesus explains that the seed is the word of God: it is scattered generously, with throwaway style, even on ground which is hard and rocky. The Palestinian farmer sowed the seed *before* he ploughed, so he could throw the seed on the pathway since the pathway was going to be ploughed up anyway. The word of God is risked even on hard ground, and Jesus never flinched from trying the word on hard hearts.

A variety of human responses to hearing the word of God are explored in the parable, from those who hear and are tempted away to those who hear and take heed. Jesus invites his hearers to pay attention to their own responses to the word of God, but if they are hard-hearted they will not understand this parable, which is the seed itself. Jesus reflects on the very processes that are going on while people listen to him speak. And he invites people to read the parable by reading where they stand in relation to the word of God.

The word of God is scattered generously, and even when it is sown in willing hearts, it takes time to grow and be seen. The sower knows that he has to wait; the process demands that he wait on the weather, the working of the soil, the slow thrust of life, before he can see the fruits of his labour. From hearing the word to letting it be seen that the word is growing, there is a time of work, of waiting, of hazard, of slow emergence. The sower cannot deny the seed the time of growth. Jesus never denies people time in working with the word. Jesus who plants the seed recognizes the particularity of planting the seed in individual people. And if individuals believed that they were growing to be nourished rather than devoured, then perhaps they would be better at nourishing the word within them. God cares what happens to people, and he expects that people will care no less for his word.

Luke 8: 16-18   Sharing the Light

> ¹⁶"No one after lighting a lamp covers it with a vessel, or puts it under a bed, but puts it on a stand, that those who enter may see the light. ¹⁷For nothing is hid that shall not be made manifest, nor anything secret that shall not be known and come to light. ¹⁸Take heed then how you hear; for to him who has will more be given, and from him who has not, even what he thinks that he has will be taken away."

Jesus continues to address his disciples on the subject of the word of God. If the word of God grows, it will be seen to have grown. Using the analogy of the light, Jesus tells his disciples not to be shy or nervous about letting their light shine. Keeping the light under the bed is a rather dangerous pastime, and a selfish one, particularly when there are people pottering around in the dark. And telling them that the underside of the bed is well-lit is a doubtful consolation. Jesus enjoins his disciples to put the light where it can be of help to all who enter, not just to those in the house. Luke, addressing his Gospel to the Gentiles, would be particularly sensitive about the light being available to those who would like to enter.

The Gospel is given as a light to be shared, not as a reserved document under the Official Secrets Act. And as the Gospel is an open book which speaks of the workings of God, so the life of the disciple must be an open book which tells a story of what the Lord has done. The best stories that are told are told as life-stories, which speak of a personal testimony about life. Better that these stories be used as lights than as secrets which come to light. Things that 'come to light' are usually forced disclosures which do not read well.

Jesus ends these saying with a paradoxical word: to him who has will more be given, and from him who has not, even what he thinks he has will be taken away. In the context of receiving the word of God which is to be shared, this word makes eminent sense. The word of God is not given as a private possession; it is not given to keep under lock and key. Those people who try to keep the word of God as their private possession will discover that they have lost even what they thought they had. The word thrives in being shared, and when it is shared with others the one who shares will be given more. And perhaps people would all risk sharing the light of God's word if they were reminded more often that the light was given as a gift to be shared in the first place. So, permission is refused for torchlight processions under the bed.

Luke 8: 19-21   Family Ties

> [19]Then his mother and his brethren came to him, but they could not reach him for the crowd. [20]And he was told, "Your mother and your brethren are standing outside, desiring to see you." [21]But he said to them, "My mother and my brethren are those who hear the word of God and do it."

In his Gospel, Mark records how Jesus' family thought him deranged in what he was saying and doing (Mk 3: 21), but Luke is silent on that point in this passage. Luke uses the visit of Jesus' family to give Jesus' axiomatic statement on the word of God: those who hear and do the word of God are members of Jesus' family. The point is of particular importance for Luke addressing his Gospel to the Gentiles: the statement underlines the point that blood relationship, the right pedigree, the right address are not access tickets to the kingdom of God. The condition for entering the kingdom is to first hear the word of God and then act on it. Fellowship in the kingdom is open to all who have ears to hear and are willing to enact the truth of what they hear in their lives. For Jesus, family ties are decided by fidelity to the word of God. Those ties do not exclude those who are born in a different place or in a different time: the family of Jesus is as wide as faithfulness to God.

Luke 8: 22-25   Master over Turbulence

²²One day he got into a boat with his disciples, and he said to them, "Let us go across to the other side of the lake." So they set out, ²³and as they sailed he fell asleep. And a storm of wind came down on the lake, and they were filling with water, and were in danger. ²⁴And they went and woke him saying, "Master, Master, we are perishing!" And he awoke and rebuked the wind and the raging waves; and they ceased, and there was a calm. ²⁵He said to them, "Where is your faith?" And they were afraid, and they marveled, saying to one another, "Who then is this, that he commands even wind and water, and they obey him?"

In the opening shipwreck scene of Shakespeare's *The Tempest*, the boatswain addresses Gonzalo, the aged member of the King's Council whose business it is to quell riots: "You are a counsellor; if you can command these elements to silence, and work the peace of the present, we will not hand a rope more; use your authority; if you cannot, give thanks you have lived so long, and make yourself ready in your cabin for the mischance of the hour, if it so hap." But old Gonzalo is powerless to quell the elements, and the ship is wrecked even though the lives of those on board are saved miraculously. The King's counsellor has no authority over the riot of the sea. Luke now tells us the story of how Jesus, when his disciples feared for their lives in the middle of a tempest, exercised his Lordship over the riot of the sea.

Jesus' reaction to the plea of the disciples is immediate: he calms the wind and the sea. It is only after that, in the midst of calm, that Jesus asks his disciples whatever happened to their faith. Perhaps it went overboard when the turbulence came, but the disciples have enough faith to appeal to Jesus in their distress. And no doubt they believed that Jesus should have been distressed too instead of sleeping his way through disaster. The incident moves the disciples to ask the question of questions: *"Who then is this?"* Who is this who has authority over nature? The answer to the question is given later (9: 20), but the answer will be understood only much later.

The experience of the disciples is a graphic one: they feel all at sea, they feel up to their neck in difficulty, they feel powerless to withstand the onslaught of the environment of threat. Again, the reaction of Jesus is generous: he is no sadist who enjoys seeing people hurting; he uses his authority for a good purpose, and in using his authority, he provokes questions about himself. Perhaps it is no surprise that it is when the disciples are courting disaster that they discover the power of the Lord over nature. And of any time to discover the Lord's power, the middle of a tempest is better than most. At least, one lives to tell the tale of the peace of the present. And the peace of the present, like all presents, is a gift.

Luke 8: 26-39   *Cure of the Demonic*

²⁶Then they arrived at the country of the Gerasenes, which is opposite Galilee. ²⁷And as he stepped out on land, there met him a man from the city who had demons; for a long time he had worn no clothes, and he lived not in a house but among the tombs. ²⁸When he saw Jesus, he cried out and fell down before him, and said with a loud voice, "What have you to do with me, Jesus, Son of the Most High God? I beseech you, do not torment me." ²⁹For he had commanded the unclean spirit to come out of the man. (For many a time it had seized him; he was kept under guard, and bound with chains and fetters, but he broke the bonds and was driven by the demon into the desert.) ³⁰Jesus then asked him, "What is your name?" And he said, "Legion"; for many demons had entered him. ³¹And they begged him not to command them to depart into the abyss. ³²Now a large herd of swine was feeding there on the hillside; and they begged him to let them enter these. So he gave them leave. ³³Then the demons came out of the man and entered the swine, and the herd rushed down the steep bank into the lake and were drowned.

³⁴When the herdsmen saw what had happened, they fled, and told it in the city and in the country. ³⁵Then people went

out to see what had happened, and they came to Jesus, and found the man from whom the demons had gone, sitting at the feet of Jesus, clothed and in his right mind; and they were afraid. ³⁶And those who had seen it told them how he who had been possessed with demons was healed. ³⁷Then all the people of the surrounding country of the Gerasenes asked him to depart from them; for they were seized with great fear; so he got into the boat and returned. ³⁸The man from whom the demons had gone begged that he might be with him; but he sent him away, saying, ³⁹"Return to your home, and declare how much God has done for you." And he went away, proclaiming throughout the whole city how much Jesus had done for him.

In this passage, Jesus witnesses his power over demons in Gentile country, the only time in this Gospel that he leaves Jewish territory. Luke, who is credited with being "the beloved physician" (Col 4: 14), gives a detailed description of the condition of a man who avoids human habitation in favour of living in a cemetery, who refuses to wear clothes, who exhibits extraordinary strength, and who frightens the people to such an extent that they put him under guard. Jesus takes the initiative to put the man to rights. If the man has experienced an invasion by the Spirit of evil, with the coming of Christ he experiences the invasion of the Spirit of God. Jesus recognizes that the power which drives the man to do as he does is the power of evil, not the power of good, and he moves to change the situation. The coming of Christ is totally opposed to the kingdom of evil: it puts the kingdom of evil into the chaos which it causes in others. And out of the chaos of the demoniac's life, Jesus brings order and peace. Creation is a continuing work to bring order out of chaos, to bring pattern out of legion. The man is no longer a borrowed battlefield for the power of evil; he is in possession of himself again. Jesus restores his power of self-possession.

Luke tells us that the evil spirits which possessed the man enter a herd of swine, which rushes over the cliff to be drowned in the lake below. Everyone present is given a clear indication of Jesus' power to banish evil. Some people have problems with the incident, arguing that Jesus' action was wasteful. It is a peculiar philosophy which argues that the right of swine to pasture peacefully is more important than the right of an individual to live peacefully. It is a peculiar community which will herd and protect swine while banishing a human being to the borders of human contempt. Jesus dismisses the swine dramatically, and focuses attention on the man. The man is the one who was in need of nurture, of care, and of protection; and he is the one who was denied that, except by Jesus.

It is little wonder that the community asks Jesus to depart from their midst. Jesus' healing care has exposed their own powerlessness; his power has made them afraid. They do not share the outright hostility of Jesus' opponents, but they do fear the power which Jesus shows. On the other hand, the cured man begs to keep the company of Jesus. But Jesus tells him to stay in his own community and witness to the wonderful work of God. Clearly, Jesus' work is the work of God. As Ellis writes: "Commanded to tell what *God* had done, the healed man proclaimed 'throughout the whole city' what *Jesus* had done."[1] Again, Jesus makes the outsider the man with the most important word in the community. The man who was an outcast now carries the most precious word that the community will ever hear. No one knows how the new prophet fared in his own community, whether he had a better reception than Jesus did in his community. Perhaps they used a similar argument against the new prophet: but we know this man well: isn't he the madman who used to hang around the graves? So, the story is told.

Luke 8: 40-56   Two Miracles for Women

⁴⁰Now when Jesus returned, the crowd welcomed him, for they were all waiting for him. ⁴¹And there came a man named Jairus, who was a ruler of the synagogue; and falling at Jesus' feet he besought him to come to his house, ⁴²for he

had an only daughter, about twelve years of age, and she was dying.

As he went, the people pressed round him. [43]And a woman who had had a flow of blood for twelve years and had spent all her living upon physicians and could not be healed by anyone, [44]came up behind him, and touched the fringe of his garment; and immediately her flow of blood ceased. [45]And Jesus said, "Who was it that touched me?" When all denied it, Peter said, "Master, the multitudes surround you and press upon you!" [46]But Jesus said, "Some one touched me; for I perceive that power has gone forth from me." [47]And when the woman saw that she was not hidden, she came trembling, and falling down before him declared in the presence of all the people why she had touched him, and how she had been immediately healed. [48]And he said to her, "Daughter, your faith has made you well; go in peace."

[49]While he was still speaking, a man from the ruler's house came and said, "Your daughter is dead; do not trouble the Teacher any more." [50]But Jesus on hearing this answered him, "Do not fear; only believe, and she shall be well." [51]And when he came to the house, he permitted no one to enter with him, except Peter and John and James, and the father and mother of the child. [52]And all were weeping and bewailing her; but he said, "Do not weep; for she is not dead but sleeping." [53]And they laughed at him, knowing that she was dead. [54]But taking her by the hand he called, saying, "Child, arise." [55]And her spirit returned, and she got up at once; and he directed that something should be given her to eat. [56]And her parents were amazed; but he charged them to tell no one what had happened.

Not all the religious leaders are hostile to Jesus. There is one, Jairus, whose responsibility it is to supervise the arrangements for the services in the synagogue, who comes to Jesus. Luke has already recorded Jesus' healing miracle in what could have been the synagogue where Jairus was an official (4: 33-37): perhaps the memory of that prompted Jairus to seek out Jesus. It is interesting to note that the two public officials who have come to Jesus so far, have come to ask for Jesus' healing help: the centurion for his servant, and Jairus for his twelve-year-old daughter. Their need for Jesus overcomes any risk of public disgrace they might have incurred through seeking out the prophet from

Nazareth. People in need tend to forget public posture: if their need is unanswered, their public posture will not save them.

On the way to Jairus's house, Jesus comes into contact with a woman who is suffering from a flow of blood, probably a menstrual disease. The disease renders her permanently unclean, which means that, for all intents and purposes, she is an outcast. She is forbidden to touch anyone, as her touch would render the other person unclean. The woman has already been busy petitioning the help of physicians, but her savings are gone, and her disease has stayed. In spite of the law of uncleanness, she decides to touch Jesus. Perhaps she thought that Jesus would never notice if she touched the hem of his garment while he was walking through a crowd; perhaps she was embarrassed at the thought of being discovered touching anyone. But Jesus notices her move of quiet desperation, and he does not permit her to go until she is touched by his love and healing power.

Jesus seems insistent in discovering who touched him. Peter makes the common-sense reply that, given the crowd which is hemming Jesus in, Jesus should not be surprised that someone came in contact with the hem of his garment. Jesus makes the observation that he has felt power go out of him. Healing costs power and energy, and Jesus feels it going. Jesus' insistence is not to embarrass the woman, or to suggest that her suffering is unimportant: it is to tell her the good news that she has been healed, not by a magical touch, but by her own faith. And Jesus, in the midst of a crowd which has been forgotten, gives her a public blessing to go in peace. The woman has received a total healing. Her faith in Jesus' healing power has been rewarded. Jesus sends her off with a blessing on her head.

Meanwhile, news arrives from Jairus' house that his daughter is dead. The messenger tells Jesus that he need trouble no further, but Jesus cancels the advice: he is going to turn the bad news into good news. When he arrives, the professional mourners are already busy about their wails, and when Jesus tells them that the girl is not really dead, they mock him. But Jesus enters the room of death with his chosen disciples and changes the atmosphere into the room of life. The Lord of the living and of the dead is present. He recalls the girl to the land of the living, and her departed spirit, not long fled, makes a surprise return. So, she is whole again, and home again. And a snack is on the way.

Jesus tells the parents not to speak of what has just taken place. Those who thought the girl was dead would probably not accept that Jesus had raised her to life. Either way the mocking mourners are confounded: if they admit that it was a miracle, they will have to laugh at themselves for mocking Jesus; if they deny a miracle and say she was sleeping all the time, their own obituary notices and wailings will look foolishly premature. But the fact that they mocked Jesus when he first appeared on the scene, suggests that they are not open to the word. A miracle will not persuade them: miracles confirm already existing faith; they do not cause faith. And no doubt the unbelievers will re-write the incident according to their prior judgements. Christ can only enter in faith, if there is a willingness to believe, if the door is left open. If there are notices of mockery on the closed door, then it doesn't matter what Christ does: entry is only with permission.

Notes

[1]E. Ellis, *The Gospel of Luke,* op cit., p. 128

Chapter Nine

Luke 9: 1-9   **The Mission of the Twelve**

9 And he called the twelve together and gave them power and authority over all demons and to cure diseases; ²and he sent them out to preach the kingdom of God and to heal. ³And he said to them, "Take nothing for your journey, no staff, nor bag, nor bread, nor money; and do not have two tunics. ⁴And whether house you enter, stay there, and from there depart. ⁵And wherevery they do not receive you, when you leave that town shake off the dust from your feet as a testimony against them." ⁶And they departed and went through the villages, preaching the gospel and healing everywhere.

⁷Now Herod the tetrarch heard of all that was done, and he was perplexed, because it was said by some that John had been raised from the dead, ⁸by some that Elijah had appeared, and by others that one of the old prophets had risen. ⁹Herod said, "John I beheaded; but who is this about whom I hear such things?" And he sought to see him.

THE GALILEAN MISSION IS COMING TO A CLOSE, and Jesus is preparing to set his face towards Jerusalem. The officials are not alone in their opposition; John the Baptist has been executed, and no doubt Jesus is aware that the same fate could befall himself. Jesus acknowledges the need of help to spread the message of his kingdom. Time is not a force which Jesus has on his side: given the menacing reaction he has received, Jesus is on borrowed time. There is a haste and a crucial urgency in proclaiming the kingdom. When he commissions his chosen twelve, they are not to be weighed down by heavy or unnecessary baggage, by anything that is superfluous. Christ gives them the theology of enough. Their baggage is the message of the kingdom which they carry in their hearts. For everything else, they must depend on the hospitality of others. The time will come soon enough when Jesus' instructions will have a more cautious tone (22: 36).

Neither are the twelve apostles to waste time with those who will not accept them. They are to travel on. It was a tradition that when the Jew left Gentile soil, he was to shake the dust from his feet, since the dust was regarded as ceremonially unclean. Likewise, the twelve are to shake "foreign" dust from their feet: foreign being those who are opposed to the message of the kingdom. What they do, they do in the name of Jesus, a name of power and authority. The instructions they receive follow the lines of Jesus' own ministry: preaching and healing. They are to announce the Gospel and to banish sickness and evil spirits. Healing has already been given as a sign of the messianic age, that the time of fulfilment is present. It is the principal sign of the arrival of the kingdom.

We are not told what actually happened on the mission: the focus is on the words of commissioning: that they are to do what the Lord has been seen to do himself. And they will experience the same reception that Jesus experiences, with the bias towards rejection. They too will have to learn when to escape, when to move on, until such times when they can do no other but be led away themselves. They will have plenty of dust to shake from their feet in the course of their ministry.

While the twelve apostles are busy about preaching and healing, Herod is asking questions about the identity of the prophet from Nazareth. Popular rumour is not short of theories. It is difficult to see how people could believe that Jesus was John the Baptist since the Jews did not have a belief in re-incarnation; but even if they had, Jesus had emerged *before* the death of John the Baptist, which would seem to render the theory insupportable. However, rumours rarely depend on reasonableness for their support. Herod wants to "see" Jesus; whether out of curiosity or murderous intent is not said. But he will not "see" Jesus until he has accepted him. No one does. Herod will be like the mourners at the house of Jairus: even when presented with a wonder, he still will not "get" who this Jesus is. Later, Luke records the words of Jesus: "And I tell you, you will not see me until you say, 'Blessed is he who comes in the name of the Lord.'" (13: 35). And Herod apears to be a long journey from that proclamation.

Luke 9: 10-17   Feeding the Hungry

¹⁰On their return the apostles told him what they had done. And he took them and withdrew apart to a city called Bethsaida. ¹¹When the crowds learned it, they followed him; and he welcomed them and spoke to them of the kingdom of God, and cured those who had need of healing. ¹²Now the day began to wear away; and the twelve came and said to him, "Send the crowd away, to go into the villages and country round about, for we are here in a lonely place." ¹³But he said to them, "You give them something to eat." They said, "We have no more than five loaves and two fish—unless we are to go and buy food for all these people." ¹⁴For there were about five thousand men. And he said to his disciples, "Make them sit down in companies, about fifty each." ¹⁵And they did so, and made them all sit down. ¹⁶And taking the five loaves and the two fish he looked up to heaven, and blessed and broke them, and gave them to the disciples to set before the crowd. ¹⁷And all ate and were satisfied. And they took up what was left over, twelve baskets of broken pieces.

The apostles return from their mission, and Jesus takes them away to a quiet place where they can be by themselves. Understandably, the quiet place is outside the territory of the man who wants to "see" Jesus, Herod Antipas. We are not told of the stories the apostles must have exchanged at that meeting, we are just told that the private seminar was interrupted. The madding crowd have a nose for hide-outs; but when they arrive, Jesus receives them with graciousness. He preaches to them about the kingdom, and he attends to those who are in need of healing. It becomes evening in the lonely place, and the people are hungry. The only thing the apostles can think of is to send the crowd somewhere else to find an answer to their hunger. The fact that the crowd would have to find lodgings suggests that they were far from their own homes.

The apostles have just returned from their mission where they would have exercised power in preaching and healing in the name of Jesus. Now, when they are confronted with the problem of feeding the crowd, Jesus throws them back on themselves: "*You* give them something to eat." If the command is more challenge than taunt, then Jesus is telling them that they have the power to nourish the hungry, to satisfy the real need of the crowd *with what they have*. Jesus focuses on what the apostles have; the apostles are aware only of what they have not; and they appeal to reasonableness in pointing out that they have only five loaves and two fish. That is all.

Christ takes the food they have. The language of Luke is heavy with the symbolism of the eucharist: he took. . . looked up to heaven. . .blessed and broke. . .and gave. Luke does not say that the loaves and the fish multiplied. What is said is that the food which the apostles have is not only sufficient for the crowd, but that it is abundantly plentiful. The people eat and they are satisfied. Luke does not mention that the crowd is astonished, or that they are filled with fear—the usual reaction of the crowd when Jesus performs a great wonder. The crowd do not register any surprise at being fed. What Jesus does is done for the crowd, but it appears as if the manner is for the apostles only.

Under the guidance and the power of Jesus, the apostles are able to give nourishment to the crowd: that is the point of the passage. Even when the apostles are confronted with the apparently impossible—the challenge to feed so many on so little—they discover that the impossible can be done in the power and in the prayer of Christ. At this event, the climax of Jesus' mission to Galilee, Luke tells us that the apostles are able to give nourishment to the legion of the hungry—even in a lonely place, which offers no fast-food stores, and no easy comfort. The miracle is that the apostles have enough to answer the needs of everyone. At their commissioning, they received the power of Christ to address the needs of the people they ministered to. Jesus asks them now to believe in that ministry.

No doubt, the apostles were surprised at what happened. Perhaps, hungry crowds are never completely surprised when they are fed; perhaps it is those who feed them who are surprised because they are aware of what appears to be a permanent short-supply—and yet it turns out as abundance. After the crowd has eaten, twelve baskets are taken up. The baskets are heavy with broken pieces. In the process of his nourishing the people, Christ will end up like the broken pieces which are left over. He will experience brokenness; he will experience what it is like to be left over. But that is to come yet. At the moment, Christ's awareness of his passion is deepening as he approaches his journey to Jerusalem. To the place of brokenness, and the place of triumph.

Luke 9: 18-27   Cross-roads

[18]Now it happened that as he was praying alone the disciples were with him; and he asked them, "Who do the people say that I am?" [19]And they answered, "John the Baptist; but others say, Elijah; and others that one of the old prophets has risen." [20]And he said to them, "But who do you say that I am?" And Peter answered, "The Christ of God." [21]But he charged and commanded them to tell this to no one, [22]saying, "The Son of man must suffer many things, and be rejected by the elders and chief priests and scribes, and be killed, and on the third day be raised."

[23]And he said to all, "If any man would come after me, let him deny himself and take up his cross daily and follow me. [24]For whoever would save his life will lose it; and whoever loses his life for my sake, he will save it. [25]For what does it profit a man if he gains the whole world and loses or forfeits himself? [26]For whoever is ashamed of me and of my words, of him will the Son of man be ashamed when he comes in his glory and the glory of the Father and of the holy angels. [27]But I tell you truly, there are some standing here who will not taste death before they see the kingdom of God."

Up to the present time, the demons are the only ones who have accurately attested to the true identity of Jesus. Herod has already asked the question, "Who is this?" and heard a variety of theories in reply. Jesus now poses the question himself: he is the man who asks the fundamental questions about himself. To Jesus' first question, "Who do people say that I am?", the disciples repeat the popular theories that Herod heard: Christ is a resurrected prophet. In this reply the focus of Christ's identity is placed in the past: Jesus is merely a modern repeat of an old story, he is an old prophet having another try. In this theory, there is no new challenge and no new message: at most, this theory presents Christ as one who comes again with an old message. The fact that popular opinion does not mention Jesus as the Messiah suggests that Jesus did not actually proclaim himself as such. So, popular opinion has him as a probable resurrection.

In his second question, Jesus addresses the heart of the individual: "But who do you say that I am?" It is the central question of all theology and all faith, a question which can only be answered in the utter honesty of a person's heart. The answer to this question is not as easy as the first: to answer the first question, one only has to listen to what others say. The second question cannot be answered by consulting public reports or opinion polls, or by searching the pages of a theological dictionary: it is irreducibly personal: "What about you: who do *you* say that I am?" In his reply, Peter proclaims that Jesus is the Christ, the promised one of God. Jesus responds to Peter's proclamation with a command to keep silent on that point. The reason is the "messianic secret" which is so constant throughout the Gospel of Mark: the kind of Messiah the people expect is not the kind of Messiah which Jesus understands himself to be.

And Jesus speaks of his own understanding of his role. He thinks through two other titles, the Son of Man and the Suffering Servant, but the cluster of titles from the past do not adequately sum up the present Christ: he is other than even these. Unlike the popular wisdom, Jesus does not locate his self-understanding in the past, but in the future. And the disciples will not fully understand the true identity of Jesus until they have received the Spirit of understanding which comes after the resurrection of Christ. Meantime, Jesus tries to introduce them to the portrait of himself as the sufferer and the outsider. Jesus is under no illusion about the suffering which he has to face: it is a suffering which, given who he is and what he stands for, cannot be avoided. It is a must. It is not the suffering of the masochist who engineers the pain; it is the suffering of a man who has to pay a price for who he is and for the values for which he stands.

Christ is keenly aware that his future involves not only suffering, but the further sting of rejection. As Moltmann says: "To suffer and be rejected are not identical. Suffering can be celebrated and admired. It can arouse compassion. But to be rejected takes away the dignity from suffering and makes it dishonourable suffering. To suffer and be rejected signify the cross. To die on the cross means to suffer and to die as one who is an outcast and rejected. If those who follow Jesus are to take 'their cross' on themselves, they are taking on not only suffering and a bitter fate, but the suffering of rejection."[1]

Christ enjoins each disciple to "take up his cross daily". Their cross will not be to join Jesus and be crucified at Jerusalem: Jesus' experience of the cross is a uniquely significant event in the story of salvation. However, the disciples will have to pay a price for witnessing to the truth of the Gospel, to having the same values as Jesus did, to favouring the same kind of people in the poor, the outcast and the rejected. If they go public on their outcast God, they will predictably experience being outcasts themselves. They will not only suffer, they will also be rejected. That is the decision the disciples have to face at the cross-roads: whether to follow the path outlined by Jesus, or decline the invitation and travel another route. The cross stands at the centre, demanding attention. Whatever the disciples decide, whichever path in life they take will involve suffering. The question is not *whether* the individual will suffer in life, the question is *for whom* or *for what*. And the promise is that if one suffers in following the Gospel of Jesus, then that suffering will be transformed like Jesus' own suffering. It will eventually be transformed into glory. But, before that happens, the cross-roads have to be faced.

Luke 9: 28-36   *The Transfiguration*

[28]Now about eight days after these sayings he took with him Peter and John and James, and went up on the mountain to pray. [29]And as he was praying, the appearance of his countenance was altered, and his raiment became dazzling white. [30]And behold, two men talked with him, Moses and Elijah, [31]who appeared in glory and spoke of his departure, which he was to accomplish at Jerusalem. [32]Now Peter and those who were with him were heavy with sleep but kept awake, and they saw his glory and the two men who stood with him. [33]And as the men were parting from him, Peter said to Jesus, "Master, it is well that we are here; let us make three booths, one for you, and one for Moses and one for Elijah"—not knowing what he said. [34]As he said this, a cloud came and overshadowed them; and they were afraid as they entered the cloud. [35]And a voice came out of the cloud, saying, "This is my Son, my Chosen; listen to him!" [36]And when the voice had spoken, Jesus was found alone. And they kept silence and told no one in those days anything of what they had seen.

Peter has just confessed that Jesus is the promised one, and Jesus has elaborated on Peter's statement to tell the disciples that the Christ must suffer before he comes into his glory. Following on the confession, Jesus' words are now corroborated in the event of the transfiguration. While Jesus is caught up in prayer, the three chosen disciples witness him in glory; they have a preview of the glory which Jesus will enjoy after his exaltation. The three disciples, who are later to be remembered for going to sleep on Jesus' suffering on the Mount of Olives, now have difficulty staying awake on the mountain to witness his glory. Heavy-eyed, they witness their Master in the company of two champions of the Old Testament, Moses and Elijah.

Some scholars argue that this account is a misplaced resurrection apparition; but, if this is so, then Peter's suggestion does not make any sense. As it stands, the story makes sense in the light of what has just taken place, and in the light of Jesus' forthcoming journey to Jerusalem, the place of his rejection and glory. Moses, representing the law, and Elijah, representing the prophets, speak of Jesus' departure. The word Luke uses is *exodos,* which literally speaks of a journey, and figuratively speaks of death. Exodus is heavy with Old Testament significance, and the presence of Moses underlines the whole experience of Israel; but Jesus' own exodus will have its climax in his death, resurrection and ascension. Now, before he sets his face towards the place of his exaltation, he experiences the confirmation of his Father; he hears the echo of the voice which recognized him after his baptism.

Popular tradition had it that Moses and Elijah were mysteriously translated to the other world at death, and were expected to re-appear at the end of the world. Popular rumour understood Jesus to be a resurrected prophet, Elijah being mentioned as a possibility. In this event, Jesus is seen in the company of Moses and Elijah, not as one who is a modern repeat of them, but as the one who supersedes them. Moses and Elijah bow out of the scene, and the focus is on Jesus. Jesus stands alone. The old order has passed away, and it gives way to the man who sums up the law and the prophets: the Christ.

As Moses and Elijah make good their exit, Peter speaks of his desire to perpetuate the moment, to tabernacle the event for posterity. Luke adds a kind note that Peter is not aware of what he is saying. Peter's heavy-eyed suggestion for architectural posterity is rebuffed by the voice of God: "This is my Son, my Chosen; listen to *him*!" Jesus is the one who has the word for the present time, not Moses or Elijah. They have already gone, and Jesus stands confirmed in his future mission. The voice of God addresses the disciples: it ratifies the word of Jesus. He is the Word. Please pay attention to him.

But perhaps it is true to say that Jesus himself needs to hear that voice which confirmed him at the beginning of his public life. Given the journey he is about to undertake, Jesus needs all the confirmation he can get. Jesus himself is struggling through the very human task to understand what it means to be himself, and the experience of the transfiguration comes at a time when Jesus is articulating as much for himself as for his disciples who he is, what is irreducibly 'him', what makes up his uniqueness. In the transfiguration Jesus is affirmed by God, and that clear affirmation by God the Father is enough to transfigure anyone. The transfiguration helps Jesus to come into touch with his true self, as the Son of God, as the Chosen One of the Father.

To experience the truth that one is the Chosen One of the Father is profoundly consoling; but when one realizes that being chosen involves suffering and rejection, that realization is profoundly terrifying. There is no separation: being the Son involves the mission of suffering and rejection; experiencing the glory of the resurrection involves the prior experience of the cross. The two are inseparable. Jesus has just been seen in his glory, but the knowledge of what the glory will involve is enough to bring the whole company down from the clouds onto solid ground. They all have to descend the mountain and face the cross; they all have to leave the heights and come down to the place where they will be transformed from dust to glory. And that journey will be hurting. The transfiguration is a preview of the glory which will eventually come. Meanwhile, the journey to Jerusalem is outstanding in the diary.

Luke 9: 37-50   *At the Foot of the Mountain*

37On the next day, when they had come down from the mountain, a great crowd met him. 38And behold, a man from the crowd cried, "Teacher, I beg you to look upon my son, for he is my only child; 39and behold, a spirit seizes him, and he suddenly cries out; it convulses him till he foams, and shatters him, and will hardly leave him. ⁴⁰And I begged your disciples to cast it out, but they could not." ⁴¹Jesus answered, "O faithless and perverse generation, how long am I to be with you and bear with you? Bring your son here." ⁴²While he was coming, the demon tore him and convulsed him. But Jesus rebuked the unclean spirit, and healed the boy, and gave him back to his father. ⁴³And all were astonished at the majesty of God.

But while they were all marveling at everything he did, he said to his disciples, ⁴⁴"Let these words sink into your ears; for the Son of man is to be delivered into the hands of men." ⁴⁵But they did not understand this saying, and it was concealed from them, that they should not perceive it; and they were afraid to ask him about this saying.

⁴⁶And an argument arose among them as to which of them was the greatest. ⁴⁷But when Jesus perceived the thought of their hearts, he took a child and put him by his side, ⁴⁸and said to them, "Whoever receives this child in my name receives me, and whoever receives me receives him who sent me; for he who is least among you all is the one who is great."

⁴⁹John answered, "Master, we saw a man casting out demons in your name, and we forbade him, because he does not follow with us." ⁵⁰But Jesus said to him, "Do not forbid him; for he that is not against you is for you."

Jesus descends the mountain of the transfiguration; he comes from the clarity of God's revelation to meet the confusion of the crowd. The time of private communion with his Father is over for the moment; now, he has to deal with the demands of the crowd and the slow understanding of his disciples. Jesus is back on the level, and it is there that he discovers anew what he is up against. A man asks Jesus to heal his only son; he has already petitioned the disciples, but they have been unable to help him. Jesus now does what the disciples were unable to do—restore the boy's lost wholeness. The crowd is astonished. They have a glimpse of the majesty which was revealed on the mountain, but their wonder and astonishment do not lead them to believe in Jesus.

In contrast to the wonder of the crowd, there is the incomprehension of the disciples. Jesus speaks for the sec-

ond time of his coming passion, and tells the disciples that
the time is coming when he will be betrayed and handed
over to others. The disciples still do not "get" what Jesus is
saying, and Luke puts in an excusing clause saying that the
meaning is concealed from them. Later, when they would
receive the Spirit of understanding, they would remember
the saying and understand its meaning; but, for the time
being, not only are they lost, but they are too afraid to ask
Jesus for enlightenment.

As if to show how far distant they are from understanding the nature of the kingdom which is the central message
of Jesus' teaching, the disciples become involved in a
fruitless discussion as to who will sit above the salt in
Jesus' kingdom. After Jesus has made it clear that suffering is on the menu, the disciples have a seminar on their
respective seating arrangements in the kingdom. Perhaps
the fact that Jesus had taken only three disciples to the
mountain and left the others, has involved the disciples in
the lethal pastime of assessing their various merits to argue
who is the greatest. Jesus is speaking of suffering and rejection, while the disciples are speaking of prestige and
power. Two viewpoints bypass each other on the plain.

Jesus tries again to make his point clear: he may be tired
of his disciples' apparent obtuseness, but he does not give
up on them. He takes a child and tells the disciples that the
child is the model for the greatest. The child, whom
everyone can afford to ignore, the one who never sits
above the salt—this is the one to whom attention must be
paid. In the upside-down world of Jesus, the little people
are the blessed people; the ones who have no obvious access to power and prestige are the ones who are crowned
the greatest. The Gospel hallows the fairy-tale to speak the
good news that the youngest and the most forgettable inherit the kingdom of God. The disciples' serious argument
as to which of them is the greatest is a boring adult
headache: being great is a gift given freely to the least likely
candidate in the land of promise, the little child.

Following on that point, John complains that there is a

stranger to their company who is driving out demons in the name of Jesus. After an incident in which the disciples have been unable to cure a boy of possession, the fact that an outsider is evidently delivering people in the name of Jesus might appear as a threat. Again, Jesus supports the one whom the disciples would gladly banish into the land of obscurity. To cast out devils in the name of Jesus is to work against the power of evil. Jesus tells his disciples that they are no exclusive group with a monopoly on the power to exorcise; the power which they have has been given to them as a gift, and they should rejoice that the healing power has not been approved through the normal channels. Exorcists who are strangers to the disciples are no strangers to God.

At the end of his Galilean ministry, Jesus still remains a sign of contradiction to the crowd and an enigma to his own disciples. The transfiguration was an exceptional event in a ministry which is heavy with misunderstanding and confusion. So, Jesus has to face not only the cross, but the real prospect that he will die with his own disciples not understanding who he really is, and what he really stands for. The disciples still show how completely wrong they can be. But Jesus still tries to bring them closer to understanding him. But the time is shortening. Jesus now moves to keep an old appointment in the city of Jerusalem. The place of the cross beckons.

Luke 9: 51-62   The Road to Jerusalem

⁵¹When the days drew near for him to be received up, he set his face to go to Jerusalem. ⁵²And he sent messengers ahead of him, who went and entered a village of the Samaritans, to make ready for him; ⁵³but the people would not receive him, because his face was set toward Jerusalem. ⁵⁴And when his disciples James and John saw it, they said, "Lord, do you want us to bid fire come down from heaven and consume them?" ⁵⁵But he turned and rebuked them. ⁵⁶And they went on to another village.

⁵⁷As they were going along the road, a man said to him, "I will follow you wherever you go." ⁵⁸And Jesus said to him,

"Foxes have holes, and birds of the air have nests; but the Son of man has nowhere to lay his head." [59]To another he said, "Follow me." But he said, "Lord, let me first go and bury my father." [60]But he said to him, "Leave the dead to bury their own dead; but as for you, go and proclaim the kingdom of God." [61]Another said, "I will follow you, Lord; but let me first say farewell to those at my home." [62]Jesus said to him, "No one who puts his hand to the plow and looks back is fit for the kingdom of God."

The time has come for Jesus to move towards his rendezvous at Jerusalem. St. Luke outlines the now urgent mission of Jesus in the context of the journey to Jerusalem, the place where Jesus will be finally rejected, and the place where he will finally triumph. Jerusalem is the holy city, the throne of David, where it was promised that the Messiah would reign. From this passage until 19:45, when Jesus is in the temple in Jerusalem, Luke uses the journey as a thematic structure for the teaching of Jesus. The journey motif does not follow any chronological sequence, nor is it routed along any map: Luke is not interested in these points: he uses the journey narrative to underline Jesus' movement towards Jerusalem. For Luke, the climax of Jesus' mission is in the ascension, when Jesus makes the return to his Father. Now, he begins the journey which will eventually lead him back to his Father.

The time has come for Jesus "to be received up". The word Luke uses is *analempsis,* which recalls the assumption of Elijah who was taken up to heaven when he completed his work on earth (2 Kings ii:9-11). The end of Jesus' journey will be when Jesus is taken up, when he is welcomed home by his Father on the completion of his quest. Jesus' whole life can be seen in the terms of the quest story: Jesus receives the commission from his Father to set out on a journey in search of man; Jesus experiences the wilderness and the trials of the classical quest story; when his mission is completed, he makes the journey of return to his Father's house. Jesus has just been confirmed in his mission in the transfiguration; he has just revealed to his disciples that he is the suffering messiah; now, he sets his face towards Jerusalem, where the suffering and the return will be accomplished.

At the beginning of this journey, Jesus travels through Samaria, which is regarded by the Jews as hostile territory. Samaria was the old capital of the northern kingdom of the Old Testament Israelites, which fell to the Assyrians in 722 B.C. The conquerers colonised the territory by importing settlers from the Mesopotamian area, who mixed and intermarried with the indigenous people. The Jews of the southern kingdom returned from exile in Babylon and began the task of rebuilding the temple in 520 B.C. By then, the Samaritans were regarded as inferiors and outsiders because of their associations with foreigners, and the Jews refused their help to build the temple in Jerusalem. The Samaritans built their own temple on Mount Gerizim, as an alternative to the temple in Jerusalem.

When Jesus travels through Samaria, the inherited bitterness and tension between the two peoples are still alive. Luke tells us that Jesus sent messengers ahead of the main company to prepare lodgings in a Samaritan village, but the villagers refused hospitality "because his face was set towards Jerusalem". According to the Samaritans, Jesus is heading for the wrong place, and they do not feel obliged to offer hospitality to someone who is travelling towards a mistake. However, Luke is later to speak kindly of the Samaritans, when he writes of the good Samaritan who helps the injured traveller (10:37), and the one leper, a Samaritan, who returns to thank Jesus (17:16).

James and John suggest that Jesus respond to the Samaritans' inhospitality by a show of consuming fire; but, happily, Jesus makes it clear that his Gospel is not involved in wiping people out by vengeance. Jesus never takes his cue for action from other people's meanness; he acts out of his own graciousness and generosity. So, as he has already instructed his apostles to do when they meet a town's hostility, the company moves on.

In contrast to the opposition of the Samaritans, three

prospective disciples now present themselves to Jesus, and Jesus warns them of the hardship that discipleship inevitably involves. Jesus speaks of himself as the itinerant of God, the wandering gypsy who has nowhere to lay his head. Given that Jesus is now on the road to Jerusalem, his self-description makes sad sense: he will not lay his head until his head is laid out in death.

To the one who wants to delay so that he can bury the dead, Jesus suggests that he leave it to the spiritually dead to bury the physically dead: those who follow Jesus are spiritually alive, and they have to concern themselves about the life-demands of the Gospel. Likewise, to the man who wants to return to say farewell, Jesus speaks of the importance of what is ahead. Discipleship has no time for looking back: it concentrates its energies on the demands of the present and of the future.

At the beginning of the journey to Jerusalem, Jesus avoids any cosmetic presentation of discipleship. He offers his disciples a harshly realistic view of what they will have to face if they become involved in the same values and passions as he is involved in. The cross is the price which Jesus has to pay for his own involvement in love and forgiveness and compassion, and the disciples will have their own bill to pick up. And only if they are willing to pay the bill are they invited to join Jesus on the long road that leads to Jerusalem.

Notes

[1] J. Moltmann, *The Crucified God,* (London, S.C.M., 1977), p. 55

Chapter Ten

Luke 10: 1-20   **The Mission of the Disciples**

   10 After this the Lord appointed seventy others, and sent
them on ahead of him, two by two, into every town and place
where he himself was about to come. ²And he said to them,
"The harvest is plentiful, but the laborers are few; pray
therefore the Lord of the harvest to send out laborers into his
harvest. ³Go your way; behold, I send you out as lambs in the
midst of wolves. ⁴Carry no purse, no bag, no sandals; and
salute no one on the road. ⁵Whatever house you enter, first
say, 'Peace be to this house!' ⁶And if a son of peace is there,
your peace shall rest upon him; but if not, it shall return to
you. ⁷And remain in the same house, eating and drinking
what they provide, for the laborer deserves his wages; do not
go from house to house. ⁸Whenever you enter a town and
they receive you, eat what is set before you; ⁹heal the sick in it
and say to them, 'The kingdom of God has come near to
you.' ¹⁰But whenever you enter a town and they do not receive you, go into its streets and say, ¹¹'Even the dust of your
town that clings to our feet, we wipe off against you; nevertheless know this, that the kingdom of God has come near.'
¹²I tell you, it shall be more tolerable on that day for Sodom
than for that town.
   ¹³"Woe to you, Chorazin! woe to you, Bethsaida! for if
the mighty works done in you had been done in Tyre and
Sidon, they would have repented long ago, sitting in sack-
cloth and ashes. ¹⁴But it shall be more tolerable in the judgment for Tyre and Sidon than for you. ¹⁵And you, Capernaum, will be exalted to heaven? You shall be brought down
to Hades.
   ¹⁶"He who hears you hears me, and he who rejects you rejects me, and he who rejects me rejects him who sent me."
   ¹⁷The seventy returned with joy, saying, "Lord, even the
demons are subject to us in your name!" ¹⁸And he said to
them, "I saw Satan fall like lightning from heaven. ¹⁹Be-
hold, I have given you authority to tread upon serpents and

scorpions, and over all the power of the enemy; and nothing shall hurt you. [20]Nevertheless do not rejoice in this, that the spirits are subject to you; but rejoice that your names are written in heaven."

JESUS IS NOW ON THE ROAD TO JERUSALEM, the place where his mission will be accomplished. But he does not have all the time in the world, and there is an urgency in the air about spreading the message. Jesus appoints and commissions seventy others to go out to heal and to preach the kingdom. The number seventy is probably symbolic: there were reckoned to be seventy Gentile nations (Gen 10); and seventy elders accompanied Moses to the holy mountain (Ex 24:11). To spread his message, Jesus needs to start a movement, he needs to gather chosen people together and move them out to spread the kingdom. He needs help. Jesus is dependent on the various talents of his chosen ones to help in the task of spreading the news of the kingdom. He needs their preaching, their prayer, their ability to communicate, their halting understanding, their quiet faith, their unformed theology, their hesitant insights, their selective moments of bravery. And he has to handle their misunderstandings, their confusion, their own preferences about how things should be done, their varied abilities in dealing with people, their fragility, their clouded memories, their relatives, their expectations, their peculiar resolves, their unspoken fears, their view of the company and its future in the real world. Jesus did not wait until all these issues were clarified and solved before he sent out his disciples: he sent them out as they were, and risked his word in their frailty.

The process of sending out the disciples continues the process of the Incarnation. Again, the Word will be risked in flesh, it will assume human form, sometimes in the most unexpected places. The expected Word takes unexpected forms: it will be born again in the most unlikely Bethlehems of a weary world. And Jesus accepts that this is the way it has to be: the birth of the Word is an ongoing event in the preaching of the disciples, and it will retain its unusual quality of unexpectedness. But Jesus is not fretful about the ability of his disciples to handle what they meet on the road: if he were, he never would have sent them in the first place. But Jesus' own time is becoming scarcer by the hour, and if his word is going to spread, then he needs an organised and concerted effort to bring it to the people. Jesus' beginning to organise his movement is not proof that he is power-conscious; it is evidence of his own powerlessness to do the task by himself. It is clearly impossible for Jesus to attend to all the speaking engagements, to attend to all the cries for healing and for help, to pay attention to all the individuals who have a story to tell. Jesus cannot even attend to all his enemies by himself, and he will receive no obvious support from his disciples in that.

For the disciples, the mission is an adventure into the unknown. They are never sure of the reception they will receive, whether they will be welcomed, or whether they will have a multitude of blessings returned to them, batted back by a disbelieving crowd. Jesus warns them about the harshness of the landscape and the predatory creatures who will be roaming it. They will enter a terrain inhabited by wolves, the pretenders of gentleness and foolishness. The disciples will discover the unfortunate truth of Jesus' saying, and perhaps only then will they realise the truth of his words. Because of the urgency of their mission, the disciples have no time for wayside formalities or casual chats: they have the peace of Christ to offer in the homes of the people. The gift they bring to the household which receives them is the precious and elusive gift of peace, a gift which will rest on each person who accepts the disciples in the name of the Lord. And the gift of the Lord's peace which brings tranquility of spirit is more precious than any casual greeting on the road of hurry. The gift of peace rests; the hurried exchange on the road disappears in the dust.

If the peace of Christ descends on all who accept him, his curse descends on the Galilean towns, Chorazin and Bethsaida, which have rejected him. Tyre and Sidon, two of the most perfidious cities of the Gentile world, will have it easier on the day of judgement because they did not have the same opportunity to repent and turn to the Lord. Capernaum is picked out for special condemnation. It now lies lost under the ruins at Tell Hum. According to Matthew 9:1, Capernaum is Jesus' "own city"; according to John 1:44, Bethsaida is "the city of Andrew and Peter" and also of Philip: Jesus and his disciples are rejected by their own towns in spite of the signs which they worked there. One can hear Jesus' tiredness and hurt at being rejected coming through these woes. The final time is upon him, and Jesus looks for community rather than individual conversion.

But there is a note of joy. When the disciples return from their mission, they rejoice in the fact that the power which they received from Christ actually works. Perhaps they would not have had reason to rejoice in that unless they had first had doubts about the power of Christ. They discover through their own experience that demons are indeed subject to the word of God. But Jesus reminds them that they are not to rejoice in their newly discovered power; they are not to have inflated ideas about themselves because they possess extraordinary power—power which they received as a gift in the first place. They are to rejoice in the graciousness of God, in the knowledge that God holds their name as precious. The disciples are to rejoice in the fact that first and last they are loved by God. Anything after that is an anti-climax.

Luke 10: 21-24   *Jesus' Prayer of Thanksgiving*

[21]In that same hour he rejoiced in the Holy Spirit and said, "I thank thee, Father, Lord of heaven and earth, that thou hast hidden these things from the wise and understanding and revealed them to babes; yea, Father, for such was thy gracious will. [22]All things have been delivered to me by my Father; and no one knows who the Son is except the Father, or who the Father is except the Son and any one to whom the Son chooses to reveal him."

[23]Then turning to the disciples he said privately, "Blessed

are the eyes which see what you see! [24]"For I tell you that many prophets and kings desired to see what you see, and did not see it, and to hear what you hear, and did not hear it."

The seventy have just returned from their mission of healing and preaching, and they have told Jesus of the success of their work. Jesus is moved to make a hymn of praise to his Father. Like Elizabeth and Mary, Jesus rejoices in the Spirit and shows his joy by his prayer of praise. Jesus does not have to be reminded of the simplicity of his own disciples, but he rejoices that the Father has elected to reveal himself to them, who, by the standards of the conventional world, are unlearned and simple. None of the disciples appears to be particularly distinguished, and Jesus compares them to the moppets of the nursery. And no one expects moppets to traffic in profundities; they are expected to keep the company of attic toys, and move easily in the kingdom of fantasy. But the light of the Gospel glimmers in the nursery of the world, and the babes are given truths too heavy for the adults to carry. And Jesus rejoices that the Gospel is preached not *in spite of* the simplicity of his disciples, but *because of* their simplicity. It is the Father's will that these little ones are chosen to share the revelation of God. God shares his secret about himself with the little people of the world, and keeps his secret from the wise and the clever.

In the first place, the Father revealed the secret in a Word, a Word which came as foolishness and was destined to be ignored. The choice of those who are to share the secret of God is in the same tradition. No doubt the disciples often wondered why they were chosen, why Jesus did not choose others who would have been better equipped for public relations, who would have had an easier facility with words, who could have mixed with effortless ease in any company, who could have avoided some of the disasters of Jesus' ministry, who could have ensured that Jesus would never expose himself to hostile crowds, who could have ensured that the wonders Jesus worked would receive

better notice. But no: Jesus goes to the nursery of the
world to choose his followers. In the upside-down kingdom which Jesus has come to establish, he chooses the
youngest sons, the forgotten people, the ones who do not
inherit the world's goods and wisdom: these are the ones
who carry his message far away. Again, the fairy-tale
choice is blessed in the Gospel.

Jesus rejoices that the Father has conferred all authority
in him, who himself is a little one. And Jesus rejoices in the
knowledge that if no one else fully understands him, his
Father does. And that is a profound consolation when he is
surrounded by inspired guesses and halting proclamations.
Because Christ is known by the Father and knows the
Father, he can reveal the Father to others. He is the only
ikon of the Father, he is the only one who can speak of the
Father in a Word. Jesus is the Word between the silence of
God and the understanding in the Spirit. To understand
the silence, the silence has to be interpreted through a
Word. And Jesus is the only Word in whom the mystery of
God can be understood.

Jesus now gives his disciples a private beatitude: they are
blessed because they have been given the gift of sight. The
prophets and the kings of old had the experience of longing, but not the experience of seeing. They never set eyes
on the sight they longed to see, they never heard the Word
they longed to hear. But the disciples have the experience
of seeing what others longed for, of hearing what others
longed to hear. The disciples are in the time of fulfilment,
and the time of fulfilment is the present. They hear the
Word which at last breaks the silence of God's secret. God
has literally given himself away in a Word—not by a mistake, or by a slip, but by the purposeful action of sending
the Word. And Jesus is the Word that breaks the silence of
ages.

Luke 10: 25-37   *The Good Samaritan*

²⁵And behold, a lawyer stood up to put him to the test,
saying, "Teacher, what shall I do to inherit eternal life?"

²⁶He said to him, "What is written in the law? How do you read?" ²⁷And he answered, "You shall love the Lord your God with all your heart, and with all your soul, and with all your strength, and with all your mind; and your neighbor as yourself." ²⁸And he said to him, "You have answered right; do this, and you will live."

²⁹But he, desiring to justify himself, said to Jesus, "And who is my neighbor?" ³⁰Jesus replied, "A man was going down from Jerusalem to Jericho, and he fell among robbers, who stripped him and beat him, and departed, leaving him half dead. ³¹Now by chance a priest was going down that road; and when he saw him he passed by on the other side. ³²So likewise a Levite, when he came to the place and saw him, passed by on the other side. ³³But a Samaritan, as he journeyed, came to where he was; and when he saw him, he had compassion, ³⁴and went to him and bound up his wounds, pouring on oil and wine; then he set him on his own beast and brought him to an inn, and took care of him. ³⁵And the next day he took out two denarii and gave them to the innkeeper, saying, 'Take care of him; and whatever more you spend, I will repay you when I come back.' ³⁶Which of these three, do you think, proved neighbor to the man who fell among the robbers?" ³⁷He said, "The one who showed mercy on him." And Jesus said to him, "Go and do likewise."

A theologian, an expert in the Jewish law, comes to Jesus to seek enlightenment. It is an unusual scenario: the lawyer playing disciple to the country prophet; but Jesus tests the authenticity of the lawyer more than the lawyer tests the wits of Jesus. The lawyer begins the exchange by asking how he is to inherit eternal life, but Jesus declines to answer his question directly; instead, he throws the lawyer back on his own knowledge of the law so that the lawyer ends up in answering his own question. The lawyer's answer echoes the classical rabbinic teaching which combines the love of God (Deut 6:5) with the love of neighbour (Lev 19:18). Jesus commends the lawyer for his answer, and enjoins him to move from the level of knowledge to the level of action and *do* what the law commands. Jesus is not so much concerned about remembering the right answer as doing the right answer; he is concerned that the lawyer not only be sincere in his answer, but serious about its fulfilment. And the answer to the question is truly discovered only at the heart of human experience. There is nowhere else to discover it.

The lawyer, after losing the first round, moves in to regain his position. He now seeks a cerebral clarification of the term "neighbour", but Jesus offers him actual involvement in being a neighbour. The lawyer sees neighbourliness in terms of legal prescription, Jesus sees neighbourliness in terms of human relationship; the lawyer regards a neighbour as a limited responsibility, Jesus regards a neighbour as a gracious supporter. The lawyer has already quoted the law which understood neighbour as the one who should be ministered to, as the object of love; but Jesus' parable switches the focus from the neighbour as the object of love to the neighbour as subject of love. In the parable, the neighbour is the one who actually ministers to the needy, the one who is engaged in love in the active tense. Jesus makes it clear in his story that the neighbour, "the one who is near", is not a matter for definition or for legal limitation; neighbour is a way of being in the world, it is a way of relating to other people and to God.

In his parable, Jesus tests the lawyer's answer. The lawyer has been focusing on the observance of the law, and Jesus' parable tells him the good news that the law which he has mentioned is enough to travel on in human life. In his story, Jesus does not concentrate on the law, he concentrates on a person who in his graciousness and concern sums up the whole of the law. And again, the person whom Jesus selects is one who is regarded as an alien and outsider by the Jews. The one whom everyone can apparently afford to neglect is the one whom nobody can afford to ignore. The outsider becomes the model for the whole law; the outcast becomes the one who enshrines Christian action. And the lawyer finds himself in the position where he has to admit that the Samaritan in the story, not the officials of religion, is the one who proves to be neighbour. The lawyer acknowledges the truth of the paradox that his own people's favourite enemy is the one who shows the way to salvation.

The scene of the story is the narrow, dangerous road

from Jerusalem to Jericho, a road of seventeen miles that was a dream to the robber and a nightmare to the traveller. A lonely traveller makes his way along the rocky ground to be ambushed by a band of robbers, who strip him and leave him half-dead. A priest passes by, notices the naked body of the traveller, but decides not to become involved and keeps to his schedule. A little later, another religious official, a Levite, notices the beaten-up body, but he too hurries on his way. Both officials give the hurt traveller a wide berth, and go their private ways. Perhaps, neither wants to become ritually defiled by coming into contact with human blood, or into contact with what they suspect could be a corpse. Whatever their reasons, they both ignore the man in the ditch.

A Samaritan is travelling the same route, and when he sees the man in need, he is moved by compassion and he moves to help the man in need. The priest and Levite are unmoved movers; the Samaritan moves to where he sees there is need. The Samaritan offers immediate first-aid in binding up the man's wounds, and then goes further, by taking the man with him to a safe lodging-place, where he can rest and become whole again. It costs the Samaritan to help the lonely traveller, but he willingly pays the price for the man's continued care, and takes responsibility for any additional costs that may accrue in his absence. Only when he is assured that the traveller will be cared for, does the Samaritan go on his way.

The religious officials are the ones who pass by the hurt and the wounded; the outsider is the one who pays attention. According to the the lawyer's outlook on life, he would have expected the priest and the Levite to stop and help and the Samaritan to hurry past; but the parable reverses the human expectations of the lawyer; it totally upsets them. The least likely of the three candidates is the one who fulfills the spirit of the law. The one who is regarded as the enemy is the one who befriends; the two who are regarded as upholders of the law are the ones who pass by its fulfilment.

To Jesus' question, "Which of the three proved neighbour?" the lawyer cannot bring himself to name the Samaritan: he describes what the Samaritan did. But the point is taken, and Jesus tells him, "Go and do likewise." Do the story, experience the truth of the story in action. Dietrich Bonhoeffer sums up the point eloquently when he writes: "We have literally no time to sit down and ask ourselves whether so-and-so is our neighbour or not. We must get into action and obey—we must behave like a neighbour to him. But perhaps this shocks you. Perhaps you still think you ought to think out beforehand and know what you ought to do. To that there is only one answer. You can only know and think about it by actually doing it."[1] The true disciple is the one who follows the injunction of Jesus: he is the one who goes his way and does the word of God. He learns the story of God by doing it, by making it happen on his own journey.

Luke 10: 38-42   *A Visit to Martha and Mary*

[38]Now as they went on their way, he entered a village; and a woman named Martha received him into her house. [39]And she had a sister called Mary, who sat at the Lord's feet and listened to his teaching. [40]But Martha was distracted with much serving; and she went to him and said, "Lord, do you not care that my sister has left me to serve alone? Tell her then to help me." [41]But the Lord answered her, "Martha, Martha, you are anxious and troubled about many things; [42]one thing is needful. Mary has chosen the good portion, which shall not be taken away from her."

The itinerant Jesus continues his journey on the road to Jerusalem, and stops in the village where Martha and Mary live. If the village is Bethany, Luke does not mention it: Bethany, being so close to Jerusalem, would not suit Luke's scheme of the journey to Jerusalem. Luke is still eight chapters in time away from Jesus' entry to Jerusalem, and Bethany is too close for his purposes. Luke portrays

Martha as the busy hostess whose only concern is to offer her guests a satisfying meal, and Mary as the eager listener to the word of the Lord. Jesus gently chides Martha for her busyness on his behalf, and tells her that the present need is not for an extravagant table to answer to his hunger, but for a generous ear in answer to his word.

The story of Martha and Mary has long been the casualty of a theological collision between various theologians who have debated the comparative merits of the active and contemplative lives. Many have argued that Martha in her busyness represents the active life of the Church, while Mary in her undivided attention to Christ represents the contemplative life. The champions of the contemplative life thought that they had struck gold in this story: here was an undeniable assertion of the supremacy of the contemplative life, where Jesus makes it clear that he prefers Mary's way to that of Martha.

By and large, that is the understanding of the story which many people have inherited: a sort of cartoon that has been paraded as the reality of the Gospel story. Martha has received an unsympathetic press from some because she is seen as the proverbial fussing aunt who sighs the sigh of the self-styled martyr; Mary has been canonized as the budding contemplative who gives a willing ear to pious ditties, who is unconcerned about the practical workings of life but is happy to hang up her brush in favour of a theological seminar while unrepentantly watching the world go by.

People secretly admire Martha, while publicly paying tribute to Mary. Like the busy pastor who might argue: "I laud Mary from the pulpit, but when it comes to choosing a housekeeper, I look for the Marthas of this world." But the story of Martha and Mary is not about prospective housekeepers or budding contemplatives: it is about the primacy of the word of God in the Christian life.

If one argues that the story is about the active and contemplative lives, then, logically, in order to let Martha represent the active life *with impunity,* one must argue that

Martha was right in carrying on with the housework while Jesus was present. But the point of the story is that Martha was wrong. Jesus says to Martha: "Martha, you are anxious and troubled about many things; one thing is needful." And Mary is doing the "needful" thing: she is listening to the word of God as it is spoken to her. What Jesus is in effect saying is that, at the present time, housework is not the needful thing, preparing a meal is not the demand of the moment. The demand of the moment is to pay attention to what the Lord wants—an attentive ear to the word which he has to speak. Mary has stopped to listen to Jesus, she has made time to spend with the Lord, she has subjected all her activity to his word. Martha has carried on with what *she* thinks is the need of the moment, and would have Mary subject to her plan of action—in which case Jesus would be left to talk to himself, and play spectator to their busyness. But Jesus has not much time left; he is on the road to Jerusalem, and he wants people to pay attention to the word which he has to say.

The story of Martha and Mary speaks of the attitude of the disciple before the presence and the word of God. The disciple should never kill the opportunity of hearing the word of God by being busy about being busy. This is not an argument to leave floors lonely for the company of a brush, or stomachs widowed for the loss of food: it is an argument for paying attention to *why* the guest has come. And the guest does not want a gastronomic extravaganza: that is not the purpose of his visit. He wants the quiet assurance that people think it worthwhile to take time to listen to what he has to say. Before his disciples are doers of the word, they are hearers of the word. For if the word of God is unheard in the disciples' lives, then it will be unspoken in their lives as well.

Notes

[1]D. Bonhoeffer, *The Cost of Discipleship* (London, S.C.M. 1978) pp. 67-68

Chapter Eleven

Luke 11- 1-4   *Prayer and Discipleship*

> **11** He was praying in a certain place, and when he ceased, one of his disciples said to him, "Lord, teach us to pray, as John taught his disciples." ²And he said to them, "When you pray, say:
> "Father, hallowed be thy name. Thy kingdom come. ³Give us each day our daily bread; ⁴and forgive us our sins, for we ourselves forgive every one who is indebted to us; and lead us not into temptation."

JESUS' OWN PRAYER MOVES ONE OF THE DISCIPLES to ask for a lesson in prayer, and Jesus happily obliges. In Matthew's account (6:9-13), the Lord's prayer is given in the context of the Sermon on the Mount; Luke's context seems more original. In his teaching prayer, Jesus reflects his own consciousness of God, he speaks through an awareness of intimacy with God whom he knows as Father, he tells of his emphasis on praise and petition. This is not a private prayer of Jesus, exclusive to him alone: the prayer is couched in the *plural,* not the singular: it is given as the prayer of the community. Jesus addresses God not in the formal terms of the traditional Jewish prayer, but in a uniquely intimate way which many people could find shocking. Jesus calls God, Father, *Abba,* which is the name a child would use to speak to his human father. *Abba* literally means daddy; it is the familiar cry of the moppet who is assured that he is speaking to a loved one, not the hesitant request of the civil servant formally seeking an audience with an anonymous power.

The prayer of Jesus summarizes Jesus' own preaching and theology; it invites the disciples to become involved in a relationship of family intimacy, of speaking to God as a generous Father with the quiet assurance of a child who has nothing to fear. The first two petitions pray for the fulfilment of God's plan on earth; the other three petitions pray for the various needs of the disciples. The prayer first proclaims the blessedness of God's name; it praises and glorifies the Father's whole being, a being called *Abba;* it asks God to act in such a way that his name will be blessed and praised among men. The prayer involves the disciples in God's passion, his kingdom, his rule of love and forgiveness, and it is that kingdom which the disciple is pledged to spread in his life and work.

The disciples are to pray for daily bread. Scholars disagree over the meaning of the word "daily": some argue that it speaks of present needs, like the daily rations of the soldier; others argue from ancient manuscripts that it is the "bread for the morrow" which speaks of the coming of the kingdom. Perhaps the two ideas are not mutually exclusive: in his commissioning of the disciples, Christ told them to depend for their daily needs on the hospitality of those to whom they ministered: if the people accepted the disciples and offered them hospitality, it was also a sign that they accepted the Lord and the message of the kingdom. For the disciple, being given daily bread was a sign of the spread of the kingdom. In that sense, when the disciple prays for daily bread, he also prays for the coming of the kingdom of God.

Jesus is a sign of God's forgiveness, and the prayer which he offers his disciples now asks for that forgiveness. God's forgiveness is not conditional on human performance: God forgives, and that is the end of the matter. But the disciple's own lack of forgiveness should not stand in the way of God's graciousness, especially if we believe that God's forgiveness works through human forgiveness— "whose sins you shall forgive, they are forgiven" (John 20:23). In that understanding, *not* to forgive others obscures the forgiving nature of the Father.

The last petition of the prayer asks the Father to "lead

us not into temptation." At first sight, the phrase would seem to imply that God could be involved in actively causing people to succumb to temptation, but the prayer is asking God to use his power so that the disciple does not succumb to temptation. Jesus is later to reflect that his own life has its "times of trial" (22:28), as he is to tell his disciples to "pray that you may not enter into temptation" (22:46). This last petition asks the Father to help the disciple in his time of trial and temptation, and again, Jesus' own experience bears out the answer to that prayer.

The whole spirit of the prayer takes its key from the first word, *Abba*. If the disciple really believes that God is a generous Father from whom there is nothing to fear, and from whom there is everything to expect, then he is challenged in whatever he does by the governing image of a generous Father. If the governing image of God is one of meanness and low expectation, of someone who does not actually *do* anything, then the disciple is likely to be the unfortunate image of that peculiar God in his own ministry. A generous image of God begets a generous image of the human; a belief in the utter forgiveness of God should animate the disciple in his own efforts at forgiveness. The prayer that Jesus offers as a model speaks of a God who cares passionately about what happens in his own family, it speaks of a God who has not fallen in love with long distance, but is as near his children as their calls for *Abba*. The Father is only a whisper away from the cradle of the world.

Luke 11: 5-13   *Prayer and Imagination*

⁵And he said to them, "Which of you who has a friend will go to him at midnight and say to him, 'Friend, lend me three loaves; ⁶for a friend of mine has arrived on a journey, and I have nothing to set before him'; ⁷and he will answer from within, 'Do not bother me; the door is now shut, and my children are with me in bed; I cannot get up and give you anything'? ⁸I tell you, though he will not get up and give him anything because he is his friend, yet because of his importunity he will rise and give him whatever he needs. ⁹And I tell you, Ask, and it will be

given you; seek, and you will find; knock, and it will be opened to you. [10]For every one who asks receives, and he who seeks finds, and to him who knocks it will be opened. [11]What father among you, if his son asks for a fish, will instead of a fish give him a serpent; [12]or if he asks for an egg, will give him a scorpion? [13]If you then, who are evil, know how to give good gifts to your children, how much more will the heavenly Father give the Holy Spirit to those who ask him!"

After giving his disciples the model prayer, Jesus now continues to speak to them about the generosity of the Father who listens to all prayers. Jesus invites the disciples to reflect on the kindness which is part of human experience and imagine a God who is infinitely kinder than anything in their experience. Jesus invites the disciples to exercise their dusty imaginations and imagine a God from whom there is nothing to fear, a God who is not in the business of putting people down or sending them off empty-handed, a God who has not barricaded himself into his remote church and put heavy locks on the stained-glass windows, a God who is not so hard of hearing that he will never bother to answer the door.

The fact that Jesus spends so much time stressing the generosity of God suggests that he had to work against a contrary impression which people had of God. Many people do believe in a God who has a gift for disaster, whose only music is the dirge, whose chief pastime seems to be the manufacturing of earthquakes and catastrophes. But this is the theology of the insurance company, in which acts of God are understood only in terms of disaster. It is a fact of life that many see God as the executioner, and themselves as the witless victims. Like Edward in *King Lear,* the theology runs thus:

As flies to wanton boys, are we to gods;
They kill us for their sport.

In this teaching on prayer, Jesus makes it clear that God is not a sadist in the sky, distributing disasters, but a Father

who passionately wants people to be nurtured in his kingdom in the knowledge that they are loved, listened to, and
attended to. Jesus asks the disciples to imagine the most
generous qualities about humans; to imagine that God is
all that and infinitely more. And then stop imagining;
because it is true. Begin to relate to God as a generous
God, and see what happens to the life-story.

To make this point, Jesus uses his own imagination to
tell a humorous story, and asks his disciples to exercise
their imaginations in listening to it. It is late one night
when the village is asleep and all is quiet. A tired and
hungry traveller calls at the house of a friend in the hope
that he will find rest and food, even in spite of the ungodly
hour. His friend does not disappoint him; he keeps alive
the old tradition of Eastern hospitality, and even though he
is caught with an empty cupboard, he goes abroad into the
night to another friend's house to borrow the three loaves
which make up a good meal. The surprised midnight host
becomes involved in letter-box diplomacy, telling of his
needs through a closed door. The householder makes it
clear that he does not want to be bothered at this hour; all
the family are abed on their shared mat, and they would all
be disturbed by the creaky drawing of the bolt. But the
midnight diplomacy continues for awhile, and eventually
the householder capitulates, not so much for the sake of
friendship, as for the simple sake of peace. The householder returns sleepily to his mat; the host returns happily
to his hungry friend.

Jesus makes the point to his disciples that if a friend can
be induced to pay attention to the needs of a midnight petitioner, how much more will God—who is *Abba,* daddy—
pay attention to the needs of his own children. Jesus
assures the disciples that God is much more gracious than
they can begin to imagine, and they should imagine him as
utter graciousness, and then start praying to him in that
understanding. If prayer is faith talking, then the disciples
should let their imaginative faith in God the Father speak
through their prayers.

Jesus tells his disciples to be unwearied in their efforts at prayer. Even if the human experience seems to be telling the disciple that he is going nowhere with his prayer, Jesus tells him that he should not let the force of that impression press him to give up. It is worthwhile to keep on asking, to keep on seeking, to keep on knocking, because God is more than silence, he is Word, and he will reply. Jesus will put his own life on the assurance that God will come and recognize the petitioner standing at the door with a voice hoarse from asking, with feet sore from seeking, with knuckles bruised from knocking. Jesus himself will get hoarse and sore and bruised, and the Father will not only recognize him, he will invite him home.

The most precious gift that the Father can give is the gift of the Holy Spirit: that will be his gift to the world when he invites Jesus home. And the gift of the Spirit is to be had for the asking; the gift of understanding is to be given to those who pray to the Father. The disciples will experience how different the world is when they receive that gift: they will still have to suffer, and to argue, and to work through their own shadowlands; but the gift of the Spirit is the constant assurance of the presence of God working at the heart of reality. And, like Jesus, it will be in that Spirit that their prayers will be made. And how can God refuse himself?

Luke 11: 14-28   The Lord of the Flies

¹⁴Now he was casting out a demon that was dumb; when the demon had gone out, the dumb man spoke, and the people marveled. ¹⁵But some of them said, "He casts out demons by Beelzebul, the prince of demons"; ¹⁶while others, to test him, sought from him a sign from heaven. ¹⁷But he, knowing their thoughts, said to them, "Every kingdom divided against itself is laid waste, and a divided household falls. ¹⁸And if Satan also is divided against himself, how will his kingdom stand? For you say that I cast out demons by Beelzebul. ¹⁹And if I cast out demons by Beelzebul, by whom do your sons cast them out? Therefore they shall be your judges. ²⁰But if it is by the finger of God that I cast out

demons, then the kingdom of God has come upon you. [21]When a strong man, fully armed, guards his own palace, his goods are in peace; [22]but when one stronger than he assails him and overcomes him, he takes away his armor in which he trusted, and divides his spoil. [23]He who is not with me is against me, and he who does not gather with me scatters.

[24]"When the unclean spirit has gone out of a man, he passes through waterless places seeking rest; and finding none he says, 'I will return to my house from which I came.' [25]And when he comes he finds it swept and put in order. [26]Then he goes and brings seven other spirits more evil than himself, and they enter and dwell there; and the last state of that man becomes worse than the first."

[27]As he said this, a woman in the crowd raised her voice and said to him, "Blessed is the womb that bore you, and the breast that you sucked!" [28]But he said, "Blessed rather are those who hear the word of God and keep it!"

Jesus exorcises a demon which is causing dumbness in a man, and the assembled people predictably marvel at the event. No one questions Jesus' evident power, but some of the onlookers accuse him of being in league with Satan, while others still await what they are pleased to call a sign from heaven. Jesus responds to the accusation that he is working for Beelzebul, the ruler of demons, with a number of telling arguments. Jesus points out that Satan is not such a dunce at the school of strategy that he would promote a civil war for the advancement of his kingdom: that would be singularly stupid. Given that his hearers take the point, Jesus takes his accusers to task on an inconsistency in their own argument: they argue that Jesus exorcises through the power of Satan, while holding that their own exorcists minister through the power of God. If they condemn Jesus, they implicitly condemn their own exorcists. Jesus has already told his own disciples that those who banish demons are not opposed to the work he is doing (9:50); now he tells his accusers that the exorcists they condemn will be justified, and their justification will be a judgement on their critics. If it is only by the power of God that demons are cast out, then it must be concluded that the presence of the kingdom is in the midst of the people. They already have their sign.

The name Jesus' accusers give to his putative patron is Beelzebul, which means "lord of the flies"—a derisory variation of the original name which meant "lord of the house". Jesus now portrays Satan as the lord of a fortified palace. The lord is a strong man whose goods are only secure because they are guarded well and because no one stronger has stormed the palace. But a stronger does come along to demolish the incumbent's trusted defences and distribute his goods. Satan is at the mercy of a stronger one, and a stronger one has come and is in the presence of the people. And Jesus makes it clear that he who does not join him against the power of evil is opposed to him, and must eventually lose because such a person is on the weaker side. As Jesus sees the conflict between good and evil as the metaphor of battle, he is in no doubt about the identity of the winner.

In the language of exorcism, the house of which Satan's power can take possession is the individual person. Jesus now emphasises the necessity of putting something in the house when Satan's power has vacated it. Nature may abhor a vacuum, but Satan has little problem with it. So, it is useless for the exorcist to banish evil and put nothing in its place. If casting out demons is a sign of the kingdom, then what should replace the presence of evil is the acceptance of the kingdom of God, of the power which moved out the evil in the first place. Jesus argues that the exorcist is doing the possessed man no favour by simply banishing the demon and leaving nothing; the nothing invites the return of more evil. And when a woman from the crowd voices a blessing on Jesus' mother, Jesus replies by underlining what he has just said: he blesses those who hear the word of God and keep it. It is the word of God which fills man's vacancy; it is keeping the word of God which will keep evil banished forever.

Jesus is clear in his own teaching that the kingdom of God is in constant battle with the kingdom of evil. The fundamental question that Jesus poses asks people which kingdom they show allegiance to, which kingdom do they allow themselves to be ruled by. In his novel, *Lord of the*

Flies, William Golding tells a story about a party of evacuated schoolboys who are marooned on a desert island, and who, by the time they are rescued, have degenerated into a group of uncaring savages. Golding explores the reality of what he sees as "the beast within" which causes the schoolboys to do such evil. One of the boys, Simon, leaves the rest of the company to go into the wilderness, where he has a conversation with the Lord of the Flies, who says: "'You knew didn't you? I'm part of you? Close, close, close! I'm the reason why it's no go? Why things are what they are?'''[2]

The message of Jesus is not a message of despair which is powerless to do anything about the destructive power which makes life "no go". The word which Jesus brings is a word which not only banishes the possessive power of evil, but keeps people in the power of good. When the Lord of the Flies is confronted with the power of the kingdom of God he is forced to abandon his possessions. And that is Gospel.

Luke 11: 29-36   *A Sign to the World*

[29]When the crowds were increasing, he began to say, "This generation is an evil generation; it seeks a sign, but no sign shall be given to it except the sign of Jonah. [30]For as Jonah became a sign to the men of Nineveh, so will the Son of man be to this generation. [31]The queen of the South will arise at the judgment with the men of this generation and condemn them; for she came from the ends of the earth to hear the wisdom of Solomon, and behold, something greater than Solomon is here. [32]The men of Nineveh will arise at the judgment with this generation and condemn it; for they repented at the preaching of Jonah, and behold, something greater than Jonah is here.

[33]"No one after lighting a lamp puts it in a cellar or under a bushel, but on a stand, that those who enter may see the light. [34]Your eye is the lamp of your body; when your eye is sound, your whole body is full of light; but when it is not sound, your body is full of darkness. [35]Therefore be careful lest the light in you be darkness. [36]If then your whole body is

full of light, having no part dark, it will be wholly bright, as
when a lamp with its rays gives you light.''

Some of the crowd listening to Jesus have already made
it known that they are waiting for a sign (v. 16), and Jesus
now addresses them directly. He tells them that the Son of
man will be a sign to the present generation in the same
way that Jonah was a sign to the people of Nineveh. But,
how was Jonah a sign? This saying of Jesus is difficult and
scholars argue about its precise meaning. They dispute
whether the sign of Jonah to the Ninevites was the
preaching of the prophet or his resuscitation after being in
the belly of the great fish; and whether the corresponding
sign to the present generation refers to the preaching of
Christ or to his resurrection after three days in a tomb. In
the record of his own preaching, Jonah does not refer to
his unusual marine hostelry; he stresses that the word of
God to the people of Ninevah is a word of destruction and
desolation which challenges them to repent. Jonah's prophecy of the coming doom does not turn out to be true,
but the point of prophecy is repentance, not accuracy. The
Ninevites heeded the word of God which they accepted as
authentic in the word of Jonah, and they repented, not
because of the wonder of Jonah's recent emergence from a
whale, but ''at the preaching of Jonah'' (v. 32). And the
Ninevites had less than Jesus' present hearers to go on; but
the Ninevites will judge the present generation who fail to
recognize a greater than Jonah in their midst.

As the Ninevites paid attention to the word of the prophet, Jonah (Jon 3), so the Queen of Sheba attended to the
word of the wise man, Solomon, and travelled great
distances to hear the word of God mediated through his
wisdom (1 Kings: 10:1 ff.). And the present generation
have a greater than Solomon in their midst. The Ninevites
and the Queen of Sheba were moved to repentance by the
authentic word of God; the present generation are ignoring
a far clearer word as it speaks to them in the life and
preaching of Jesus. They wait for a sign, while the sign

stands before them. The present generation are treating
signs as spectacular events which will induce wonder,
whereas they herald the messianic age which aims to
awaken repentance. Jesus never admonishes the crowd for
not reacting to signs with wonder—people can wonder all
their lives and commit themselves to nothing; but he does
reproach the people for not responding to his signs with a
life of repentance. Repentance is the true response to the
sign of Jonah.

Luke gives a series of Jesus' sayings which use the
metaphor of light. The question for those who listen to the
word of God is whether they are going to be touched and
moved by the light before them, or remain wrapped and
isolated in their own darkness. If they become enlightened
people, they will dispel the dullness and the darkness
within and around them. Light is not private energy; it is
for sharing with others; it is for banishing the darkness
over the face of the deep. And if there is darkness over
anyone's deep, it will communicate itself to others. If the
person is alive with the light, a light that has been lighted
within, that light will give clarity and warmth and comfort
to those who sit in darkness, to those who wander in the
shadows in search of a glimmer of light.

Jesus speaks of the eyes as the lamp of the body. Con-
versational usage speaks of eyes in terms of light—of eyes
which shine, sparkle, flash, dazzle, glimmer, glitter,
twinkle, glisten, gleam. In Shakespeare's *Troilus and
Cressida,* Ulysses says of Cressida:

> There's language in her eye, her cheek, her lip,
> Nay her foot speaks; her wanton spirits look out
> At every joint and motive of her body.

> (IV, v, 55)

Eyes which sparkle speak as a joyful sign; eyes which are
vacant and lifeless tell their own tale. People who hear the
word of God and act on it are in turn expected to be signs
to others, signs which clearly communicate the good news

which has been first received as gift. The whole person is a sign to others—so if many of the others are in darkness, it helps if the sign is well lighted. The alternative is darkness speaking to darkness about the energy crisis.

Luke 11: 37-54   *Criticism of the Pharisees and the Lawyers*

[37]While he was speaking, a Pharisee asked him to dine with him; so he went in and sat at table. [38]The Pharisee was astonished to see that he did not first wash before dinner. [39]And the Lord said to him, "Now you Pharisees cleanse the outside of the cup and of the dish, but inside you are full of extortion and wickedness. [40]You fools! Did not he who made the outside make the inside also? [41]But give for alms those things which are within; and behold, everything is clean for you.

[42]"But woe to you Pharisees! for you tithe mint and rue and every herb, and neglect justice and the love of God; these you ought to have done, without neglecting the others. [43]Woe to you Pharisees! for you love the best seat in the synagogues and salutations in the market places. [44]Woe to you! for you are like graves which are not seen, and men walk over them without knowing it."

[45]One of the lawyers answered him, "Teacher, in saying this you reproach us also." [46]And he said, "Woe to you lawyers also! for you load men with burdens hard to bear, and you yourselves do not touch the burdens with one of your fingers. [47]Woe to you! for you build the tombs of the prophets whom your fathers killed. [48]So you are witnesses and consent to the deeds of your fathers; for they killed them, and you build their tombs. [49]Therefore also the Wisdom of God said, 'I will send them prophets and apostles, some of whom they will kill and persecute,' [50]that the blood of all the prophets, shed from the foundation of the world, may be required of this generation, [51]from the blood of Abel to the blood of Zechariah, who perished between the altar and the sanctuary. Yes, I tell you, it shall be required of this generation. [52]Woe to you lawyers! for you have taken away the key of knowledge; you did not enter yourselves, and you hindered those who were entering."

[53]As he went away from there, the scribes and the Pharisees began to press him hard, and to provoke him to

speak of many things, ⁵⁴lying in wait for him, to catch at something he might say.

Jesus accepts an invitation to dinner. His host is a Pharisee, who betrays his surprise that Jesus feels free to ignore the ritual washing of the hands before the beginning of the meal. Jesus has already publicly ignored the Pharisaic rules for observing the sabbath and keeping a distance from sinners, and now he continues to make it clear that he does not feel bound to follow the Pharisaic interpretations of the law. Again, Jesus is provoked before he says his piece, and Luke uses the occasion to give Jesus' collected criticisms of the Pharisees and the lawyers. Jesus addresses three woes to the Pharisees, criticizing them for their practice of the law; he addresses three woes to the scribes, criticizing them for their attitude to the law. Manson argues that Jesus is not placing his argument with the whole body of the Pharisees and the lawyers because: "The Pharisaic ideal was a genuine religious ideal; and the men who gave themselves to it were mostly sincere and earnest. To maintain that all Pharisees were *ipso facto* hypocrites is as absurd as a claim that they were all saints."³ One can take Manson's point, and at the same time acknowledge from human experience that when people are in conflict situations where they are provoked to voice criticism, imprecise generalisations are often thrown in for good measure. Conflict situations are not famous as parade grounds for dictionary precision; and Jesus shows his own frustration in the language which he uses.

Jesus accuses the Pharisees of paying attention to the externals of religion, while selectively ignoring the heart of religion. Jesus compares them to the pots and pans which are clean on the outside, but which, on closer inspection, turn out to be soiled because the inside is unclean. The God who makes the outside makes the inside also; and, of necessity, it is the inside which must be clean. In his woes, Jesus notes that the Pharisees are happy to pay tithes on herbs which are not tithed in order to cover themselves:

they are busy students of the theology of "just in case", and non-starters at the school of love and justice. In their focus on the externals, the Pharisees are happy to be acknowledged publicly for what they are not privately. Jesus compares them to unseen graves. Graves were whitened to warn people away because contact with the dead meant ritual defilement (Num 19:16). Jesus compares the Pharisees to unwhitened graves, which do not warn people of the inner decay which they house. So, people are contaminated for coming into contact with the Pharisees— the very people who regard themselves as so clean.

Not surprisingly, one of the lawyers notes that Jesus' wide-ranging criticism includes his group, the experts in the interpretation of the law. When Jesus speaks, he proves how right the lawyer is in his observation. Jesus has already made it clear that he does not feel obliged to follow interpretations of the law which hamper the spirit of the law, and he now arraigns the scribes for imposing heavy burdens on people, while absolving themselves from helping those who fall under the weight. Their practice of over-burdening people with laws obscures the image of the Father which Jesus has already disclosed—of a Father who passionately cares what happens to his people. Jesus reminds the lawyers that their own ancestors were respon-sible for killing the prophets; and he tells them that by their own attitude to prophecy they make certain that the work of the prophets remains entombed with their bones. For the lawyer, the only good prophet is a dead prophet. And Jesus goes on to say that the present generation will be held responsible for the death of the prophets; in rejecting the message of the kingdom, they are responsible for the conti-nuing persecution of the prophets.

In the third woe against the lawyers, Jesus accuses them of keeping the kingdom of God closed to those who want to enter. As experts of the law, the lawyers claim to have the key of understanding; they claim to be able to unlock the truth of the word of God, but all they do in their precious and burdensome interpretations is throw away the key. They stand before a locked door. The custodians whose duty it is to welcome people to the word of God, now stand before that word to tell the people that there is no entry. By their own attitude to the law, they have dishonoured their privileged calling.

The lawyers and the scribes react to Jesus' sweeping criticisms by trying to catch him out. Jesus has displayed his own tiredness with their misplaced enthusiasm which exerts so much energy on the minutiae of the law, while leaving the heart of the law a casualty dying from neglect. They are forever reminding people what the law is and forever forgetting what the law is for. They use the law as a weapon to bludgeon others, and as a shield to protect themselves. And they do not thank Jesus for pointing this out to them. As teachers, they are the last to be taught themselves; so, perhaps it is no surprise that Jesus gives them a verbal thrashing.

Notes

[1]Cf. J. Jeremias, *The Lord's Prayer,* (Philadelphia, 1964), pp. 6-15

[2]W. Golding, *Lord of the Flies* (London: Faber and Faber, 1970), p. 158

[3]T. W. Manson, *The Sayings of Jesus* (London: S.C.M., 1971), p. 99

Chapter Twelve

Luke 12: 1-12   Fear and Security

12 In the meantime, when so many thousands of the multitude had gathered together that they trod upon one another, he began to say to his disciples first, "Beware of the leaven of the Pharisees, which is hypocrisy. ²Nothing is covered up that will not be revealed, or hidden that will not be known. ³Whatever you have said in the dark shall be heard in the light, and what you have whispered in private rooms shall be proclaimed upon the housetops.

⁴"I tell you, my friends, do not fear those who kill the body, and after that have no more that they can do. ⁵But I will warn you whom to fear: fear him who, after he has killed, has power to cast into hell; yes, I tell you, fear him! ⁶Are not five sparrows sold for two pennies? And not one of them is forgotten before God. ⁷Why, even the hairs of your head are all numbered. Fear not; you are of more value than many sparrows.

⁸"And I tell you, every one who acknowledges me before men, the Son of man also will acknowledge before the angels of God; ⁹but he who denies me before men will be denied before the angels of God. ¹⁰And every one who speaks a word against the Son of man will be forgiven; but he who blasphemes against the Holy Spirit will not be forgiven. ¹¹And when they bring you before the synagogues and the rulers and the authorities, do not be anxious how or what you are to answer or what you are to say; ¹²for the Holy Spirit will teach you in that very hour what you ought to say."

AFTER HAVING ARRAIGNED THE SCRIBES and the Pharisees for their lack of integrity, Jesus now instructs his own disciples in the presence of large crowds in an address which moves from admonition to encouragement. He warns his disciples against the hypocrisy of the Pharisees, against the essential pointlessness of deceptions which must eventually lead to disclosure. Jesus has no time for the theology of cover-up, for a studied plan which has more interest in enclosing the truth in a maze of peripheral detail than disclosing the truth in all its clarity. Hypocrisy by definition is not a private affair: it engages other people in its conspiracy, it pollutes the whole human environment, and it cripples right judgement. Hypocrisy needs many disguises, and when it takes refuge in a law or a doctrine or a system, it borrows the wardrobe of the reasonable so that it can become theoretically defensible. Indifference masquerades as innocence; what is legal wears the make-up of what is legitimate; opportunism puts on the apparel of kindness; murder wears the mask of political necessity. All this cannot come about without appalling consequences to the climate of human endeavour; and Jesus makes it clear that the whole masquerade will not go unheeded. The pretenders will eventually be exposed, the secrets that have kept people bound will eventually be disclosed for all to see. In short, hypocrisy is destined to fail. And if it fails sooner than eternity, all the better.

Often, hypocrisy only survives because people are afraid of those who use it as their base of power; but Jesus tells his disciples not to fear those whose power is limited to the destruction of the body. The disciples have more reason to fear the one who has the complete power to cast into hell. But Jesus then changes his heavy tone to tell the disciples that they have no reason to fear God. The worthless bird of the market-place was the sparrow, but the sparrow is an important creature in the eyes of God. Again the disciples are asked to imagine a God from whom there is nothing to fear; they are asked to imagine a rather comical scene of a God who keeps a reckoning of everyone's hair count, which, given the sparse number of some, might not be heavy arithmetic. In the knowledge that there is a God who cares, the disciple can rejoice in a fearlessness which is born of faith. Fear of man is a fear that binds; fear of God is a fear that liberates because God does not manipulate human fear, he disposes of it. Fear, like vengeance, should be left to God because he will do nothing about it. He banishes it from the kingdom.

Jesus speaks of the future judgement of the Son of Man, although it is unclear whether he consciously identifies himself with the title here. The important thing is that people acknowledge Jesus in the present time, and they can be assured of his reciprocal acknowledgement before the angels of God. Forgiveness can always be given to those who, without faith, deny the Son of Man. Faith and truth are gifts of the Spirit, and they make a claim on the individual: they demand to be recognized and enacted. Those who fail to enact the truth which they recognize and those who falsify what they know to be true make a nonsense of forgiveness because there is no recognition of repentance. Repentance demands a recognition of the truth: that is its primary condition for action. As for his own disciples, Jesus tells them again that they are not to fear: they are not to be anxious about their speeches for the defence, for the Holy Spirit will be their real counsel. In times when they will need the word of defence, they will receive the words they need through the power of the Spirit.

Jesus assures his disciples that in spite of the suffering and the hurt which they will experience in the course of their discipleship, they do indeed have a God from whom there is nothing to fear. Jesus does not simply tell his disciples that they have nothing to fear; he gives them reason not to fear. Fear is never banished by proclamation or by persuasion; it has to be replaced with a stronger force—in this case, the image of a God who will support and encourage the true disciple. But, throughout the history of religions, fear has been no stranger to the human scene. Traditionally, religion has been one of the most powerful forces for combating fear, while at the same time fear has been one of the main roots of religion. Religion can lock itself into its own bind and create as much fear as it banishes. Ideas and actions which were originally inspired to repel fear can themselves become charged with

fear, with the sad result that aberrations in dogmatic formulae or creed can be punished by fearful threats. Fear can
cause alienation and disintegration in the Christian churches;
and that is not Good News. Christ underlines the positive
in Christianity when he tells his disciples that the Christian
follower has nothing to fear; and if Christianity induces
fear instead of banishing it, then it becomes rightly suspect. The Father wants to be acknowledged by love, not
fear. And it is the love of God, nothing else, which makes a
nonsense of fear.

Luke 12: 13-21   The Rich Fool

 [13]One of the multitude said to him, "Teacher, bid my
brother divide the inheritance with me." [14]But he said to
him, "Man, who made me a a judge or divider over you?"
[15]And he said to them, "Take heed, and beware of all covetousness; for a man's life does not consist in the abundance of
his possessions." [16]And he told them a parable, saying, "The
land of a rich man brought forth plentifully; [17]and he
thought to himself, 'What shall I do, for I have nowhere to
store my crops?' [18]And he said, 'I will do this: I will put down
my barns, and build larger ones; and there I will store all my
grain and my goods. [19]And I will say to my soul, Soul, you
have ample goods laid up for many years; take your ease,
eat, drink, be merry.' [20]But God said to him, 'Fool! This
night your soul is required of you; and the things you have
prepared, whose will they be?' [21]So is he who lays up treasure
for himself, and is not rich toward God."

A man asks Jesus to pass a favourable judgement in a
legal dispute over a family inheritance. Although it was
customary for the rabbis to dispense legal judgements on
domestic matters, Jesus refuses to be entangled in a family
dispute over who is to possess what. Jesus focuses on what
caused the dispute in the first place; he concentrates on the
reason why two brothers are distanced from each other
over possessions: the desire to have. Rather than support
the man's claim, or keep the conversation at the level of

legal niceties, Jesus invites the man to a deeper grappling with the root of the dispute: covetousness. And Jesus makes his point in the parable of the rich fool.

Jesus tells the story of the rich man who has an uncommon problem: he has such an abundance of crops that he has run out of storage space. The question of sharing the abundance does not arise, and the rich man decides to pull down his existing barns and build larger ones to accommodate his grain and his goods. The rich man then has a conversation with himself and assures himself that he has plenty of goods for the future, so he can now relax and enjoy himself. But, in a moment of the night, God puts into question the rich man's life. And God asks the rich man the sad question: whose shall they be now? So, the same story is true of any man who is busy about getting rich in things which God does not treasure at all.

The story of the rich man is heavy with possessive pronouns, and there is no doubt what forms the focus of his world. No one else appears in the story: the rich man is unrelated and alienated: he speaks only to himself, and only about his possessions. He believes that because he has enough possessions for the future, that the future itself is in his possession. He identifies himself so much with what he has, that when what he has is taken away, not only does he have nothing, but it appears by his own definition of life that he is nothing.

In his book, *To Have or To Be?*, Erich Fromm discusses two fundamental modes of living in the world: having and being. He writes:

> The manner of the having mode of existence follows from the nature of private property. In this mode of existence all that matters is my acquisition of property and my unlimited right to keep what I have acquired. . . .In the last analysis, the statement 'I (subject) have O (object)' expresses a definition of *I* through my possession of *O*. The subject is not *myself,* but *I am what I have.* My property constitutes myself and my identity. The underlying thought in the statement 'I am I' is '*I am because I have X*''[1]

That describes accurately the existence of the rich man, a man who describes who he is by what he has. Fromm articulates the ultimate question:

If I am what I have and if what I have is lost, who then am I?[22]

Jesus answers that question in the parable: a fool. Only a fool finds the reason for his existence in something which is transitory, in something which must pass. Only a fool is happy in the knowledge that his heart's desire finds its total fulfilment in a barn full of grain.

Only a fool imagines that he can image his Creator by hoarding grain for himself—grain which by its very purpose is grown for sharing in the breaking of bread. When God asks him: "The things you have prepared, whose will they be?" there is no answer. Given the style of the rich man's conversation, he could only say: "Not mine." He did not keep his goods for the purpose of sharing them, only for himself. Not only does he not share his goods, but, more fundamentally, he does not share himself with others. And that is his real poverty. He invests all his creative energy in perpetuating his solitary existence: nothing of himself goes out to other people. Even his conversation is directed to himself.

Jesus will later go on to speak about the real treasure of the heart. Jesus' listeners might have questioned whether the rich man in the parable had a heart. Throughout the Gospel story, Jesus shares the treasures of his own heart with every person he meets, and his most precious treasure is the kingdom of God. And that treasure is not a matter of having, it is a way of being. It is a way of being which will never be destroyed by midnight visits, by catastrophes, by death or by judgement. Having as a way of life will disappear; being as a way of life in the kingdom of God is present forever.

Luke 12: 22-34   *Anxiety and Release*

[22]And he said to his disciples, "Therefore I tell you, do not be anxious about your life, what you shall eat, nor about

your body, what you shall put on. ²³For life is more than food, and the body more than clothing. ²⁴Consider the ravens: they neither sow nor reap, they have neither store-house nor barn, and yet God feeds them. Of how much more value are you than the birds! ²⁵And which of you by being anxious can add a cubit to his span of life? ²⁶If then you are not able to do as small a thing as that, why are you anxious about the rest? ²⁷Consider the lilies, how they grow; they neither toil nor spin; yet I tell you, even Solomon in all his glory was not arrayed like one of these. ²⁸But if God so clothes the grass which is alive in the field today and tomor-row is thrown into the oven, how much more will he clothe you, O men of little faith! ²⁹And do not seek what you are to eat and what you are to drink, nor be of anxious mind. ³⁰For all the nations of the world seek these things; and your Father knows that you need them. ³¹Instead, seek his kingdom and these things shall be yours as well.

³²"Fear not, little flock, for it is your Father's good pleasure to give you the kingdom. ³³Sell your possessions, and give alms; provide yourselves with purses that do not grow old, with a treasure in the heavens that does not fail, where no thief approaches and no moth destroys. ³⁴For where your treasure is, there will your heart be also.

Following on his parable of the rich fool, Jesus now speaks to his disciples on the subject of anxiety and discipleship. He tells his disciples not to be anxious about food or clothing, because life is much more than these. Anxiety about these things restricts the field of their con-cern, and a look at the natural world will assure them how God takes care of these matters. God even makes provision for the ravens, which were regarded as unclean; and if he does that for the birds of the air, surely he can be trusted to do much more for his own disciples. And perhaps that is the fundamental question which underlies discipleship: can God be really trusted? Jesus answers the question affir-matively, and tells his disciples to live in that trust.

Jesus speaks about the folly of *merimnao,* an attitude of anxious thought, an outlook on life which cannot generate anything but more anxiety. Worrying about life does not add a moment to the life-span; it serves to cast a shadow over the whole of the life story. Anxiety and its close relative, fear, are constrictive rather than constructive:

they close the disciple in on his minor concerns rather than releasing him in his task of building the kingdom of God. In seeking the kingdom of God, the disciple is released from being locked into concerns about food and clothing: God will take care of those needs. Jesus develops the priority which he taught the disciples in his prayer: first, pray for the kingdom of God: the daily bread comes after that.

Jesus assures his disciples that it is the Father's "pleasure to give you the kingdom." The Father does not give the kingdom reluctantly: he takes pleasure in being gracious and generous, and Jesus enjoins his disciples to give graciously themselves. They should act out the image of their gracious Father, and if they do that, they will provide themselves with a real treasure that age will not tarnish, that will be safe from any thief, that no moth can destroy. And when the disciple seeks first the kingdom above all else, his heart is in the right place. His heart is at home in the kingdom of his Father.

Jesus offers his followers a release from anxiety in trusting in the Father. Anxiety is imprisonment; it offers no release from its confines. As Kurt Riezler writes about the psychological effects of anxiety: "The German *Angst,* the French *angoisse,* the English *anguish,* and the Latin *angustiae* all stem from a root which connotes 'pressure,' 'narrowness.' The corresponding word in Greek, used with some emphasis by the Christian fathers, is *stenochoria,* 'the narrow space.' Man's chest feels constricted. Anxiety closes walls in on man".[3] Jesus wants to break down the walls and offer release from that prison. No disciple should be confined in anxiety; no follower of Jesus should allow himself to be manipulated by the thinking and advertising which capitalizes on human anxiety. Jesus offers the alternative: trust in a Father whose message does not imprison or confine, but which liberates the individual. And that is true release.

Luke 12: 35-48   *Time of Crisis*

[35]"Let your loins be girded and your lamps burning, [36]and be like men who are waiting for their master to come home from the marriage feast, so that they may open to him at once when he comes and knocks. [37]Blessed are those servants whom the master finds awake when he comes; truly, I say to you, he will gird himself and have them sit at table, and he will come and serve them. [38]If he comes in the second watch, or in the third, and finds them so, blessed are those servants! [39]But know this, that if the householder had known at what hour the thief was coming, he would not have left his house to be broken into. [40]You also must be ready; for the Son of man is coming at an unexpected hour."

[41]Peter said, "Lord, are you telling this parable for us or for all?" [42]And the Lord said, "Who then is the faithful and wise steward, whom his master will set over his household, to give them their portion of food at the proper time? [43]Blessed is that servant whom his master when he comes will find so doing. [44]Truly, I say to you, he will set him over all his possessions. [45]But if that servant says to himself, 'My master is delayed in coming,' and begins to beat the menservants and the maidservants, and to eat and drink and get drunk, [46]the master of that servant will come on a day when he does not expect him and at an hour he does not know, and will punish him, and put him with the unfaithful. [47]And that servant who knew his master's will, but did not make ready or act according to his will, shall receive a severe beating. [48]But he who did not know, and did what deserved a beating, shall receive a light beating. Every one to whom much is given, of him will much be required; and of him to whom men commit much they will demand the more.

After telling his disciples not to be anxious about wordly goods, Jesus now instructs them to be vigilant and alert in preparation for the coming of the Son of man. Scholars disagree about the meaning of the passage: some argue that Jesus never used the title 'Son of man' of himself, and, further, that because talk of the parousia would have been meaningless to Jesus' hearers, Luke's text is adapted to the theology of the early Church; some argue that the imminent crisis Jesus refers to is within the orbit of the disciples' experience—namely, the crucifixion. Certainly, the crucifixion plays a fundamental part in the critical experience of the disciples, for, with the resurrection and the ascension, it forms the departure of Jesus from the earth. Between the departure of Jesus and the coming of the Son of man in the parousia, there is the in-between time; and in both parables, Jesus stresses the absence of the master and the time before his delayed return—which is consistent with the idea of Jesus' own ascension and the eventual coming of the Son of man.

As he often does, Jesus makes his point through imagery. The people of Jesus' time wore long flowing robes which were tucked under the girdle to make work and travel easier. Jesus uses the image to speak of a permanent state of readiness for those who await the return of their master. And the promise is that when the master returns to find his servants awake and ready to welcome him he will do something totally unexpected: he will reverse the roles, and minister at table to them in recognition of their faithfulness during his absence. The fidelity of the disciple will be rewarded by the unexpected gratitude of the master; the master will be present to the servant in a surprising way. He will play servant to the servants. Then, in a switch of imagery, Jesus makes the point that if burglars sent visiting cards to announce their intended visit, the householder would make sure that he was at home. But burglars do not practice this gracious habit—so the disciples are to be ready when the coming crisis arrives unannounced.

Peter asks Jesus whether this parable refers to the Twelve or to everyone. Jesus declines to answer, but offers another parable which speaks not of a servant but of a steward. The steward was in fact a servant who had charge of all the other servants, and was in total charge during the absence of the master. Here Jesus refers to the religious leaders and to the special authority and responsibility which are committed to their care. Responsibility goes with the privilege of leadership, and the leaders have to account for their use of authority. Leaders of God's people are expected to be trustworthy stewards: they were found worthy of trust to be appointed, and they must live worthily of the trust. Those who abuse that trust will be punished, just as those who honour it will be rewarded. But there is no one in the service of the Lord, least of all the leaders, who is unaccountable.

But the underlying good news in all this is that the disciples are indeed trusted in the first place. Jesus does trust them, and when he will be with them no longer, he will continue to trust them to be faithful to his memory, to be faithful in their own stewardship. Like the servants in the parable of the talents, not only have the servants been given talents, but more importantly, they have been *trusted* to use the talents wisely. Again, the image is of a gracious God who does not act out of suspicion but out of trust. And the trust will be unexpectedly rewarded when Jesus, in the image of the messianic banquet, will serve his faithful servants at his own table. The master will hold a heavenly Feast of Fools and play servant to the servants of God. And that is no mean image of God.

Luke 12: 49-53   *Decision and Conflict*

⁴⁹"I came to cast fire upon the earth; and would that it were already kindled! ⁵⁰I have a baptism to be baptized with; and how I am constrained until it is accomplished! ⁵¹Do you think that I have come to give peace on earth? No, I tell you, but rather division; ⁵²for henceforth in one house there will be five divided, three against two and two against three; ⁵³they will be divided, father against son and son against father, mother against daughter and daughter against her mother, mother-in-law against her daughter-in-law and daughter-in-law against her mother-in-law."

In the thoughts which he now shares with his disciples, we have a rare insight into the inner conflict which Jesus experiences on the road to Jerusalem, a conflict between fidelity to his mission and the natural movements of his own heart. John the Baptist had prophesied that Jesus would baptize "with the Holy Spirit and with fire" (3:16), and Jesus now speaks about his own approaching baptism in the crucifixion. At the opening of his public life, Jesus was baptized in a public event which marked the beginning of his mission: now the mission is coming to a head, and Jesus wishes that it was all over. Jesus has already been acknowledged by the Spirit after his baptism, but he still has to face the coming fire in the experience of the crucifixion. Understandably, he shows his own impatience to get it all finished. His own crisis looms large.

The imagery of fire was a traditional Old Testament image for judgement and testing. Likewise, the image of water was not a soft and safe image, but one which spoke of a person being so involved in something that he was "up to his neck in it". So:

we went through fire and water (Psalm 66, v. 12)

Save me O God!
For the waters have come up to my neck. (Psalm 69, v. 1)

Jesus himself has to first undergo the water and the fire: he does not inflict the process on others and play the observer, untouched by the pain of involvement. Jesus first travels the route of fire and water; he has to handle the opposition to his values and cherished beliefs—an opposition which culminates in his crucifixion. The opposition is mounting and Jesus senses the coming crisis when he will be up to his neck in things. And when God is up to his neck in it, even God has to pay a price.

Jesus warns of the division which will take place in his wake; division which will respect no sacred places and which will insinuate itself into close family relationships. If the stories which he tells, the claims which he makes, the love which he gives, the values which he shares, the forgiveness which he offers, all move people to eliminate him, then his own disciples must be prepared for similar treatment if they go public on his way of life. Jesus is torn in the recognition that his way of life will be the cause of such division, but if he is to be unerringly faithful to his mission, then that division has to be handled honestly rather than wished away. Jesus admits that he is not overly keen on the fire which he has to undergo, but he knows that the fire is neither dispensable nor incidental to the fulfilment of his mission. The cross is crucial. When his followers have to make crucial choices, they will have to take sides; and they should not be surprised to see familiar faces on the opposite side. Jesus saw a few familiar faces opposed to him, and the sight was not easy to behold. He bled at the sight because he knew that he could do no other than be true to himself. But if that is frightening, the alternative is more so.

Luke 12: 54-59   *The Signs of the Times*

⁵⁴"He also said to the multitudes, "When you see a cloud rising in the west, you say at once, 'A shower is coming'; and so it happens. ⁵⁵And when you see the south wind blowing, you say, 'There will be scorching heat'; and it happens. ⁵⁶You hypocrites! You know how to interpret the appearance of earth and sky; but why do you not know how to interpret the present time?

⁵⁷"And why do you not judge for yourselves what is right? ⁵⁸As you go with your accuser before the magistrate, make an effort to settle with him on the way, lest he drag you to the judge, and the judge hand you over to the officer, and the officer put you in prison. ⁵⁹I tell you, you will never get out till you have paid the very last copper."

Jesus now turns to the crowds and points out to them the profound discrepancy between their sensitivity in reading the weather signs in the sky and their insensitivity in failing to read the religious signs in their midst. They can read the signs of the sky and of the earth, and yet they are unwilling rather than unable to pay attention to the signs before their very eyes. Jesus clearly believes that the signs which they ignore are not esoteric riddles which only a

select minority can understand, but signs which can be
discerned by a person who puts himself honestly before
God. The whole point of any sign is that it can be read and
understood without recourse to a dictionary; Jesus says
that his signs can be read and understood by the average
person who is not enclosed in his own hypocrisy. And
Jesus expects people not only to read the signs but act on
what they say.

Jesus continues his point in telling a parable of crisis. In
the story which he tells, Jesus suggests that the man is actually guilty of the crime of which he is accused. In his
desperate situation, it would be folly for the accused to go
to a court which would surely commit him to prison. The
thing for him to do would be to act in his own interests and
use his time of freedom to settle the issue out of court. If
he does not, and is committed, he will be imprisoned, and
be in the tortuous position of being unable to work to pay
off the debt. And he will have to stay in prison until the
debt is completely discharged.

In this eschatological parable, Jesus invites his hearers to
see themselves in this time of crisis as the ones who are on
their way to the court. They are foolish not to use the present time, when they are still free, to settle their affairs with
God and put themselves right in his sight. If they are right
in the sight of God, then no accuser has any case against
them. But if the present generation do not use the present
time to settle their affairs with God, then the future looks
bleak indeed. It would be foolish not to make the effort,
because what is at stake is not money, but a life of peace in
the presence of God.

Again, Jesus feels constrained to underline the urgency
of the present moment to tell people that they should use
the present as a gift, which is a favour to them. If people
stop playing the hypocrite, and look honestly into their
own hearts, they will acknowledge their guilt and do something about it. People's guilt is not the end of the story:
they still have time to change their standing before God.
Jesus has tried in his own words and works to tell the peo-

ple of the coming crisis, and he passionately believes that the language he uses is not beyond anyone's range of understanding. The farmer pays attention to the weather signs so that he can act on what they tell him; all the more so should people act on what the present signs tell them. The only time for repentance is the present. Tomorrow is another tense.

Notes

[1] E. Fromm, *To Have to To Be?* (London, Abacus, 1979) p. 82

[2] Ibid., p. 111

[3] K. Riezler, "The Social Psychology of Fear" in *Identity and Anxiety*, edited by Stein, Vidich, and White (New York, Free Press, 1960), p. 146

Chapter Thirteen

Luke 13: 1-9   *Timely Repentance*

13 There were some present at that very time who told
him of the Galileans whose blood Pilate had mingled with
their sacrifices. ²And he answered them, "Do you think that
these Galileans were worse sinners than all the other
Galileans, because they suffered thus? ³I tell you, No; but
unless you repent you will all likewise perish. ⁴Or those eighteen upon whom the tower in Siloam fell and killed them, do
you think that they were worse offenders than all the others
who dwelt in Jerusalem? ⁵I tell you, No; but unless you repent you will all likewise perish."

⁶And he told this parable: "A man had a fig tree planted in
his vineyard; and he came seeking fruit on it and found none.
⁷And he said to the vinedresser, 'Lo, these three years I have
come seeking fruit on this fig tree, and I find none. Cut it
down; why should it use up the ground?' ⁸And he anwered
him, 'Let it alone, sir, this year also, till I dig about it and put
on manure. ⁹And if it bears fruit next year, well and good;
but if not, you can cut it down.'"

JESUS CONTINUES ON THE THEME OF REPENTANCE and
enjoins his hearers to heed his warnings about the urgency
of the task which confronts them: repentance before it is
too late. Some of Jesus' audience tell of an incident, which
could have taken place at the time of Passover, when an
unspecified number of Galileans were killed while they
were offering sacrifice. No source other than Luke's
Gospel attests the historicity of this event; but, given
Pilate's undisguised hatred for the Jews, and given the
Galileans' record for resistance, the incident could well
have happened. We do know of Pilate's practice of sending
his soldiers, disguised in long cloaks, into the crowds so
that when the people did become unruly, the soldiers could

disperse them with clubs. Josephus testifies to the brutal efficiency of Pilate's soldiers, and, although he does not mention the incident referred to here, it is in keeping with his account. However, it cannot be ruled out of consideration that Jesus' interrogators made up the story to test Jesus' response to Roman occupation and possible revolt. Whatever the motives for the question, Jesus uses it to make his own point about the need for repentance.

Jesus shares his own reflection about an incident in which eighteen people were killed in a building accident, and makes the point that they were no worse than other Galileans in their sinfulness. Jesus rejects outrightly the old equation between sinfulness and suffering. Disasters and accidents are not inflicted on people by God as a punishment for sin: that reasoning suggests that those who happen to be living are, therefore, less sinful. More importantly, Jesus rejects the image of God which sustains that peculiar outlook. Jesus makes it clear that the God he believes in does not relate to people through the medium of disaster and accident, that God does not prove he is God by manufacturing a liturgy of sadism whereby he can be acknowledged. That is a terrible image of God which is hardly different from the Greek's Medusa, whose peculiar talent was for petrification. A theology which makes that image of God the prevalent religious image also makes that kind of religion profoundly unnecessary. The God whom Jesus speaks about does not have a charism for disaster; he is a God who wants people to turn to him and discover their true selves. Jesus argues that everyone shares a basic similarity with those who were executed and those who suffered the accident: everyone is a sinner who is in need of repentance. And unlike the people caught in disaster, the present generation are being forewarned to prepare themselves.

Jesus now illustrates what he has said in the parable of the barren fig tree. Joachim Jeremias argues that in this parable Jesus makes use of an old folk-tale which dates back to before the fifth century B.C. and which was in use in Jesus' time. The climax of the tale of Ahiquar occurs with the judgement: "My son, you are like a tree which yielded no fruit, although it stood by the water, and its owner was forced to cut it down. And it said to him, Transplant me, and if even then I bear no fruit, cut me down. But its owner said to it, When you stood by the water you bore no fruit, how then will you bear fruit if you stand in another place."[1] If Jesus did use this story as the inspiration of his own parable, then he reversed the ending from one of closed judgement to one of possible change. The thrust of Jesus' parable is that there is still time for change.

In the parable, the owner has gone into the vineyard in the expectation that this year the fig tree will have produced fruit. However, he meets disappointment again. The tree is yielding nothing; it is merely taking up useful space. The tree consumes, but it does not produce; it is a parasite, a hanger-on, and the owner has now run out of patience. He no longer holds out any hope for fruit so he sees no other option but to cut the tree down. The vinedresser plays the role of counsel for the defence, and pleads for a stay of execution. He promises to tend the fig tree himself, but he does take the owner's point that there is a time limit on the matter, and he acknowledges that if the tree does not bear fruit the following year it should be cut down. But, perhaps the vinedresser argued the same argument last year, and the year before. It is interesting that the vinedresser does not say that *he* will cut the tree down: he tells the owner that he can do it himself.

Unlike the image of God underlying the first question, Jesus presents a generous image of a patient God who is willing to wait. But if God has all the time in the world, human beings do not: time, by definition, limits human action, and Jesus urges his hearers to use the time they have to repent. Barrenness is no boast for a tree which exists to bear fruit; sinfulness is no boast for a person who exists to be good. And to mix the metaphors: if barrenness is brought about by unwillingness to produce fruit, then the tree is 'responsible' for its barrenness and it cannot put the blame on bad placement, inclement weather, or neglect. The tree has within it the seeds of its own fruit and the seeds of its own disintegration. Jesus wants people to make the effort now to turn to God. Now is the time of the patient vinedresser, but even all his attention and energy cannot totally replace native effort. The growth must come from within.

Luke 13: 10-21   *Healing and the Kingdom*

¹⁰Now he was teaching in one of the synagogues on the sabbath. ¹¹And there was a woman who had had a spirit of infirmity for eighteen years; she was bent over and could not fully straighten herself. ¹²And when Jesus saw her, he called her and said to her, "Woman, you are freed from your infirmity. ¹³And he laid his hands upon her, and immediately she was made straight, and she praised God. ¹⁴But the ruler of the synagogue, indignant because Jesus had healed on the sabbath, said to the people, "There are six days on which work ought to be done; come on those days and be healed, and not on the sabbath day." ¹⁵Then the Lord answered him, "You hypocrites! Does not each of you on the sabbath untie his ox or his ass from the manger, and lead it away to water it? ¹⁶And ought not this woman, a daughter of Abraham whom Satan bound for eighteen years, be loosed from this bond on the sabbath day?" ¹⁷As he said this, all his adversaries were put to shame; and all the people rejoiced at all the glorious things that were done by him.

¹⁸He said therefore, "What is the kingdom of God like? And to what shall I compare it? ¹⁹It is like a grain of mustard seed which a man took and sowed in his garden; and it grew and became a tree, and the birds of the air made nests in its branches."

²⁰And again he said, "To what shall I compare the kingdom of God? ²¹It is like leaven which a woman took and hid in three measures of meal, till it was all leavened."

Luke now tells us of the last occasion Jesus taught in the synagogue. The officials are increasing their critical watch on Jesus, and, in this incident on the sabbath, they publicly criticise him for disregarding the law. Having already asserted his authority over the sabbath (6:1-11), Jesus now uses the occasion of healing to give a teaching on the meaning of the sabbath. Jesus notices a woman who has been crippled for eighteen years with a bent back. Jesus takes the initiative—again he is moved to minister personally to the afflicted one. He calls her publicly, and tells her the good news that she is freed from her illness. He lays his hands on her, the healing takes place, and the woman responds by praising God. The leader of the synagogue takes issue with Jesus' defying the law of the sabbath in the synagogue, but he directs his comments to the assembly rather than to Jesus. He tells the people that they should come for healing on the six working days of the week, but not on the sabbath. For this man, healing people from their pain is not a ministry to be exercised on the holy day.

Jesus contests the argument, and he points to the discrepancy in an attitude which justifies attention to the needs of animals while ignoring the needs of human beings. A law which promotes that kind of tortuous reasoning is rightly suspect. Jesus says that he must (*dei*) heal the woman: the matter is not open to dispute. Jesus was obviously aware of the legal disputes about what kind of knots could be tied and untied on the sabbath, but he has no time for a theology of knots which can justify the release of an animal, and keep a woman bound in her affliction. His opponents do not see the Lord of the sabbath who liberates those who are bound; they only see a man who has broken the law. Again, his opponents ignore the signs which are under their noses.

Jesus goes on to tell his hearers two parables which speak of the kingdom of God in their midst. In telling people about a reality that is unfamiliar to them, Jesus uses familiar images of the land and of the kitchen to put his hearers in contact with the truth of what he is saying. In the prophecy of Ezekiel, the imagery of the fully grown tree is used to speak of the universal salvation of God:

All the birds of the air
  made their nests in its boughs;
under its branches all the beasts
  of the field
  brought forth their young;
and under its shadow
  dwelt all great nations.

(Ezek 31:6)

The tiny mustard seed which Jesus speaks of could grow into a large plant, big enough to be called a tree. The tree would become a home for *all* the birds of the air, and offer them shelter and nourishment. From a tiny seed there grows greatness, a greatness which is shared with those who care to come and enjoy it.

Jesus makes a similar point in the parable of the leaven. There is a quiet overnight transformation in the kitchen when the woman mixes the yeast in with the dough and leaves it until morning when a small amount of leaven has transformed a mass of dough. The process is hidden and quiet; it is an 'inside job', but the effects of the domestic drama are not beyond anyone's range of understanding. Anyone who cares to notice can see that a small amount of yeast has permeated the whole of the dough, and now it is "all leavened."

So the kingdom grows in the midst of the familiar and makes its presence known in small ways. The kingdom too travels the route from insignificance to greatness, a movement which is taking place at this very moment. From the small beginnings in the ministry of Jesus—his healing the afflicted, his sayings, his quiet transformations, his unusual company of disciples, his even more unusual crowd of followers—there is arising the greatness of the kingdom of God. And this movement is taking place in the heart of the familiar, where birds play suitor to trees, where little miracles happen in the quiet of the family kitchen. It is the familiar which is the locus of the kingdom, and Jesus invites his hearers to please notice

what is happening in their midst. At the heart of their own
experience, the kingdom is happening. The mustard seed
grows; the leaven rises; the kingdom of God increases—
and all that is going on at this very moment. Now.

Luke 13: 22-30   Who's in, Who's out

> ²²He went on his way through towns and villages,
> teaching, and journeying toward Jerusalem. ²³And some
> one said to him, "Lord, will those who are saved be few?"
> And he said to them, ²⁴"Strive to enter by the narrow door;
> for many, I tell you, will seek to enter and will not be able.
> ²⁵When once the householder has risen up and shut the door,
> you will begin to stand outside and to knock at the door, saying,
> 'Lord, open to us.' He will answer you, 'I do not know where
> you come from.' ²⁶Then you will begin to say, 'We ate and
> drank in your presence, and you taught in our streets.' ²⁷But
> he will say, 'I tell you, I do not know where you come from;
> depart from me, all you workers of iniquity!' ²⁸There you
> will weep and gnash your teeth, when you see Abraham and
> Isaac and Jacob and all the prophets in the kingdom of God
> and you yourselves thrust out. ²⁹And men will come from
> east and west, and from north and south, and sit at table in
> the kingdom of God. ³⁰And behold, some are last who will be
> first, and some are first who will be last."

Luke continues the journey narrative with a reminder
that Jesus is still on the way to Jerusalem, the place where
his mission will be completed. Luke does not chart the
journey through geographical terrain, which is of little interest to him or his readers, but through Jesus' own
teachings and pronouncements, through the signs which he
works, through the stories which he tells, through his
growing awareness of what his mission involves, through
his coping with the mounting opposition which he meets.
And as he is on the road to the cross, someone asks him
whether those who are to be saved are few in number.

In answer, Jesus declines to engage in a statistical
theology which involves speculating about the numbers of
those saved; instead, he brings the discussion down to

earth by focusing on the present need for everyone to strive for salvation. Jesus underlines the need for personal effort, for personal striving: the Greek word, *agonizomai,* speaks of struggle and exertion and contention; it is the source word of the English word, agony. Rather than getting involved in cerebral speculation about numbers, Jesus speaks of the agonizing struggle that every individual has to undergo if he is to enter the narrow door to the house of salvation. To get into the household of God is not an easy task: it is not a matter of trying to slip in with the right crowd; it is not a question of being carried along by the right movement: entrance is granted only after a personal agonizing struggle. It costs to enter; and the price is to be paid personally, not by any group account.

In a short parable, Jesus reflects on the experience of those who will find themselves on the wrong side of the door. The image is now changed from a narrow door to a closed door: there is a time-limit involved in the story of salvation. Jesus summarizes the kind of defence people will use to persuade the householder to allow them in. First, there is the straightforward plea for the householder to change his mind, but he states that he has no knowledge of the petitioners: they are strangers to him. The people try to counter this by reminding the householder that they ate and drank with him, and that they remember the time he taught in their streets. The householder is not too impressed with the presumed advantages of a physical proximity which does not add up to commitment. Eating out in the same restaurant, drinking in the same pub, hearing the same sermon do not necessarily argue to sharing the same values. The people may have hung around the householder, but they were not for him; and it is that personal commitment which the householder recognizes.

Jesus goes on to speak of the despair and the frustration which people will experience when they see the patriarchs and the prophets in the kingdom, while discovering themselves on the outside. Not only will they see their fathers in faith, but people from the four corners of the world who will find fellowship at the messianic banquet. Enjoying the heavenly banquet is a result of the favour of God and personal struggle; nobody is seated at the table because he persuaded the host he had the right pedigree or dined out at the right address. Those who find themselves excluded from the banquet will have their own expectations turned upside-down when they see that the outsiders are in, and the so-called "in" people are outside. When it comes to the messianic banquet, there is no telling who will be coming to dinner.

In this passage, Jesus develops the theme of the urgency of the present time in the argument against presumption: the narrow door eventually becomes the closed door, and no one can presume that he will find himself on the warm side of the door. It is folly to spend time speculating about the arithmetic of salvation; one can only act on the truth of the Gospel here and now, and leave the arithmetic to God.

In Shakespeare's *King Lear,* old Lear eventually finds himself the prisoner of Edmund, so he consoles his daughter, Cordelia, with the thoughts:

Come, let's away to prison;
We two alone will sing like birds i' the cage:
When thou dost ask me blessing, I'll kneel down,
And ask of thee forgiveness: so we'll live,
And pray, and sing, and tell old tales, and laugh
At gilded butterflies, and hear poor rogues
Talk of court news; and we'll talk with them too,
Who loses and who wins; who's in, who's out;
And take upon's the mystery of things,
As if we were God's spies: and we'll wear out,
In a wall'd prison, packs and sects of great ones
That ebb and flow by the moon.

(V, iii, 8-18)

From his own experience, Lear reflects on the transience of court favour, and invites Cordelia to imagine what it would be like to understand God's ways as if they saw through his eyes—then he and Cordelia, even in prison, could outlast the "in" groups at court who are in and out of favour like the changes of the moon. Who's in and who's out at court depends on the fleeting fashions of the day; who's in and who's out in the kingdom of God does not depend on shifting fancies, but on the favour of God and the honest struggle of those who follow his ways. The kingdom of God is given to those who take upon themselves "the mystery of things" to see the world as God sees it. And even in a walled prison, that is good news.

Luke 13: 31-35   *Lament over Jerusalem*

[31]At that very hour some Pharisees came, and said to him, "Get away from here, for Herod wants to kill you." [32]And he said to them, "Go and tell that fox, 'Behold, I cast out demons and perform cures today and tomorrow, and the third day I finish my course. [33]Nevertheless I must go on my way today and tomorrow and the day following; for it cannot be that a prophet should perish away from Jerusalem.' [34]O Jerusalem, Jerusalem, killing the prophets and stoning those who are sent to you! How often would I have gathered your children together as a hen gathers her brood under her wings, and you would not! [35]Behold, your house is forsaken. And I tell you, you will not see me until you say, 'Blessed is he who comes in the name of the Lord!'"

Luke connects this passage with the previous section which opened with a reminder of Jesus' journey to Jerusalem. Now, Jesus receives a warning from some Pharisees that because Herod Antipas wants to kill him, he must leave Herod's territory without delay. Jesus is decisive in his reply, and makes it clear that he is not going to be intimidated by an insignificant tetrarch or banished by his whim: when Jesus leaves, it will be because his mission requires him to go to Jerusalem. Josephus records that Herod was a ruler who wanted desperately to avoid any conflict within his domain;[2] but a man who disposes of John the Baptist as a domestic favour, and who depends on rumour or borrowed messengers to communicate his wishes can hardly be credited with much political finesse in coping with his opponents. In contrast to a vacillating Herod, Luke presents Jesus as a strong figure who is in possession of himself and in control of his fate, and who speaks publicly about his future plans.

It is not clear from the text whether the Pharisees came to Jesus out of genuine concern for his safety or whether they were being used, wittingly or unwittingly, by Herod to frighten Jesus out of the territory: their motivation can only be guessed at. However, there is no doubt about Jesus' own feeling towards Herod: he castigates him as "that fox". As Manson writes: "'Fox' in Jewish usage has a double sense. It typifies low cunning as opposed to straightforward dealing, and it is used in contrast to 'lion' to describe an insignificant third-rate person as opposed to a person of real power and greatness. To call Herod 'that fox' is as much as to say he is neither a great man nor a straight man; he has neither majesty nor honour."[3]

Jesus sends the message back to Herod that he will continue with his work of opposing the power of evil and the hold of sickness until such times as his mission is completed. Jesus is certain that he will complete his mission in Jerusalem, not in Herod's territory. Jerusalem is seen as the summary of the people of Israel, and Jesus reminds his hearers of how Jerusalem has acted towards the prophets: it has played the role of executioner, so it is only appropriate that it should not be deprived of playing that role to the most important prophet of all time. Herod cannot enter the drama now and alter the fatal relationship between Jerusalem and Jesus, between the executioner and the victim. And in this case, the victim is travelling to keep an ancient appointment with the executioner.

In his moving lament over Jerusalem, Jesus speaks in the language of Wisdom and recalls the repeated attempts by God to send messengers to the people of the city, only to be met with violence and murder. God was moved to act out of concern; the people were moved to act out of murder and contempt. And they will do likewise to the prophet who is now on his way to the fateful city. The lament contains an image of a tender God, a God seen in the image of a caring mother who wants to gather her little ones under the protection of her wing. But the little ones are not interested—perhaps because they have long since ceased to be little ones. The image is of a God who wants to gather his people into the kingdom, but the people want nothing to do with God and take steps to make that known. So, there is the image of a God who is alone and lonely for his own children, and who is strong enough to allow his own vulnerability to be known. A God who speaks of his own failure to gather his people together can only do so if he hopes that things will turn out differently.

In its hostility to the prophets and to Jesus, Jerusalem is a forsaken place which speaks more of the absence of God than of his presence. It is not that God has abandoned the city; it is that he has been banished from it repeatedly. And it will remain so until the people acknowledge the one who comes in the name of the Lord. If this is a reference to the final coming of the Messiah, then the acknowledgement will be too late. As Jesus points out in the previous section, acknowledgement before a closed door is decidely late. If the judgement suggests that there is still time to proclaim Jesus as the one who has come in the name of the Lord, then the time is now, and there is still hope for the people of Jerusalem. But future events are not kind to this interpretation.

In the liturgy of the Sacred Triduum, the ancient reproaches recall Jesus' lament over Jerusalem:

> My people, my people, what have I done to you?
> How have I offended you?
> Answer me, answer me.

The reproaches have Jesus pleading for a reason why the people have conspired against him when he has done them only kindness. Of course, Jerusalem does not and did not answer. Certainly, Luke presents Jesus as a man who is fixed on Jerusalem, who is very much aware of the terrible record it has, but still feels compelled to have his final days there. Probably, Jesus is aware of the profound ambiguity of the expression framed in the passive tense: I will be finished in Jerusalem.

Notes

[1] J. Jeremias, *The Parables of Jesus*, (London, S.C.M. Press, 1978) p. 170

[2] Cf. Josephus, *Antiquities*, 18, 7, 2

[3] T. W. Manson, *Sayings*, op cit., p. 276

Chapter Fourteen

Luke 14: 1-6   Healing the Man with Dropsy

14 One sabbath when he went to dine at the house of a ruler who belonged to the Pharisees, they were watching him. ²And behold, there was a man before him who had dropsy. ³And Jesus spoke to the lawyers and Pharisees, saying, "Is it not lawful to heal on the sabbath, or not?" ⁴But they were silent. Then he took him and healed him, and let him go. ⁵And he said to them, "Which of you, having a son or an ox that has fallen into a well, will not immediately pull him out on a sabbath day?" ⁶And they could not reply to this.

JESUS ACCEPTS THE INVITATION TO DINE on the sabbath. His host is said to be a ruler, probably a leading Pharisee, possibly a member of the Sanhedrin. Luke uses the setting of the meal as the context for a healing and for a group of Jesus' sayings which relate to feasting. At the very beginning of his account, Luke puts us in touch with the atmosphere around the table, one which is anything but relaxed and sympathetic. Jesus is being scrutinised by his table companions, who seem to be waiting like birds of prey to pounce at the first opportunity. The opportunity soon comes, but none of the watchers makes a move.

While all eyes are on Jesus, a man who suffers from dropsy suddenly appears on the scene and stands before Jesus. The man's body would have been bloated from the disease, which was understood by many to be venereal. If the Pharisees understood dropsy to come from immoral contact, the man's disease would have been a powerful argument in favour of the school which argued that suffering resulted from sinfulness. But Jesus has already disposed of that argument, and he does not refer to it here.

It is conceivable that Jesus' table companions had arranged the man's entry to test Jesus' reaction; it is also possible that the man heard that Jesus was dining at the house of a well-known man and invited himself to attend in the hope that he would be healed. Whatever the exact reason for his being at the meal, the text does not tell us. The man does not appeal to Jesus, and Jesus does not address him; instead he initiates a debate with the Pharisees and the lawyers and asks them the general question whether it is lawful to heal on the sabbath. The professional debaters are suddenly afflicted with silence and they do not answer Jesus' question. Strict rabbinic teaching stated that healing could take place only when human life was endangered: perhaps, those around the table disagreed in their own interpretations; perhaps they did not want to appear inhuman by giving an unqualified no; perhaps they were moved to see the essential fatuity of engaging in a seminar on healing while an afflicted man stood before them in need of help.

No one takes the opportunity to answer the point, and Jesus heals the man of his sickness and lets him go. No conversation is recorded between the man and Jesus; perhaps it was unnecessary that any take place. After the healing, Jesus continues with his point by asking his hearers to admit that they would free one of their own animals if it fell into a well on the sabbath: and if they would free an animal from distress, would they not all the more so liberate a human being from his bondage of sickness. If Jesus is expecting a reply to his question, then he is disappointed. Again, there is a grand silence over the dinner table, but this time the silence is interpreted. It is the silence which possesses the atmosphere when the truth is seen but not acknowledged; it is the silence which follows after a debate when one side realizes that it has nothing to say, except to admit that it is wrong. So, the silence continues.

In making his own argument, Jesus does not place his appeal before the law; he makes his appeal personal to his hearers in calling upon *their* best human instincts: "Which of you. . ." If people disagree in their interpretations of the law, Jesus is hoping that they will be more likely to agree in their shared compassion for one of their own animals in need of help. The expected answer to Jesus' question is that nobody in his right sense would abandon one of his animals in a pit because it happened to be the sabbath. His human instinct would instruct him to help the animal out, and no doubt, he would reconcile that with the law later. Also, the fact that Jesus' hearers admitted that a man could be healed on the sabbath if his life was in danger already recognized the principle that in certain cases compassion took precedence over the requirements of the law. Jesus argues for the extension of compassion, so that a man should not be left in his disease or affliction because it happens to be the sabbath. In effect, Jesus is inviting his hearers to *trust* their human instincts in the matter of mercy—and travel on them.

Luke 14: 7-14   *On Not Standing on One's Dignity*

⁷Now he told a parable to those who were invited, when he marked how they chose the places of honor, saying to them, ⁸"When you are invited by any one to a marriage feast, do not sit down in a place of honor, lest a more eminent man than you be invited by him; ⁹and he who invited you both will come and say to you, 'Give place to this man,' and then you will begin with shame to take the lowest place. ¹⁰But when you are invited, go and sit in the lowest place, so that when your host comes he may say to you, 'Friend, go up higher'; then you will be honored in the presence of all who sit at table with you. ¹¹For every one who exalts himself will be humbled, and he who humbles himself will be exalted."

¹²He said also to the man who had invited him, "When you give a dinner or a banquet, do not invite your friends or your brothers or your kinsmen or rich neighbors, lest they also invite you in return, and you be repaid. ¹³But when you give a feast, invite the poor, the maimed, the lame, the blind, ¹⁴and you will be blessed, because they cannot repay you. You will be repaid at the resurrection of the just."

In the narrative setting of a meal at a Pharisee's house, Luke continues Jesus' discourse on matters connected with feasting. Jesus tells a parable which none of his hearers would have difficulty in understanding. The parable seems to stay at the level of worldly advice on how to get to the top of the table by starting at the bottom, and how to avoid starting at the top only to find oneself ushered to the bottom; but if that were the sum of Jesus' teaching it would hardly be a parable. The story moves from the familiar to the unfamiliar; Jesus takes his hearers through the metaphor of the marriage feast to glimpse a truth about the kingdom of God, to understand how honour is conferred by God on those who are truly humble.

The advice which Jesus offers is simple and direct: when you are invited to a marriage banquet, do not rush to take the place of honour at the top of the table: the honoured guests will arrive later, and you will have to make way for them; then you will find yourself in the embarrassing situation of having to pass all the other places that have been taken, and take your seat at the lowest place of the table. Instead of assuming a position of focus and honour, take the lowest place so that when the host enters and sees you, he will honour you in front of the assembly by moving you higher. Since you are a guest at the banquet, leave it to the host to decide who is worthy of the places of honour: since it is *his* party, that is his privilege.

At first reading, Jesus' saying seems to offer a calculated and cunning device which guarantees that you will get to the top if you play the right power game: play Uriah Heep, and not only will you get to the top, but everyone will see you rise to the top. Then you can sit above the salt and quietly congratulate yourself on your strategy. The next saying, however, flattens this interpretation: he who exalts himself—whether he does it crudely by takeover or subtly by insinuation—will be humbled. So, if a man takes the lowest place not because he believes it is rightly his but as a calculated posture to influence his host to move him higher, that man will find himself in the embarrassing posi-

tion of being left where he is—in the lowest place. Humility
is not a matter of playing the right power game; it is a matter of acknowledging the truth that since we are favoured
in the first place with an invitation, we should regard it as a
privilege *to sit at the table at all.* And it is God's part, not
ours, to confer the honours on who sits where.

Jesus is not giving a summary course in etiquette at banquets; he invites his hearers to move through the familiar
ground of the banquet to an understanding of honour in
the kingdom. The man who will be exalted in the kingdom
will not be the man who has engineered his way to the top,
but the man who acknowledges that honour in the kingdom comes when the *host* recognizes it, not when the guest
assumes it. Honour in the kingdom is conferred along the
lines already expressed in the *Magnificat:*

> he has scattered the proud in the imagination of their
> hearts,
> he has put down the mighty from their thrones,
> and exalted those of low degree;
> he has filled the hungry with good things,
> and the rich he has sent empty away.
>
> (1:51b-53)

The theme of the *Magnificat* continues to echo when
Jesus tells his host the kind of people he should invite to his
dinner-parties. The proud, the mighty and the rich do not
appear on Jesus' guest-list; instead, the poor, the maimed,
the lame and blind are the ones who are invited to join the
party. It is interesting to remember that at the dinner which
Jesus is now attending, an uninvited guest, who suffered
from dropsy, has already made an appearance—one which
provoked no response from the Pharisees and the lawyers.
Even if the man had been planted by the Pharisees, he was
not invited to share the meal: now Jesus tells his host that
he ought to have invited guests like that man. Jesus literally
turns the tables on his host and gives him a lesson from the
etiquette of the kingdom of God. The guest-list should not

be made up of those who are going to return the invitation: that is merely the practice of exchanging favour for favour. People should be invited who cannot return the invitation; and they are the people who really need a dinner and all that goes with it. The people Jesus mentions are people who need food because they are hungry, who need company because they are outcast, who need rejoicing because they know sadness, who need sharing because they are isolated in their sickness. All this is normally denied them, and Jesus enjoins his host to give it freely and without charge.

Those who offer a hospitality that cannot be returned on this earth will have their reward at the resurrection of the just. If people are kind to the outcasts and the cripples by sharing their table with them, the Lord will remember their kindness and hold it in their favour. And as Jesus will develop in the next parable, it is the beggar and the cripple who are invited to the kingdom of heaven. If people share their table with the crippled, then they, as crippled hosts, will be honoured in the kingdom of heaven. It is not a matter of the clean inviting the unclean, of the healthy inviting the crippled: it is more a matter of the crippled sharing their table with the crippled, of beggars sharing their food with other beggars. For when it comes to the kingdom of God, who can assume the place of honour at the table? Who can suppose that they do not belong to the large human company of the maimed, the lame and the blind?

Luke 14: 15-24   *The Great Banquet*

[15]When one of those who sat at table with him heard this, he said to him, "Blessed is he who shall eat bread in the kingdom of God!" [16]But he said to him, "A man once gave a great banquet, and invited many; [17]and at the time for the banquet he sent his servant to say to those who had been invited, 'Come; for all is now ready.' [18]But they all alike began to make excuses. The first said to him, 'I have bought a field, and I must go out and see it; I pray you, have me excused.'

¹⁹And another said, 'I have bought five yoke of oxen, and I go to examine them; I pray you, have me excused.' ²⁰And another said, 'I have married a wife, and therefore I cannot come.' ²¹So the servant came and reported this to his master. Then the householder in anger said to his servant, 'Go out quickly to the streets and lanes of the city, and bring in the poor and maimed and blind and lame.' ²²And the servant said, 'Sir, what you commanded has been done, and still there is room.' ²³And the master said to the servant, 'Go out to the highways and hedges, and compel people to come in, that my house may be filled. ²⁴For I tell you, none of those men who were invited shall taste my banquet.'"

Jesus concludes his discourse at the Pharisee's dinner with a parable which sums up what he has been saying. Jesus uses the traditional image of the banquet which would be familiar to his hearers as an Old Testament image which marked the inauguration of the messianic age. The banquet was to be prepared by God himself, and shared with those who were numbered among the faithful. The party is foretold by Isaiah:

On this mountain,
Yahweh will prepare for all peoples
a banquet of rich food, a banquet of fine wines,
of food rich and juicy, of fine strained wines.
The Lord Yahweh will wipe away
the tears from every cheek;
he will take away his people's shame
everywhere on earth,
for Yahweh has said so.   (Is 25:6, 8)

The image is immensely joyful and consoling of a God who graciously invites all people to come and share his banquet, where there will be gastronomic delights to gratify the most fastidious, and where God himself will ensure that tears are wiped away and shame is banished from the land.

One of the guests makes a pious remark about the happiness of the man who will share in the heavenly banquet. If the man was imagining that he was as good as there, then he was in for a disappointment. Jesus makes it clear that the image of the banquet is not one which can be applied only to the last day; the image of the banquet speaks to the *present* time. The invitations have already been sent out, and the servant is now calling the people to take their places at the banquet. If they now refuse the invitation to come, then they will miss the banquet and others will take their place. The invitation cannot be postponed to some future date; it has to be answered in the present tense. Now.

In the story which Jesus tells, a man gives a large banquet for many people. It was an oriental custom for upper-class people to send out two invitations: the first invitation was to announce the banquet, and the second invitation was to tell those who had accepted that the banquet was now ready. To accept the first invitation and refuse the second was regarded as a flagrant discourtesy and an insult to the host. The three men mentioned in the parable tell the servant who has called to summon them that they cannot accept because they are too busy to come. All three regard what they have to do as more important than honouring the invitation.

The servant returns with his disappointing news and the host is angry. But he is not going to be at a loss for dinner company. The servant is told to comb the streets and alleyways of the city and find guests among the poor, the maimed, the blind and the lame. The servant does this, but there is still room for more people at the party. This time the master sends his servants outside the boundaries of the city walls to search the highways and hedgerows for the vagrants and the tramps who might be roaming and finding shelter there. The servant is to "compel" them to come. This is not to bludgeon them into agreement: gentlemen of the road would naturally be suspicious of a sudden invitation from a stranger to attend a banquet, so the servant has to persuade them gently that he will not take no for an answer. The master makes it clear that those who refused the invitation will not taste of the banquet: they have excluded themselves from the festivities.

Without pressing the analogical interpretation to its

limits, one can see a historical parallel between the first invited and the people of Israel, between the crippled within
the city walls and the Jewish tax-collectors and sinners,
and between those outside the city walls and the Gentiles;
but the main point of the parable is neither the refusal of
the first invited nor the kind of people who eventually sit at
table: the focus of the parable is on the graciousness of the
host. The underlying image which Jesus presents is of a
gracious God who takes delight in throwing a banquet. He
is a God who wants the company of others, and who is not
unaffected when the guests refuse to come and feast with
him. There is the image of a God who is hungry for table-
company, a God who will not sit down at table and start
the banquet until all the places have been filled.

Unlike Dives in the parable of the rich man, the host is
not someone who is happy to feast sumptuously at his
table while ignoring the cripple at his gate. God does not
care for dining alone; he is concerned to have table fellowship with others, and so he is generous in his invitations.
He is moved to invite, to send his servant to the shabby and
the broken, to those who are regarded as ritually unclean
because of their physical deformities, to persuade those
who take refuge in the shadows and the forgotten alleyways of the world to come home and join his company. He
is God who is lonely in his kingdom for the company of
others to share his table. And a God who is hungry for
human company, who will postpone the party until all the
places have been filled, is a tender God. And the good
news is that no one has to wait until the last day before he
can relate to God as a concerned and gracious host; Jesus
asks everyone to relate to God in that image *now*.
Somewhere, there is a God who is waiting for his invitations to be honoured if people could see that they are invited to the banquet. Now.

Luke 14: 25-35   *Calculating the Cost*

²⁵Now great multitudes accompanied him; and he turned
and said to them, ²⁶"If anyone comes to me and does not

hate his own father and mother and wife and children and brothers and sisters, yes, and even his own life, he cannot be my disciple. ²⁷Whoever does not bear his own cross and come after me, cannot be my disciple. ²⁸For which of you, desiring to build a tower, does not first sit down and count the cost, whether he has enough to complete it? ²⁹Otherwise, when he has laid a foundation, and is not able to finish, all who see it begin to mock him, ³⁰saying, 'This man began to build, and was not able to finish.' ³¹Or what king, going to encounter another king in war, will not sit down first and take counsel whether he is able with ten thousand to meet him who comes against him with twenty thousand? ³²And if not, while the other is yet a great way off, he sends an embassy and asks terms of peace. ³³So therefore, whoever of you does not renounce all that he has cannot be my disciple.

³⁴"Salt is good; but if salt has lost its taste, how shall its saltness be restored? ³⁵It is fit neither for the land nor for the dunghill; men throw it away. He who has ears to hear, let him hear."

Great crowds accompany Jesus on the road to Jerusalem, a road that will take him to the place of trial and triumph. In spite of all the enthusiasm and the apparent support, Jesus is in no doubt about the ordeals which face him at the place of appointment. When Jesus speaks his mind on the cost of discipleship, he is in serious and sober mood: he knows that he himself will have to pay a heavy price for who he is and for what he stands, and he knows that those who follow him will have to meet a similar challenge. He is careful to avoid giving a false impression of discipleship, of building it up like some architectural prospect designed to evoke feelings of awful grandeur; instead, he paints a picture of discipleship as a very serious calling which demands unhurried thought and unqualified commitment. As always, Jesus avoids making the Gospel into an elegant conceit which does not take account of the opposition and the experience of suffering which are involved when it is taken seriously. Jesus wants people to follow him wholeheartedly or not at all.

When he commands his followers to hate their own relatives and their own life, Jesus is not proclaiming a Gospel of active hatred. Jesus has already told people to love their enemies (6:27) and he is not violating his own ethic in this passage. The construction which Jesus uses was a Semitic way of underlining one priority over another; instead of saying that the disciples must love the kingdom more than their own lives and relations, the saying makes the same point in a comparison of extremes. Deuteronomy 21:15 uses the construction, with hatred meaning a lesser degree of love. The point is that Jesus asks a total commitment to the kingdom of God, and all other commitments are of subordinate importance.

Jesus goes on to impress on his hearers that no one can be his disciple if he does not bear his cross. For Jesus' hearers, the image of a man carrying a cross meant only one thing: since crucifixion was a Roman punishment, usually for highway robbery or sedition, and was a familiar sight in Palestine, Jesus' audience would think of a man being led by Roman soldiers on a one-way journey to execution. The normal Jewish method of execution was by stoning; the Romans used crucifixion to execute slaves and foreigners. So, Jesus' picture of the disciple is of one who will have to cope not only with decisions which will affect his family and his own life, but also with decisions which will involve his being at variance with the authorities.

Jesus develops his thoughts on discipleship in a set of twin parables. He asks his hearers to agree that if one of them were to enter into a contract to build a tower, he would first sit down—not a posture of impatience—and calculate whether he could finish the task. If he were to start the building but could not complete it, he would have earned a reputation as a man who had built a monument to testify to his stupidity. Likewise, any king whose intelligence reports told him that his forces were outnumbered two to one would sit down and think seriously whether his military strategy could overcome the numerical advantage of his enemy. And he would do the thinking before he engaged his enemy in battle. If he decided that the military arithmetic was too heavy for comfort, he would send his ambassadors to negotiate for peace while the enemy was still at a safe distance. And a long way off is the only safe distance between opposing armies of vastly different strengths.

Jesus is not putting such a high price on discipleship that no one can afford to value it; he is emphasizing that anyone who is interested should first take the time to sit down and see whether he is equal to the task. Jesus does not want people to become disciples under false pretences; he does not want to give people the impression that his company is casual and easy-going, one into which people can shuffle their way when the mood takes them. Jesus is in a serious frame of mind: as he nears his own death, his own thoughts are clarified; and he does not need qualified commitments or momentary enthusiasms which exhaust themselves when the night comes. Jesus knows well that membership in his company does not mean that everything will be heavenly clear and uncomplicated: his disciples will be no strangers to hesitation and doubt; but, for the moment, he wants them to be as sure as possible what they are getting themselves into.

Jesus sums up his points by saying that the disciple is called to preserve life, to help it grow, to give it flavour. When the salt loses its taste it is only fit for throwing out; when the disciple loses the heart of discipleship then he is of help to nobody. The disciples will discover soon enough how people will smart at what they say and at what they do in the name of Christ. But when people smart at the disciples it suggests that something is happening, that some dynamic is taking place. For when the disciple loses his ability to make people smart then he has lost the edge of his discipleship.

Chapter Fifteen

Luke 15: 1-10   **The Lost Sheep and the Lost Coin**

15 Now the tax collectors and sinners were all drawing near to hear him. ²And the Pharisees and the scribes murmured, saying, "This man receives sinners and eats with them."

³So he told them this parable: ⁴"What man of you, having a hundred sheep, if he has lost one of them, does not leave the ninety-nine in the wilderness, and go after the one which is lost, until he finds it? ⁵And when he has found it, he lays it on his shoulders, rejoicing. ⁶And when he comes home, he calls together his friends and his neighbors, saying to them, 'Rejoice with me, for I have found my sheep which was lost.' ⁷Just so, I tell you, there will be more joy in heaven over one sinner who repents than over ninety-nine righteous persons who need no repentance.

⁸"Or what woman, having ten silver coins, if she loses one coin, does not light a lamp and sweep the house and seek diligently until she finds it? ⁹And when she has found it, she calls together her friends and neighbors, saying, 'Rejoice with me, for I have found the coin which I had lost.' ¹⁰Just so, I tell you, there is joy before the angels of God over one sinner who repents."

JESUS HAS JUST INVITED THOSE WHO HAVE EARS to hear to listen to what he has to say. The tax-collectors and the sinners, those who are summarily dismissed as outcasts by religious orthodoxy, take the advice of Jesus and approach him to hear what he has to say. The Pharisees and the scribes, those who pride themselves in keeping a safe distance from sinners, are in a different mood: they are busy murmuring their complaint that Jesus receives sinners and eats with them. Not only does he not avoid their company, but he shares table companionship with them. Jesus answers his critics with the twin parables of the Lost Sheep

and the Lost Coin, in which he suggests that if he is disregarding the law which forbids associating with sinners,
then he is in good company—for God himself actively
seeks out the company of sinners and rejoices when they
repent.

In the two parables, Jesus addresses the profound problem behind the murmuring—the Pharisees' mean image of
God. The Pharisees automatically presume that God wants
no dealings with sinners, that he does not want to risk involvement, that he is nervous in their company. Jesus' image of God is a world apart: Jesus' God is not closeted in
hurt bewilderment, wondering when the sinner is going to
change his ways, but a God who wants the sinner to share
the joy of heavenly company, and takes the initiative to
seek him out and make that joy possible. Jesus invites the
Pharisees and the scribes to change their way of relating to
sinners because it has nothing to do with God's way of
relating to sinners. And Jesus exemplifies God's way.

Jesus appeals to the human experience of his listeners with
the format: "What man of you. . .does not?" and invites
them to imagine that if they found themselves in circumstances similar to the people in the parables they would
act no differently. Not only that, but Jesus questions
whether they act likewise *now*. Jesus invites his hearers to
agree that when they do experience loss they are moved to
do something about it: they do not simply ignore it. In
both parables, there is the experience of loss, the movement of search, and the joy of discovery. The story is from
loss to discovery, and the movement is only possible
because of a search. And, as in the next parable of the
Father and Two Sons, the emphasis is on the joy which is
experienced and shared when the lost is found.

In the first parable, the shepherd discovers, probably
after the evening count, that one of the sheep is missing.
Head downwards, a sheep can easily nibble its way into the
kingdom of the lost to become a soft target for the wolf.
Alone, a sheep will surely perish, and the only thing it does
is lie down, immobilised with fear. When the shepherd

discovers that he is less one, he does not write it off as an inevitable loss, as "one of those things that happen". He leaves the other sheep, probably in the care of another shepherd, and goes off in search of the lost one. When he finds the lost sheep, he carries it on his shoulders, rejoicing. But his rejoicing is not solitary; he wants others to share it. Jesus tells his hearers that the same story is told in heaven when a sinner repents: there is joy and happiness when a sinner—one whom the Pharisees want nothing to do with—is brought home.

The second parable speaks of a woman who loses one of her ten silver coins. The coin Luke refers to is the drachma, which was the normal wage for a day's work. In Arab Palestine, when a girl was married, part of her dowry was a head-dress strung together with coins—something which was regarded as so precious that it could never be taken off or exchanged. The coin could have been one of the drachmae from the head-dress, or it could have been part of the savings of a poor woman. Whatever its significance, its loss was not unimportant. The woman lights a candle so that she can see in the dark house, and sweeps the floor. She searches until she can see a glint of the coin by candle-light or hear it tinkle against the stone floor. Her delight at finding it is such that she is moved to ask her friends and neighbours to celebrate with her. Like the shepherd, she wants others to share the joy of finding what was lost and precious. The loss is solitary, but the joy is communal.

If a man and a woman will go to such lengths to recover lost property, will God not go to lengths to recover the lost sinner? If a man and a woman act on their wish to share the joy of their find with others, will God not share the joy of a repentant sinner? Jesus asks his hearers to give God the credit of measuring up to the best of human behaviour, rather than attributing to him the worst of human behaviour. If one's image of God is that he does not even act well according to human criteria of generosity and care and sensitivity, then what characterizes one's image of God is its very absurdity. Jesus tells his hearers that reflection on their own behaviour to recover lost property can tell them something about God's concern for the sinner. And the image of God which should emerge from that reflection should be of a God who seeks out the company of sinners to bring them home.

Jesus is clear in his own mind that God is not inclined to tell sinners to "get lost" but is keen on seeking them out. The image of God as the one who does not just welcome the returning sinner but seeks him out had no rabbinic equivalent, and was good news to Jesus' hearers. Jesus claims familiarity with God's way of dealing with sinners, and takes his own cue from that knowledge. Jesus seeks out the company of sinners because God seeks out the company of sinners. So, the sinner is not one who has been abandoned in the kingdom of the lost and who has no hope of being found. Jesus tells whoever has ears to hear that God is searching in the kingdom of the lost for those who have wandered and strayed. When he has found them, they will be lost no more. And there will be a party to celebrate the homecoming.

Luke 15: 11- 32   *A Father and Two Sons*

[11]And he said, "There was a man who had two sons; [12]and the younger of them said to his father, 'Father, give me the share of property that falls to me.' And he divided his living between them. [13]Not many days later, the younger son gathered all he had and took his journey into a far country, and there he squandered his property in loose living. [14]And when he had spent everything, a great famine arose in that country, and he began to be in want. [15]So he went and joined himself to one of the citizens of that country, who sent him into his fields to feed swine. [16]And he would gladly have fed on the pods that the swine ate; and no one gave him anything. [17]But when he came to himself he said, 'How many of my father's hired servants have bread enough and to spare, but I perish here with hunger! [18]I will arise and go to my father, and I will say to him, "Father, I have sinned against heaven and before you; [19]I am no longer worthy to be called

your son; treat me as one of your hired servants.'" [20]And he arose and came to his father. But while he was yet at a distance, his father saw him and had compassion, and ran and embraced him and kissed him. [21]And the son said to him, 'Father, I have sinned against heaven and before you; I am no longer worthy to be called your son.' [22]But the father said to his servants, 'Bring quickly the best robe, and put it on him; and put a ring on his hand, and shoes on his feet; [23]and bring the fatted calf and kill it, and let us eat and make merry; [24]for this my son was dead, and is alive again; he was lost and is found.' And they began to make merry.

[25]"Now his elder son was in the field; and as he came and drew near to the house, he heard music and dancing. [26]And he called one of the servants and asked what this meant. [27]And he said to him, 'Your brother has come, and your father has killed the fatted calf, because he has received him safe and sound.' [28]But he was angry and refused to go in. His father came out and entreated him, [29]but he answered his father, 'Lo, these many years I have served you, and I never disobeyed your command; yet you never gave me a kid, that I might make merry with my friends. [30]But when this son of yours came, who has devoured your living with harlots, you killed for him the fatted calf!' [31]And he said to him, 'Son, you are always with me, and all that is mine is yours. [32]It was fitting to make merry and be glad, for this your brother was dead, and is alive; he was lost, and is found.'"

"There was a man who had two sons" begins one of the most touching and exquisite short stories in the pages of world literature. Alone among the evangelists, Luke gives us the story of a father and two sons, a story which speaks to us of the boundless mercy and understanding of God. Traditionally, the story is known as the parable of the Prodigal Son, but this title does scant justice to a tale which tells us of the extravagant love of the father, the self-righteous posturing of the elder son, and the journey from folly to wisdom of the younger son. The parable is told by way of reply to the scribes and the Pharisees who have been complaining about Jesus' lax attitude towards sinners: "This man receives sinners and eats with them" (v. 2). Jesus tells the parable, as he did the parables of the Lost Sheep and the Lost Coin, to justify God's attitude to sinners, an attitude which Jesus himself exemplifies in his own behaviour. The parable goes further to challenge Jesus' critics to change their attitude to sinners from one which is characterized by its hostility to one which is characterized by its hospitality. Reaching out is more God-like than keeping away; association is more God-like than segregation.

The story is told of a father who has two sons and who loses them both: one is lost in a far country, and the other is lost in the wilderness of his own hostility. One leaves home in the fond hope that he will find happiness in the experience of the unfamiliar only to discover that it is found at the heart of the familiar. One stays at home but is such a stranger to the love and joy which surround him that he might as well be an alien in a foreign land. They are a mixed human family in which tenderness, selfishness and hostility all vie with each other for possession. By the end of the story, tenderness has won over selfishness; but it is unclear whether hostility will stay out in the cold.

The younger son leaves home, and not until he becomes a self-confessed failure does he make a journey which brings him the happiness he has been so eagerly seeking. It appears that the younger son has gone on a fruitless journey to end up where he started, but if the geography of the journey's end is the same as the starting-point, the traveller is different. The journey has been a profound learning experience for the younger son: he is a man of new insight at journey's end. The elder son does not leave home, but by the end of the story proximity to his father has not led him to insight. The elder brother does not move—he does not move to welcome his lost brother, he does not move to rejoice with his father. He has barricaded himself in his own no-go area, where self-righteousness reigns; where dancing and music are sounds to be justified rather than entered into; where the return of a lost brother is an occasion for practising the precise arithmetic of fidelity.

The younger son yearns for a life different from that experienced at home. He leaves home and discovers that his promised land is barren of hope. He experiences failure but his failure is not unimportant. The experience of failure forms the *krisis,* the turning-point in the story of the younger son. He reflects on his situation and admits to himself that his present situation is hopeless; but this realisation is a positive discovery—in the terms of Socrates, there is the knowledge of ignorance. But if the present situation is hopeless, the future is seen differently because the younger son remembers what happens at home. He makes the journey of return, and is welcomed home to feasting and merrymaking. There is a progressive psychological movement in the younger son's story:

1. Dissatisfaction with home; urge to travel
2. Withdrawal from home
3. Discovery of the hopelessness of present situation
4. *Experience of failure*
5. Remembering home, which makes possible anticipation of better future
6. Journey of return
7. Welcome home and party

In the structure of development, there is a parallelism and antithesis between the various parts of the story. The original dissatisfaction and yearning are balanced by the welcome home; the withdrawal eventually leads to the journey of return; the *awareness* of present hopelessness is saved through *memory* of a kinder past and *anticipation* of a kinder future. The experience of failure forms the pivotal point of the story, while the merrymaking forms the climax. It is doubtful whether the merrymaking would have taken place without the experience of failure, but that paradox is only a reflection of the truth that resurrection is possible only after death, and that being found is possible only after being lost.

The younger son's journey shares the ancient structural composition of setting out and coming home, which is a central theme in myth and religion. At the beginning of the journey, the son is no hero; but when he makes his return his father is happy to give him a hero's welcome. The fact that he has returned shows that he has come to some insight on the journey. He now sees differently. T. S. Eliot captures the dynamic of the circuitous journey in *Four Quartets,* "Little Gidding":

We shall not cease from exploration
And the end of all our exploring
Will be to arrive where we started
And know the place for the first time.

In the opening of the story, the younger son asks for his share in the property. It is generally supposed that he was about seventeen years old: the story suggests that he was unmarried, and most male Jews married between the ages of eighteen and twenty. According to the Jewish law of inheritance, the first son would receive two-thirds of the property, double what the younger son would receive. The transaction normally took effect on the death of the father, but even if the father deeded the property to his sons during his life-time, the sons would normally have the right of possession, but not the right of disposal, since the father retained the use and enjoyment of the property. The younger son in the parable asks for the right to dispose of his share, which the father legally grants, but the father still has a right to future income from that disposal. When the father gives the younger son his portion of the property, he also gives the remainder to the elder son. That is why he can say to the elder son: "All that I have is yours" (v. 31). When the younger son leaves home he has no further claim on the home property, but he does have the obligation of supporting his father in his need.

A few days after the settlement is made, the younger son heads for a far country, putting as much distance as possible between himself and home. In his new surroundings, the younger son lives loosely and spends freely. He runs out of money and runs into famine, and the unhappy combination of these two events forces him into a double degradation: he accepts employment from a Gentile and finds himself in the field tending swine. He is a long way from home and from the fulfilment of his dream. If he had made any friends, they have already bowed out of the scene for no one gives him anything. He is so hungry that he would gladly eat the husks from the carob tree.

Things have turned out badly, but the Gospel story tells us that "he came to himself". After a long journey, the younger son eventually comes to himself. In the midst of his failure he sees a way out. His memory saves him, and allows him to imagine a future different from the present. Remembering how well the servants at home are treated, he makes the decision to return to his father's house. He starts preparing a boring speech for the benefit of his father, but his memory of his father is less than accurate if he thinks his father's attitude of generosity is dependent on eloquence. No doubt on the return journey, he rehearses the finer points of his speech.

And then there is the twist in the story: the father's attitude is totally unexpected and conflicts with the son's reading. In the East, it was regarded as undignified for an old man to run, but the father is not loaded down with his own dignity, he is free to love and show that love freely. The father's love totally overshadows the son's recently acquired sense of unworthiness. The father is neither interested in hearing speeches from the counsel for the defence nor in making them for the counsel for the prosecution. His instinct is for forgiveness and acceptance, and everything else falls away as unimportant. The younger son starts in on his speech, but all the rehearsals were in vain. The father is busy telling the servants to bring the best robe, a symbol of status; the ring, a symbol of authority; sandals, which were worn only by freemen, and in the house were worn only by the host. The fatted calf is called upon to grace the table. And the cry goes out to "make merry". There has been a resurrection and a find. The lost son is home.

While all the drama of the homecoming is going on at

the house, the elder brother has been working in the field. The story picks up with his making his way home after a day's labour. When he approaches the house, he hears music and dancing. Rather than hurry in to see what the rejoicing is about, he keeps his distance and calls a servant to explain the reason for the merrymaking. The servant gives an unvarnished account of what has happened, and the elder brother reacts with anger. Unlike his father, he does not have the generous instinct to rush to meet the younger brother. He refuses to move. His own anger immobilises him. Now, he is the one who is far from home. He is the "separated one".

For the second time, the father comes out to meet one of his sons. The father has to involve himself in the tortuous position of having to explain why one son should rejoice with another, but all he receives in return is another boring speech. Throughout his speech, the elder son, unlike his younger brother, never calls his father, 'Father'. Like the younger son, the elder son calls on his memory, but unlike the memory of the younger son, it is not a happy one and it does not bring him nearer to his father. He uses the occasion to lecture his father on his past service and obedience, and to chastise his father for not giving him a kid to make merry with his friends. A son who needs to wait on his father's initiative before he can rejoice with his friends is taking the issue from where it is (with himself) and placing it where it is not (with his father). The elder brother goes on to disown his brother, calling him "this son of yours", and proceeds to inform his father how the younger son spent his time in a far country, making sure that the account is suitably seedy. With every word, the elder brother distances himself more and more from his father and his brother, and from the touch of humanity and tenderness.

The father is not going to cancel the merrymaking or question his own generous instincts in order to please his son. The father puts the problem back where it belongs — with the elder brother. He addresses his son, *teknon,* which is an affectionate term, "my dear son". The father's own generosity to his elder son is unchanged and unaffected by the meanness which confronts him. He simply repeats what he said to the servants—who seem to have had no trouble understanding what the elder brother finds difficult: it is fitting to make merry. And the father corrects the elder brother's earlier disowning of his brother: "for this your brother was dead, and is alive; he was lost and is found."

The story ends there. Did the father go back to the merry-making alone? Did the brother change his mind and go into the house to rejoice with his brother? Was the elder brother moved by the compassionate plea of his father? Jesus does not say. Perhaps the story of the elder brother is still being told.

Chapter Sixteen

Luke 16: 1-13   The Clever Steward

16 He also said to the disciples, "There was a rich man who had a steward, and charges were brought to him that this man was wasting his goods. ²And he called him and said to him, 'What is this that I hear about you? Turn in the account of your stewardship, for you can no longer be steward.' ³And the steward said to himself, 'What shall I do, since my master is taking the stewardship away from me? I am not strong enough to dig, and I am ashamed to beg. ⁴I have decided what to do, so that people may receive me into their houses when I am put out of the stewardship.' ⁵So, summoning his master's debtors one by one, he said to the first, 'How much do you owe my master?' ⁶He said, 'A hundred measures of oil.' And he said to him, 'Take your bill, and sit down quickly and write fifty.' ⁷Then he said to another, 'And how much do you owe?' He said, 'A hundred measures of wheat.' He said to him, 'Take your bill, and write eighty.' ⁸The master commended the dishonest steward for his prudence; for the sons of this world are wiser in their own generation than the sons of light. ⁹And I tell you, make friends for yourselves by means of unrighteous mammon, so that when it fails they may receive you into the eternal habitations.

¹⁰"He who is faithful in a very little is faithful also in much; and he who is dishonest in a very little is dishonest also in much. ¹¹If then you have not been faithful in the unrighteous mammon, who will entrust to you the true riches? ¹²And if you have not been faithful in that which is another's, who will give you that which is your own? ¹³No servant can serve two masters; for either he will hate the one and love the other, or he will be devoted to the one and despise the other. You cannot serve God and mammon."

THE PARABLE OF THE CLEVER STEWARD is acknowledged to be one of the most difficult parables to interpret, and commentators seeking to make sense of it have offered a litany of interpretations. The parable is sometimes referred to as the story of the Dishonest Steward, but this title seems unfortunate. Although the steward is dishonest, it is his ingenuity and resolute action which are commended— not his dishonesty. To focus on his dishonesty is to make interpretation of the parable doubly difficult, since it is to move the spotlight of attention away from the main point of the parable, which is how one man turns personal disaster into shared opportunity. There is dispute about where the parable ends and the commentary begins; whether the *kyrios* of v. 8a refers to the master or to Jesus; whether the verses after the parable are by way of comment or appended sayings with only tenuous links to the parable. The parable itself is addressed to the disciples, although the Pharisees are within hearing (v. 14) and react unfavourably to what is said.

The parable opens with a rich man who hears accusations that his steward has been mismanaging the affairs of the estate. The master of the house believes the reports to be true so he calls his steward, asks him for a final account, and gives him a notice of dismissal. The fact that the steward is dismissed makes it unlikely that he is a servant: servants were disciplined, not discharged. The steward reflects on his new situation of crisis and thinks how he can face the future now that he is unemployed and has no further income. He does not spend long discounting digging and begging as possible means of income, so he hits on the idea of calling in his master's debtors so that he can reduce the total they owe. He calls them in one by one: secrecy is part of his plan. And he wants to be able to depend on their future kindness: after the transaction, they are in his debt.

There are two basic interpretations of the steward's action. The first interpretation holds that the steward called in his master's debtors and engaged each of them in a conspiracy to fraudulently deprive the master of the house of his rightful income. This reading argues that the transactions were dishonest, even if the outcome was favorable to the steward and the debtors. In the light of this, v. 8a makes for difficulty: how could the master or Christ commend such a transparently discreditable transaction? The difficulty is not insurmountable since what is commended is not the wrongdoing, but the determined action of the steward in a time of crisis to secure future employment or support. Thus in telling the parable, Jesus is not offering uncritical support of "cooking the books"; he focuses on the urgency and the energy with which a worldly man secures his future at a time of reckoning, with the argument that the children of the light should learn from that and ensure that their own future is not in jeopardy.

The second interpretation, which owes much to the research of J. M. Derrett,[1] argues that the action of the steward was legal and worthy of praise. The argument is based on the Jewish law forbidding usury, and the commercial custom of the time. By law, Jews were forbidden to take interest on loans to fellow Jews (Lev 25:36). However, the Pharisees had managed to discover a way of upholding the letter of the law while still making money from loans by arguing that the law was meant to protect the poor from exploitation but did not prohibit payment of interest when the transaction was financially beneficial to both parties. The argument was that if a man actually possessed a little of the commodity he wished to borrow then he could not really be regarded as destitute. Since almost everyone had a little wheat and a little oil, whatever was borrowed was restated in terms of wheat and oil and the interest was then added on. The whole arrangement was a legal fiction, but it was the commercial practice at the time. The bonds were made out in terms of wheat and oil, and although the business was usurious, the bonds did not show this.

In this interpretation, the steward in the parable takes the bond which gives the total owed, including interest, and tells the debtor to rewrite the bond and reduce it by the amount of the interest due on the transaction. In this light, the steward would be acting legally and morally, he would be helping the debtors, and he would be presenting his master as one who was gracious and who obeyed the law of God which forbade usury. The master was thus in no position to recall the original bond and cancel what the steward had done: this would have incriminated him in entering a usurious transaction. The best the master could do would be to capitalise on the deal and present himself as a faithful observer of the law. Thus, all the parties are seen as conforming to the law of the Lord—and all because of the steward's dismissal. One commentator, Fitzmyer, argues that the interest on usurious transactions was the steward's commission, so that the steward would be forfeiting his own claim to the money, and the master would be losing nothing.[2] Thus the steward would be accepting a present loss in the hope that it would turn out to be a future investment.

The collected sayings which follow the parable are connected to each other with the link word *mamom,* which literally means "that in which you put your trust". Jesus does not argue that as a worldly man can purchase friends will ill-gotten gains, so disciples can "buy" their way into heaven: people enter heaven because of the graciousness of God. Money should be used to benefit people, not manipulate them; and since it is given as a trust in the first place, it should be used in the service of discipleship. If a man can be trusted to use wealth wisely, then he can be trusted with the real wealth of the kingdom. Finally, Jesus emphasises the absolute claim of God on the disciple: there must be no rivals to God. He requires total fidelity.

As in many of his stories, Jesus invites his hearers to attend to what is going on in the world around them and learn from their observations. Even in worldly transactions, where a man can turn a private affliction into a shared triumph, there is a teaching. The disciples are enjoined to put their trust in God who has favoured them with trust in the first place. Return trust for trust. And that is a fair deal.

Luke 16: 14-18   *The Law and the Kingdom*

¹⁴The Pharisees, who were lovers of money, heard all this, and they scoffed at him. ¹⁵But he said to them, "You are those who justify yourselves before men, but God knows your hearts; for what is exalted among men is an abomination in the sight of God.

¹⁶"The law and the prophets were until John; since then the good news of the kingdom of God is preached, and every one enters it violently. ¹⁷But it is easier for heaven and earth to pass away, than for one dot of the law to become void.

¹⁸"Every one who divorces his wife and marries another commits adultery, and he who marries a woman divorced from her husband commits adultery.

The Pharisees respond with disdain to the teaching of Jesus on the right use of wealth, and Jesus addresses them directly. Although the Pharisees did not have the Sadducees' reputation for accumulating wealth, they did have the convenient belief that prosperous living was a sign of God's favour. This attitude was contrary to Jesus' teaching which stressed the folly of putting trust in riches rather than in God. Jesus makes his own position clear when he criticizes the practice of the Pharisees which seeks justification in the eyes of men: almsgiving may appear a laudable deed, but it is not enough in itself. No one can move from performance to justification and bypass the heart. God can see into the hearts of men, and it is what resides there that is important to him.

The next three sayings are linked together by the word law. Jesus named John the Baptist as a significant figure in the development of God's plan: before him, the law and the prophets were in possession; after him, God's plan takes shape in the preaching of the kingdom. The meaning of "everyone enters it violently" is disputed. Whether it means that, like the steward in the previous parable, everyone should act with urgency and energy when confronted with the pressing reality of the kingdom, or whether it means that most people are in fact oppressing the kingdom and its truth³ is still unclear. In both interpretations, there is a pressing reaction to the kingdom rather than one of indifference.

Verse 17 is not free of difficulty. There is a question whether Jesus is being ironical or whether he is unambiguously upholding the permanency of the law. The "dot" is the small projection which distinguishes a Hebrew letter, or it can be a scribal ornamentation. Is Jesus ironically saying that the world could be collapsing around the heads of the scribes while they are engrossed in ornamenting the minutiae of the law? Will heaven and earth pass away before the scribes see the purpose of the law? If even the dot cannot be changed, does Jesus appear to ignore his own advice in the next saying, when he changes the Mosaic Law on divorce? Given Jesus' continued emphasis on the supremacy of the kingdom of God, perhaps this saying is an emphatic testimony to the importance of the kingdom as the reality within which the law must be interpreted. In that sense, the kingdom is the cognitive field, within which the law must be seen and understood.

The saying on divorce would appear to support the latter view. In the context of the kingdom, Jesus clarifies the teaching on marriage. It had become the practice for men to divorce women for the flimsiest of reasons: Rabbi Hillel permitted a man to divorce his wife if she did not produce gastronomic delights to his taste, or if she spoke to a strange man; Rabbi Akiba permitted a man to divorce his wife if he discovered someone prettier—which by the law of averages would destroy every marriage. In his teaching, Jesus *brings* the law into the kingdom, where it has its true setting.

Luke 16: 19-31   *The Rich Man and Lazarus*

[19]"There was a rich man, who was clothed in purple and fine linen and who feasted sumptuously every day. [20]And at his gate lay a poor man named Lazarus, full of sores, [21]who desired to be fed with what fell from the rich man's table; moreover the dogs came and licked his sores. [22]The poor

man died and was carried by the angels to Abraham's bosom. The rich man also died and was buried; [23]and in Hades, being in torment, he lifted up his eyes, and saw Abraham far off and Lazarus in his bosom. [24]And he called out, 'Father Abraham, have mercy upon me, and send Lazarus to dip the end of his finger in water and cool my tongue; for I am in anguish in this flame.' [25]But Abraham said, 'Son, remember that you in your lifetime received your good things, and Lazarus in like manner evil things; but now he is comforted here, and you are in anguish. [26]And besides all this, between us and you a great chasm has been fixed, in order that those who would pass from here to you may not be able, and none may cross from there to us.' [27]And he said, 'Then I beg you, father, to send him to my father's house, [28]for I have five brothers, so that he may warn them, lest they also come into this place of torment.' [29]But Abraham said, 'They have Moses and the prophets; let them hear them.' [30]And he said, 'No, father Abraham; but if some one goes to them from the dead, they will repent.' [31]He said to him, 'If they do not hear Moses and the prophets, neither will they be convinced if some one should rise from the dead.''

Still addressing the Pharisees, Jesus tells his tale of the rich man and Lazarus. Since H. Gressman's scholarly work on this text,[4] most commentators acknowledge the affinity between this parable, which is peculiar to Luke, and an old Egyptian folk-tale which tells the story of Si-Osiris who travels to the land of the dead where he witnesses the reversal of fortunes of two people who were buried on the same day. The man who was rich on earth is now in torment; the man who suffered poverty and hardship on earth is now in bliss. The tale ends: "He who has been good on earth will be blessed in the kingdom of the dead, and he who has been evil on earth will suffer in the kingdom of the dead." A Jewish version of the story in the form of a poor scholar and a rich publican, Bar Ma'jan, was current in the time of Jesus, and it carried the same moral: what happens to people in the next world depends on what they do on earth.

Some scholars dispute the unity of the parable as presented by Luke, arguing that the second section was later added by the early Church upon learning of the failure by the Jews to believe in the resurrection, and hence their failure to believe in anything *because* of it. However, if the structural unity of the Egyptian folk-tale and its Jewish counterpart remains uncontested, there is no logical necessity to question the unity of Jesus' version of the same story. In fact, the parable makes more sense as a pre-resurrection story since it emphasizes the sufficiency of God's revelation at any given time, and man's capacity to respond to a message in his own time, without waiting for visitors from another world. The parable also makes the point that resurrection is valueless as a persuasive means in leading people to change their lives. Jesus' listeners have Moses and the prophets in their tradition, and they have Lazarus on their doorstep. And that is enough to be going on.

The rich man in the parable is portrayed as a figure who makes a vocation out of self-indulgence. With outer garments dyed purple from the very expensive dye from the shellfish murex, and undergarments of fine linen, the rich man wears one of the most expensive outfits known in the ancient world. He dines sumptuously—not once a week, but every day—and it appears that he hardly comes up for air given his obsessive commitment to feasting. The rich man is probably a Sadducee, not only because Sadducees were among the few people who could afford such a life-style, but because we learn later that the rich man and his brothers did not believe in an after-life which was connected with life on earth. The Sadducees did not believe in the resurrection, but in the Old Testament idea of Sheol, the Hebrew equivalent of Hades, which was a shadowy underworld where everyone, good and bad, went after death. It was a neutral place which had no pain and no hope. It was a place of no accountability; just blankness. Given this convenient belief, the rich man in the parable believes that his present life is the only one, and that he will not be held accountable for his life when he dies. But a surprise awaits him.

In contrast to the rich man who feasts in company every day, Lazarus is portrayed as a helpless, lonely beggar who receives nothing but the unwanted attention of stray dogs. He is the only person who is named in any of Jesus' parables: his name, from the Hebrew, Eleazar, means "(He whom) God helps". The name makes sad sense, since no one appears on the scene to care for him. Lazarus is covered in ulcers, and he is so weak that he cannot even ward off the scavenging dogs. They make a pitiful sight at the gate of the rich man's house. Lazarus has been educated to have humble hopes: he does not expect to dine at the rich man's table; he would be happy to eat the pieces of bread on which the guests wipe their fingers. Lazarus hopes for the fingered rejects of the dinner-table. And so, he waits. And waits.

The scene shifts to the next world where we witness a reversal of fortunes. On his death, Lazarus receives an angelic escort to the heavenly banquet where he reclines his head on the bosom of the father patriarch; he is no longer the outsider and the forgotten one, but the favoured guest. The rich man discovers that Hades is not the neutral territory he had believed, but Gehenna, the place of torment. He recognizes Lazarus and refers to him by name—so the rich man did know the identity of the beggar at his gate. But there is not a word of apology to the man he constantly ignored. The rich man calls Abraham "Father", but this late recognition is not sufficient for salvation. The rich man's first instinct is for his own lost comfort, and he arrogantly assumes that he can call on the service of Lazarus to minister to him. When that fails, he thinks of his brothers who shared his belief in the nature of Hades, and hopes that Lazarus will play messenger to inform his brothers that they are wrong. The rich man implies that he had insufficient information about the nature of the afterlife, with the further implication that if he had known, he would have acted differently. However, Abraham replies that since there is enough in Moses and the prophets—the books which the Sadducees accept—and since heavenly visitors are not knock-down arguments, there is nothing further to do. The brothers have enough in the witness of the prophets, and in the need of their fellow-men.

While on earth, the rich man had accepted the poverty, the pain, and the isolation of Lazarus as an acceptable part of the human landscape. He knew Lazarus by name, but he did nothing to alleviate the affliction that was before his eyes. The rich man did not assault or abuse Lazarus: he did nothing, and that was his crime. He treated Lazarus as if he were already dead; he forgot about Lazarus; and Lazarus died of his forgetfulness. It was the rich man's apathy, his insensitivity, which proved ground enough for damnation. It was his so-called 'innocence' which constituted his crime. As Dorothee Solle has written: "When you look at human suffering concretely you destroy all innocence, all neutrality, every attempt to say, 'It wasn't I; there was nothing I could do; I didn't know.' In the face of suffering you are either with the victim or the executioner—there is no other option."[5] And God is clearly on the side of the victim.

Notes

[1]Cf. J. D. M. Derrett, *Law in the New Testament* (London, 1970) pp. 48-77

[2]Cf. J. A. Fitzmyer, "The Story of the Dishonest Manager" in *Theological Studies* 25, 1964, pp. 23-42

[3]Cf. M. Black, *An Aramaic Approach to the Gospels and Acts,* (Oxford University Press, 1967) p. 84

[4]H. Gressman, *Von reichen Mann und armen Lazarus* in the *Abhandlungen* of the Prussian Academy (phil.-hist. Kl., 1918, no. 7)

[5]D. Solle, *Suffering,* (Philadelphia, Fortress Press, 1975) p. 32

Chapter Seventeen

Luke 17: 1-10   Forgiveness and Faith

17 And he said to his disciples, "Temptations to sin are sure to come; but woe to him by whom they come! ²It would be better for him if a millstone were hung round his neck and he were cast into the sea, than that he should cause one of these little ones to sin. ³Take heed to yourselves; if your brother sins, rebuke him, and if he repents, forgive him; ⁴and if he sins against you seven times in the day, and turns to you seven times, and says, 'I repent,' you must forgive him."

⁵The apostles said to the Lord, "Increase our faith!" ⁶And the Lord said, "If you had faith as a grain of mustard seed, you could say to this sycamine tree, 'Be rooted up, and be planted in the sea,' and it would obey you.

⁷"Will any one of you, who has a servant plowing or keeping sheep, say to him when he has come in from the field, 'Come at once and sit down at table'? ⁸Will he not rather say to him, 'Prepare supper for me, and gird yourself and serve me, till I eat and drink; and afterward you shall eat and drink'? ⁹Does he thank the servant because he did what was commanded? ¹⁰So you also, when you have done all that is commanded you, say, 'We are unworthy servants; we have only done what was our duty.'"

IN THIS PASSAGE, Luke gives us Jesus' advice to his disciples in a series of collected fragments, which have no particular context and no obvious connection. Firstly, Jesus talks about the inevitability of temptation as part of the human drama, something which he himself has experienced in his own story. He warns those who play the role of tempter and are responsible for misleading the lowly ones that they would have fared better in the depths of the sea. The tempter is one of the traditional images of Satan, and it is not the vocation of the follower of Christ to take a lead from that quarter and allure innocents away from the presence of God. The true disciple puts people in contact with God by the integrity of his own life.

Jesus goes on to counsel honesty and forgiveness in human relationships. He argues to an openness in dealing with others whereby disciples should have the courage and the concern to tell others of their wrongdoing. This openness avoids the harbouring of wrongs; it avoids nursing old griefs; it avoids leaving people cloistered in their own wrongdoing. In effect, Jesus tells his disciples to speak words of encouragement because their words offer release in forgiveness. Everyone must be offered the opportunity of repentance, the chance to say "I am sorry". And when that is done, the matter is ended. No recriminations; no postmortems. The matter ends with forgiveness, and forgiveness must be proferred as many times as repentance is promised. There is no arithmetical limit to forgiveness; there is no last time for human forgiveness.

If the next verse comments on the disciples' reaction to what Jesus has just said, then their request for an increase in faith is understandable. But Jesus' reply moves away from considering faith as a quantity which one should have more of, to say that the quality of faith as small as a mustard seed can do wonders. Again, Jesus underlines the greatness of littleness. In the context of Jesus' image, he is hardly advising his disciples to plant sycamine trees in the sea: that activity is sufficiently pointless to counter that suggestion. What Jesus does emphasize is that faith makes limitless forgiveness a real human possibility—and that, rather than decorating the sea with trees, will always be a profound benefit to the world.

Finally, in a small parable peculiar to Luke, Jesus buries the notion that good works put God in the ungodly position where he owes the disciple. That scenario is an ingenious human conceit. Jesus makes it clear that a religious attitude which owes much to arithmetic and selective bookkeeping (like that of the elder brother in an earlier parable) has nothing to do with the kingdom of God.

Nobody has a claim on God. The foundation of Christianity is in the acknowledgement that man is favoured by God in the first place, not vice-versa. God is the one who favours, and no matter how good any individual is, he is always the favoured one. However, in his own teaching, Jesus does not portray God as the master who waits to be served, but as the king who does not sit at table until an odd assembly are brought in from the highways and byways to share the banquet. But that is God's privilege, not man's right. The human task, in the word of Ignatius of Loyola's *Prayer for Generosity*, is:

To give and not to count the cost;
To fight and not to heed the wounds;
To toil and not to seek for rest;
To labour and not to ask for any reward
Save that of knowing that we do Thy will.

Luke 17: 11-19   *The Ten Lepers*

[11]On the way to Jerusalem he was passing along between Samaria and Galilee. [12]And as he entered a village, he was met by ten lepers, who stood at a distance [13]and lifted up their voices and said, "Jesus, Master, have mercy on us." [14]When he saw them he said to them, "Go and show yourselves to the priests." And as they went they were cleansed. [15]Then one of them, when he saw that he was healed, turned back, praising God with a loud voice; [16]and he fell on his face at Jesus' feet, giving him thanks. Now he was a Samaritan. [17]Then said Jesus, "Were not ten cleansed? Where are the nine? [18]Was no one found to return and give praise to God except this foreigner?" [19]And he said to him, "Rise and go your way; your faith has made you well."

Luke again alludes to his journey motif by recalling that Jesus is still on the way to Jerusalem, although it does not appear from the geographical information that he is making much progress. While some scholars go to pains to make sense of Luke's geographical plotting,[1] their attempts often seem more ingenious than helpful. The governing factor

to take into account is Luke's concern for logical development rather than chronological or geographical exactitude.

As he approaches an unidentified village, Jesus is met by
ten lepers. The law required that lepers live away from centres of population (cf. Lev 13:46), but they usually stayed
near towns and villages so that they could beg easily. The
lepers keep the required distance from Jesus; they recognize
him, call him by name, and appeal for mercy. Jesus does
not cure their affliction immediately, but tells them to go
and present themselves to the priest—which was a legal requirement since the priest was the equivalent of the health
officer who had to confirm the cure before the leper was
allowed to return to the normal life of the community.

The lepers take Jesus at his word and go on their way, and
it is while they are on the way that they are cured. As the ten
lepers lift up their voices to appeal to Jesus for mercy, one
of them lifts up his voice to praise God for the healing.
Although Jesus charged all the group to go to the priests,
for one of the group it is more important to travel on his
human instinct to say thank-you than to have his cure certi-
fied by the proper authorities. So, a solitary figure makes a
journey of return and prostrates himself before Jesus in a
prayer of thanksgiving. He is a Samaritan—with the presumption that the others are Jews. Again, there is the reversal of expectations: it is the outsider who becomes the model
of gratitude and faith. Although Jews and Samaritans
would never normally be seen in each other's company, it
seems unremarkable if they are lepers. Affliction knows no
boundaries. But now that all ten are cured, separation
returns immediately—and it is the outcast who makes the
move in favour of Jesus.

Jesus responds to the Samaritan's return with three
questions—all of which testify to his personal hurt at people's ingratitude. It seems as if Jesus is checking his
memory, and is pained by its accuracy. Were not ten
cleansed? Whatever happened to the other nine? It appears
as if Jesus is beginning to doubt whether ten were *really*
cleansed, whether the healing *really* worked since the

human response is so shabby and mean. Apparently, ingratitude can make the giver doubt himself, or at least doubt whether his own faith in people is justified by events. If ten were cleansed, why were they unmoved to praise the power of God which made their cure possible? Why is a foreigner the only one who does what the others are taught by their tradition to do? Do you have to be taught to say thank-you? Why does meanness characterize some people when they are gifted? If healing costs Jesus in his own faith and energy, what does it cost someone to acknowledge it?

In his commentary on the response of the ungrateful nine, George McCauley reflects how people become like that: "Despite cures, some people are going to go on feeling like lepers, anyway. They cannot be touched by sentiments of gratitude because they cannot see any sentiment capable of penetrating the hard and fixed coating of their unworthiness. . .We often do favours for the wrong reasons (one-upmanship, showing off, an obsessive need to look good, guilt, controlling others, pity, etc.). So, we think others are acting just as aggressively or obliquely when they do us favours. Kindness, we suspect, is a contest, and the one who has to say thank you has already lost. Or, we fear that to show gratitude is to compromise our independence."[2] Whatever the explanation for the attitude of the ungrateful nine who did not thank Jesus, Jesus is hurt by the experience. And he is obviously less interested in the cure, than in the teaching which emerges from it.

Jesus' final word to the Samaritan is to commend him for his faith. It is not that the other nine had no faith, since they did take Jesus' word that they would be cured; but they did not respond with their own word of thanks. Their faith lacked an essential quality in gratitude. So, Jesus sends the Samaritan on his way with the assurance that he is well—not just physically, but in the sight of God. Gratitude does that.

Luke 17: 20-37   *The Day of the Son of Man*

²⁰Being asked by the Pharisees when the kingdom of God was coming, he answered them, "The kingdom of God is not coming with signs to be observed; ²¹nor will they say, 'Lo, here it is!' or 'There!' for behold, the kingdom of God is in the midst of you."

²²And he said to the disciples, "The days are coming when you will desire to see one of the days of the Son of man, and you will not see it. ²³And they will say to you, 'Lo, there!' or 'Lo, here!' Do not go, do not follow them. ²⁴For as the lightning flashes and lights up the sky from one side to the other, so will the Son of man be in his day. ²⁵But first he must suffer many things and be rejected by this generation. ²⁶As it was in the days of Noah, so will it be in the days of the Son of man. ²⁷They ate, they drank, they married, they were given in marriage, until the day when Noah entered the ark, and the flood came and destroyed them all. ²⁸Likewise as it was in the days of Lot—they ate, they drank, they bought, they sold, they planted, they built, ²⁹but on the day when Lot went out from Sodom fire and sulphur rained from heaven and destroyed them all—³⁰so will it be on the day when the Son of man is revealed. ³¹On that day, let him who is on the housetop, with his goods in the house, not come down to take them away; and likewise let him who is in the field not turn back. ³²Remember Lot's wife. ³³Whoever seeks to gain his life will lose it, but whoever loses his life will preserve it. ³⁴I tell you, in that night there will be two in one bed; one will be taken and the other left. ³⁵There will be two women grinding together; one will be taken and the other left." ³⁷And they said to him, "Where, Lord?" He said to them, "Where the body is, there the eagles will be gathered together."

This passage on the presence of the kingdom of God and the future coming of the Son of Man is heavy with textual difficulties, not least because the sayings themselves warn against seeking observable signs where none are to be found.³ So, we have to try to make sense of sayings which point to the futility of trying to make sense of present or future events by seeking for signs. The question of time is paramount in the passage: the Pharisees want to know *when* the kingdom is coming; the disciples want signs to forewarn them *when* the coming of the Son of Man will take place. In his reply to both parties, Jesus underlines the folly of the question and points out that just as no warning signs were given to announce the coming of the kingdom, so no preliminary signs will warn people of the second coming of the Son of Man. People are not going to be given the striking signs which *they* seek. Undaunted, the disciples have another try, and this time ask *where* the coming is going to take place, but Jesus keeps to his previous warning that although no one will know beforehand when or where it will happen, everyone will certainly know when it does. The coming of the Son of Man will be unmistakable.

That the Pharisees are still asking for signs of the coming of the kingdom is evidence that they have not recognized the reality of the kingdom in their presence. They are waiting for something which is already present; and if they cannot recognize Jesus' own witness and ministry, what purpose signs? There is an unresolved dispute over the translation of v. 21b: is Jesus saying to the Pharisees that the kingdom of God is "within you" or "in your midst"? The usual translation of the Greek word, *entos*, is 'within', but it does seem unlikely that Jesus is telling the hostile Pharisees that the kingdom is within them. Manson puts the matter concisely when he writes: "The conclusion is that even if it be admitted that 'within' is the natural and proper translation of the probable original Aramaic, which would equally well be translated by an *en meso,* 'among.'"⁴ Also, since the Pharisees' question is about time—not about the interiority or exteriority of the kingdom—it would seem to make more sense if Jesus' answer is understood in the context of time: the kingdom of God is among you at this moment.

Jesus now turns to the disciples and addresses them in a series of apocalyptic sayings. He warns that the day will come when they will seek signs to tell them of the arrival of the parousia, but that day will come unannounced. It is unclear why Luke uses the phrase "the days of the Son of

Man" unless it is to make a literary balance with "the days of Noah" and "the days of Lot". The coming of the Son of Man is not a period which can be measured in days; it is the end moment of time itself in the arrival of the new age. But because this day is unpredictable, the disciples will be tempted to believe those who claim to see signs of it. But, if there are going to be no signs, there can be no accurate reading: there is nothing to be read. It is a pointless exercise to be concerned about the timing; when it does happen—as when lightning flashes in the sky—there will be no doubt in anyone's mind that it is the real thing. And Jesus turns his own concern back to present times, and, as he has done before, warns that the Son of Man must suffer at the hands of a generation which fails to recognize the most important sign under their noses.

Jesus enjoins his disciples to pay attention to the lessons of the story of salvation and learn from past events. When tragedy comes, it hits at the heart of the familiar. But people believe that they are immune and need not pay attention. Like the people in Noah's day who were engaged in the normal business of eating and drinking and marrying— but that normal business of life had no future because the people were ignoring something more important than eating or drinking. Although it might have appeared at the time that Noah was just a harmless eccentric preparing for an imaginary catastrophe, and people could regard it all with patronizing indifference, it was not Noah who was unprepared when the catastrophe struck. So, in the days of Lot, destruction came when people were engaged in the litany of the ordinary and paid no attention to the example of Lot. The same will happen at the coming of the Son of Man, and people are being given warning now.

When the day of the Son of Man arrives it will be too late for the man relaxing on his housetop and the man working in the fields to make a dash for their possessions. Their·possessions will not need saving; it will be they themselves. The time will come when time itself will be no more, when there will be no time left. Again, Jesus takes an example from a past event: learn from the story of Lot's wife who discovered too late that there is an end-date to lingering and longing, that the day comes when time is a luxury which no one can afford. When that time comes, there will be a separation between those who are ready and those who are unready, even though they occupy the same bed, or grind at the same mill. Proximity to others is no protection, any more than being with one's possessions.

The disciples respond by asking where all this will take place as if it will be geographically limited like the destruction of Sodom. But the day of the Son of Man will come as an ubiquitous event, and everyone will know of it. The margin translation of v. 37b speaks of vultures rather than eagles, and this would appear to make more sense, given the catastrophic imagery which has been used. Eagles do not eat carrion, nor do they gather together in flocks. The image would seem to be that, just as the exact location of carrion is clear to the onlooker from the hovering presence of vultures, so the presence of the Son of Man will be clear to everyone when he comes.

In this passage, Luke presents Jesus' involved reflections on time within the thematic setting of the presence of the kingdom and the future coming of the Son of Man. Jesus recalls the past, he anticipates the future, and he does this to heighten people's awareness of the importance of the present. The present is always the time of judgement. Although the imagery which Jesus uses seems weighted with disaster, he does offer a prescription for recovery. The only way to prepare for an unpredictable event is to make the present a time of fidelity and integrity. Then there is nothing to fear. In the face of indifference and misunderstanding, and in the face of his own oncoming crisis, Jesus becomes more pressing in his argument. Jesus has not so much time left himself; even he cannot bargain with time, and perhaps that realisation compels him to portray the importance of the present time as forcefully as he can. And it is in the midst of the ordinary, in eating and drinking and marrying, that people must come to a decision.

As Chekhov wrote: "People eat their dinner, just eat their dinner, and all the time their happiness is being established or their lives are broken up." People might accept that as a true observation of the present; but Jesus' question stands: are they going to *act* on it?

Notes

[1] H. Conzelmann, *The Theology of Saint Luke* (London, Faber and Faber, 1969), pp. 68-73

[2] G. McCauley, "The Word" in *America,* October 1, 1977

[3] For an excellent summary of the state of the question, cf. I. H. Marshall, *The Gospel of Luke: a Commentary on the Greek Text,* (Exeter, The Paternoster Press, 1978) pp. 652-669.

[4] T. W. Manson, *The Sayings of Jesus,* op cit., pp. 303-304

Chapter Eighteen

Luke 18: 1-8   The Unjust Judge

18 And he told them a parable, to the effect that they ought always to pray and not lose heart. ²He said, "In a certain city there was a judge who neither feared God nor regarded man; ³and there was a widow in that city who kept coming to him and saying, 'Vindicate me against my adversary.' ⁴For a while he refused; but afterward he said to himself, 'Though I neither fear God nor regard man, ⁵yet because this widow bothers me, I will vindicate her, or she will wear me out by her continual coming.'" ⁶And the Lord said, "Hear what the unrighteous judge says. ⁷And will not God vindicate his elect, who cry to him day and night? Will he delay long over them? ⁸I tell you, he will vindicate them speedily. Nevertheless, when the Son of man comes, will he find faith on earth?"

JESUS CONTINUES TO ADDRESS HIS DISCIPLES and encourages them to persevere in prayer without losing heart. Jesus summarises his teaching in the form of a parable, which is followed by an application. The parable is peculiar to Luke, but it does have affinities with the story of the insistent night caller (11:5-8). Commentators dispute whether v. 8b is a Lucan addition or an original Son of Man saying: whichever it is, it fits easily into a teaching which exhorts the disciples to pray—and to be found praying in faith when the Son of Man comes.

The judge is portrayed as a man who has no fear of God and no regard for man: the only thing left for him is to attend to his own precious counsel. The peace of the judge's world is being threatened by the continued protestations of a widow who persists in demanding her rights under the law. The Jewish law demanded that judges be particularly concerned for the rights of certain people: the stranger, the sojourner, the widow, the orphan and the poor—all those who had no powerful source of protection other than the right of their cause (Cf. Ex 22:22; Deut 10:18). But a judge who by his own admission has neither fear of God nor regard for man is unlikely to honour the law of God which favours the legion of the fragile. Although it is not stipulated that the judge is Jewish, it cannot be discounted by the argument that Jewish law demanded three judges in matters of arbitration: as Jeremias points out, one judge was regarded as sufficient in a dispute over money or inheritance.[1]

In all his deliberations, the judge did not reckon on the persistent resolve of the widow. The judge's convenient wisdom is no match for the widow's inconvenient sense of justice which eventually wins the day. The widow does not ask for a favour; she insists on her rights under the law. Probably her adversary was rich and had already paid the price for a favourable decision, a practice which was as common as unjust judges. The judge eventually relents, not out of any high motive, but because he is weary of the tireless widow. Verse 5 is translated as "she will wear me out", but the literal translation would read "she will give me a black eye". It is doubtful whether the judge feared physical assault; Derrett argues in favour of a metaphorical reading, namely, that the judge was afraid of his character being blackened.[2] But a judge who has no regard for man is unlikely to change because of possible disgrace. It is more likely that he was tired of all the fuss and bother caused by the widow and acceded to her demand in order to get rid of her and regain his lost peace.

The widow is a figure of powerlessness in the midst of power, she is one of the little people who seems destined to lose; but, as so often happens in the Gospel of Luke, there is a reversal, and littleness is favoured. The widow is steadfast; she does the judge an unusual favour and exhausts him into justice. She knows exactly what she wants, and she does not rest until her petition is answered.

Jesus goes on to apply the parable to the prayer life of

the disciples in a message of profound comfort. If an unjust judge of this world can be pressured into paying attention to the nagging of a widow who is a stranger, how much more will God vindicate his own people? One of the Old Testament titles for God was "protector of widows" (Ps 68:5); now Jesus makes it clear that God will protect and care for all those who cry to him day and night. In the parable, God is not being compared to his discredit with the judge; rather God's willingness to help is being contrasted with the judge's reluctant justice. The judge delayed right judgement; God will answer speedily.

The elect of God will have reason to call on his name night and day, since living a life of fidelity will bring with it suffering and trial and persecution. The disciples will have to face all these at close quarters in the near future. No doubt, there will be times when they will wonder why justice always seems so long in coming; why justice seems to be a permanent late-comer on the human scene. People's patience and endurance will be tested, but Jesus gives the assurance that God does not ignore the cries of his own people. The question is whether when the Son of Man does come he will find his followers living a life of faith in the promise of God. As at the end of the parable of the father and two sons when Jesus left his hearers with a question about whether they would act like the elder son, so Jesus concludes his teaching on this parable with a question to his hearers: will they follow the example of the persistent widow and continue in their prayer, or will they give up their life of faith as a lost cause?

Luke 18: 9-14   The Pharisee and the Tax Collector

⁹He also told this parable to some who trusted in themselves that they were righteous and despised others: ¹⁰"Two men went up into the temple to pray, one a Pharisee and the other a tax collector. ¹¹The Pharisee stood and prayer thus with himself, 'God, I thank thee that I am not

like other men, extortioners, unjust, adulterers, or even like this tax collector. ¹²I fast twice a week, I give tithes of all that I get.' ¹³But the tax collector, standing far off, would not even lift up his eyes to heaven, but beat his breast, saying, 'God, be merciful to me a sinner!' ¹⁴I tell you, this man went down to his house justified rather than the other; for every one who exalts himself will be humbled, but he who humbles himself will be exalted."

The previous section finished with the question about who would be found faithful when the Son of Man comes. In the parable of the Pharisee and the tax collector, Jesus gives the example that justification before God depends on humble acknowledgement in faith rather than self-righteous claims on God based on legal observance. The parable is addressed to those who share the outlook of the Pharisee in the story; it questions their whole spirituality and judges it as unacceptable to God.

In the parable, two men go up to the temple to pray, but only one of them actually prays. The contrast is made between one who focuses on his own performance and one wno realises the folly of that exercise; between one who proclaims the "I", and one who shelters his "me" in the mercy of God; between a speech of self-congratulations, and a telegram for help; between one who is busy marking up points in his favour, and one who realizes that he has nothing to mark up; between one who has a precise memory of what he has done, and one who remembers only that God is merciful. In the eyes of Jesus, the contrast adds up to unacceptable and acceptable prayer.

The Pharisee goes up to the Temple and prays "with himself"—a good translation which suggests that there was too much of the self in the Pharisee's prayer. He mentions God, and dwells on himself. It appears as if God is incidental to a drama in which the Pharisee has clearly cast himself in the lead role. The Pharisee notices the tax collector only to dismiss him as a worthless figure against whom he can shine. Others are hauled on the stage so that they can be spurned by the protagonist. The Pharisee goes on to mention how he goes beyond the requirements of the law to do extra good works. The Pharisee floats on his self-satisfaction. He is a bore.

The tax collector is no saint and knows it; he realises that he cannot afford to dwell on his own performance. His virtue does not lie in not being a saint, but in not being insufferable. He avoids any kind of comparison: no doubt he is aware that there are legions of people who are better and worse than himself, and that salvation does not come because one can discover people whose performance is meaner than one's own. The tax collector looks only at himself, and knows one thing for certain—that he is a sinner. And he acknowledges that in the presence of God. He also knows that God is a merciful God, so he makes a prayer when he puts God's mercy first and his own sinfulness in second place. It makes good Christian sense to hold that the former can overshadow the latter. The tax collector's words are few, but the attitude of his heart is the one which is pleasing to God.

Given the audience, Jesus is not so much asking them to interpret the parable as asking them to allow themselves to be interpreted by the parable, allow the parable to comment on their own spirituality. In that sense, the parable is more threat than comfort; it questions rather than confirms the attitudes and expectations of the hearers. Jesus' hearers would normally expect that the prayer of the Pharisee would be accepted and that the prayer of the tax collector would be rejected, but there is a double reversal. What is being questioned is not whether Pharisees are good and tax collectors are bad, but the fixed attitude which makes them so. The point of the parable is not to make the Pharisees into villains and tax collectors into heroes—that is just to reinstate the hearer's prejudices with different actors; but to unsettle people's own biases about the kind of people whose prayers are acceptable to God. The parable shows clearly that it is not a certain type of *person* whose prayer is accepted, but a certain type of *prayer* itself.

Scholars argue whether v. 14 is a Lucan addition. Certainly, this is the only instance where "justified", *dedikaiomenos,* is used in the Gospels, and it is understandable why some commentators argue that it is Pauline; but others argue that the language is clearly not based on Paul. Paul's own doctrine of justification has its basis in the teachings of Jesus,[3] and there is no conclusive argument which states that v. 14 could not have been an original saying of Jesus. Even though the verse was a floating saying which was placed here, it does make an appropriate comment on the parable. It is not that God demands that people flatten themselves or verbally abuse themselves before they are attended to: that is to make a theology of creeping self-disparagement and argue to the superiority of inferiority. That is to join the Pharisee's camp, which has already been judged as unacceptable. Jesus is arguing for a profound honesty before God, an honesty which not only acknowledges that the mercy of God is all-embracing, but an honesty which admits that God in his wisdom has judged mankind to be *worth* saving in the first place. And that is good news.

Luke 18: 15-17   *Children and the Kingdom*

[15]Now they were bringing even infants to him that he might touch them; and when the disciples saw it, they rebuked them. [16]But Jesus called them to him, saying, "Let the children come to me, and do not hinder them; for to such belongs the kingdom of God. [17]Truly, I say to you, whoever does not receive the kingdom of God like a child shall not enter it."

At 9:50, Luke parted company with Mark's account and used source material which also appears in Matthew and material peculiar to himself. Luke now rejoins the Marcan source, and makes a good connection between his own story of the Pharisee and the tax collector and the Marcan story of the little children by linking the two with the common theme of humility.

In the previous story, the Pharisee made a speech of self-congratulations in which he compared himself to lesser mortals, in particular the tax collector. In his own teaching on the parable, Jesus condemned the Pharisee for his presumptuous attitude and made it clear that no one could do anything which would add up to an indisputable claim on God. Jesus now takes little children, who clearly cannot do anything to merit the kingdom of God, and offers them as models for those who would enter the kingdom. The little ones who are regarded as unimportant in an adult society are held up as the ones to whom the kingdom of God belongs.

In a story which ignores the solemn posturing of adults to gain the attention of God and focuses on the natural ability of children to gain access to God, Jesus takes the little ones as the serious example of discipleship. No doubt the disciples thought they were doing Jesus a favour by trying to protect him from infants; but Jesus declines the protection of adults in favour of the presence of children. If Jesus needs protection from anyone it is not from children. He invites the children to come to him and forbids anyone to hinder their approach. And then Jesus reverses the situation: the people who would dismiss the children are the ones who must imitate them if they are to be true disciples of Jesus. The little ones whom it was presumed could be dismissed are suddenly the ones whom no one can afford to ignore.

Again, as he often does, Jesus holds up the one whom everyone thinks he can forget about, the little one, the unimportant one, as the one whom people must attend to. The child's own dependence and trust and receptivity, which exist at the heart of a relationship, are held precious in the sight of God. The child is the one who says "Abba" naturally and easily, and it is to such that the kingdom of God is given as a gift. In order to enter the kingdom, everyone must have the receptivity of the child, must be able to receive an unmerited gift which reflects the gratuitousness of God. And whoever does, will have unobstructed access to the presence of Jesus and the kingdom of God.

Luke 18: 18-30   Riches and the Kingdom

¹⁸And a ruler asked him, "Good Teacher, what shall I do to inherit eternal life?" ¹⁹And Jesus said to him, "Why do you call me good? No one is good but God alone. ²⁰You know the commandments: 'Do not commit adultery, Do not kill, Do not steal, Do not bear false witness, Honor your father and mother.'" ²¹And he said, "All these I have observed from my youth." ²²And when Jesus heard it, he said to him, "One thing you still lack. Sell all that you have and distribute to the poor, and you will have treasure in heaven; and come, follow me." ²³But when he heard this he became sad, for he was very rich. ²⁴Jesus looking at him said, "How hard it is for those who have riches to enter the kingdom of God! ²⁵For it is easier for a camel to go through the eye of a needle than for a rich man to enter the kingdom of God." ²⁶Those who heard it said, "Then who can be saved?" ²⁷But he said, "What is impossible with men is possible with God." ²⁸And Peter said, "Lo, we have left our homes and followed you." ²⁹And he said to them, "Truly, I say to you, there is no man who has left house or wife or brothers or parents or children, for the sake of the kingdom of God, ³⁰who will not receive manifold more in this time, and in the age to come eternal life."

In contrast to the child who is offered as the natural model for those who would enter the kingdom, a rich ruler now approaches Jesus to discover what he must do to inherit eternal life. Jesus now begins his reflections by questioning the ruler's use of the word "good", an epithet which was usually reserved for God. Jesus is not questioning his own goodness or indirectly hinting at his divinity; it seems more likely that he is criticizing the casual way the ruler has addressed him, a criticism which is justified when the ruler fails to take the advice of the "good teacher".

As he did with the lawyer in a similar situation (10:25), Jesus refers the ruler to the law, and reminds him of those commandments which regulate his relationships with other people. The ruler replies confidently that he has observed all these. Given that he has, he has experienced the insufficiency of the law to gain eternal life, the acknowledgement of which led him to Jesus in the first place to ask the opening question. Jesus neither questions nor applauds the reply;

instead, he offers a challenge and an invitation to the ruler to sell all that he has and follow the teacher.

The ruler's enthusiasm now moves into sadness, for he is very rich. He has nothing more to say; he no longer talks about what he does, but remembers what he has. The promise which Jesus holds out to him pales beside the reality of his own security and riches. He has many possessions, but the reverse is also true: his possessions seem to have him, for they bind his sense of identity to what he has, rather than to who he is. He is offered what Jesus offered very few of his contemporaries—a personal call to follow him. But the ruler must first exercise a final authority over his possessions by disposing of them, and proving to himself and to God that his real treasure is in heaven. But it is all too much for the ruler, and his possessions are in possession.

In Mark's account of the story, the young man whom Jesus "looked on and loved" now takes his leave sorrowfully, and Jesus turns to address the disciples (Mk 10:22). In Luke's account, Jesus continues to talk to the ruler. He tells him that it is very hard for the rich to enter the kingdom of heaven, which reflects on the ruler's original question. With sad humour, Jesus gives the example of a camel attempting the impossible—going through the eye of a needle. Some commentators have tried to explain the saying by making it reasonable and humourless, but the image captures the point Jesus is making. It is easier for a limousine to get through revolving doors than for a rich man to enter the gates of heaven. But perhaps, no one gets the joke; perhaps, no one feels like laughing.

Certainly, Jesus' hearers are not amused, and they ask who can be saved. In a culture where riches were often seen as God's blessing, the rich were seen as favoured by God. But, if they with their advantages could not be saved, what chance had anyone else? Jesus has already stated that riches are to be disposed of, not cherished as a sign of God's favour. In his response, Jesus does modify his earlier remark by saying, "What is impossible for men is possible for God." God can save the rich; but it takes God to do it.

Peter reminds Jesus that the disciples have already fulfilled the command that the ruler declined to follow, and Jesus' reply continues in a humorous vein. The disciples may indeed have given up house, prospects of marriage, family, for the sake of the kingdom, but in so doing they inherit a much bigger family than they left. The disciples have not said goodbye to caring and ministering to others; in following Christ, they will be reaching out to a family whose members will be beyond any particular race, whose number will be beyond count, and whose needs will be beyond measure. That might appear a strange bargain to any disciple, but Jesus says it is one which has eternal life as its final reward. And that is no mean exchange.

Luke 18: 31-34   Prediction of the Passion

[31]And taking the twelve, he said to them, "Behold, we are going up to Jerusalem, and everything that is written of the Son of man by the prophets will be accomplished. [32]For he will be delivered to the Gentiles, and will be mocked and shamefully treated and spit upon; [33]they will scourge him and kill him, and on the third day he will rise." [34]But they understood none of these things; this saying was hid from them, and they did not grasp what was said.

Jerusalem has always figured largely in Jesus' own thinking as the place where his mission will be accomplished. The time is now approaching when Jerusalem must be faced, and Jesus warns his chosen twelve of the nature of the things to come. At the transfiguration, Moses and Elijah spoke of Jesus' *exodus,* a figurative reference to his death, which was to take place at Jerusalem (9:31). Now, the time is coming when the prophecies and the predictions will be fulfilled, and the saving purpose of God will be accomplished. At Jerusalem, Jesus will come to the end of his journey and to the place of his destiny.

Jesus predicts his own coming suffering, the shameful treatment which he will receive at the hands of the Gentiles, his own death and resurrection. In his own comment,

Luke notes that the twelve did not understand what Jesus
was talking about. If the prediction was to help prepare
them for what was to come, it failed; when the time of trial
comes, it will find the apostles completely unprepared. At
the moment, it would appear that Jesus is talking to
himself; certainly, there is no comfort in the response of
the apostles. But, as Leany writes: "Luke's representation
of the Apostle's dullness enhances the moments of the
enlightenment in chapter xxiv. . .and helps to explain the
contrast before and after the resurrection."⁴ For the moment, enlightenment is far away, and the apostles just do
not see what is before them.

Luke 18: 35-43   *The Faith of a Blind Man*

³⁵As he drew near to Jericho, a blind man was sitting by
the roadside begging; ³⁶and hearing a multitude going by, he
inquired what this meant. ³⁷They told him, "Jesus of
Nazareth is passing by." ³⁸And he cried, "Jesus, Son of
David, have mercy on me!" ³⁹And those who were in front
rebuked him, telling him to be silent; but he cried out all the
more, "Son of David, have mercy on me!" ⁴⁰And Jesus stopped, and commanded him to be brought to him; and when he
came near, he asked him, ⁴¹"What do you want me to do for
you?" He said, "Lord, let me receive my sight." ⁴²And Jesus
said to him, "Receive your sight; your faith has made you
well." ⁴³And immediately he received his sight and followed
him, glorifying God; and all the people, when they saw it,
gave praise to God.

By way of contrast to the apostles who could not see the
meaning of Jesus' prediction of the passion, Luke now
presents us with the episode of a blind man who miraculously receives his sight from Jesus, and who then follows
him. Jesus is on his way to keep an old appointment in the
city of Jerusalem, and he travels by way of Jericho, which
is about seventeen miles east of Jerusalem. In Mark's account, the blind man is called Bartimaeus, and the healing
takes place as Jesus leaves Jericho. Luke, with his concern

for thematic arrangement, locates the miracle on the approach road to Jericho, and then moves into the city for the Zacchaeus story and the related parable, which form the climax of this section.

The road to Jerusalem would be busy with travellers making their way to Jerusalem for the feast of the Passover. It was customary for the people to travel by caravan for safety's sake, and it was an accepted practice for a rabbi to teach the group as it made its journey to the holy city. Jesus is using the occasion as an opportunity to teach whoever would give an ear to his word. He would have a motley following: his own disciples, the legion of the curious, the professional hangers-on, the critics interested in making a killing, stray people and stray dogs. Jesus has already made a reputation for himself as a teacher and a healer, one which is about to be called upon.

A blind man is sitting by the roadside and hears the noise of the approaching gathering. He asks what is happening, and is told that the prophet from Nazareth is passing by. The blind man does not want Jesus to pass by; he has more than a curious interest in Jesus, for he has waited a long time to escape from his world of darkness and now the man who can release him is within shouting distance. So, the blind man shouts, and he calls Jesus by the Messianic title of Son of David, a title calculated to stop any group. The people around the blind man are not pleased with the commotion he is causing so they try to quieten him. But the blind man is persistent; he has everything to lose by keeping quiet; he must get Jesus to pay attention to his plight. Now he has to compete not only with the noise of the passing crowd, but with the noise of the surrounding protestors. The blind man initiates a one-man uproar: he screams the scream of desperation in the belief that the Son of David will indeed have mercy on him. It is a scream of desperation but not of despair; it is a scream of faith.

Jesus has shown throughout his ministry that he is not embarrassed by the cry of the outcast or by the appeal of the afflicted, and, unlike the present protestors, he knows that peace will not be made by covering up human distress. Jesus breaks off the teaching. The roadway seminar can wait; the roadside healing has waited long enough. Jesus has the blind man brought to him and invites him to articulate his own need in the presence of all those gathered. In admitting his need, the blind man also expresses his faith in Jesus as Lord, and Jesus tells him that his faith has made him well. When the blind man receives his sight he comes face to face with Jesus for the first time. He sees Jesus, and he uses his sight to follow Jesus, where before he could only wait for him.

Luke concludes the episode with a familiar note: the healed man gives glory to God, and the people join him in their praise of God. The power of God has been manifested in their midst, and when this is done the natural response is the praise of God. The healed man is a mobile argument for the powerful concern of God for the afflicted. And given the crowd that follows Jesus, a mobile emergency ward of the afflicted and the hurt, there is reason to praise a God who attends to the cries of the wounded.

Notes

[1]Cf. J. Jeremias, *The Parables of Jesus,* op cit., p. 153

[2]Cf. J. D. Derrett, "Law in the New Testament: The Parable of the Unjust Judge" *New Testament Studies* 18, 1971-72, pp. 178-191

[3]Cf. A. M. Hunter, *Gospel According to St. Paul,* (London, 1966)

[4]A. R. C. Leaney, *The Gospel According to St. Luke* (London, 1971) p. 239

Chapter Nineteen

Luke 19: 1-10   Zacchaeus

[19]He entered Jericho and was passing through. [2]And there was a man named Zacchaeus; he was a chief tax collector, and rich. [3]And he sought to see who Jesus was, but could not, on account of the crowd, because he was small of stature. [4]So he ran on ahead and climbed up into a sycamore tree to see him, for he was to pass that way. [5]And when Jesus came to the place, he looked up and said to him, "Zacchaeus, make haste and come down; for I must stay at your house today." [6]So he made haste and came down, and received him joyfully. [7]And when they saw it they all murmured, "He has gone in to be the guest of a man who is a sinner." [8]And Zacchaeus stood and said to the Lord, "Behold, Lord, the half of my goods I give to the poor; and if I have defrauded any one of anything, I restore it fourfold." [9]And Jesus said to him, "Today salvation has come to this house, since he also is a son of Abraham. [10]For the Son of man came to seek and to save the lost."

IN CHAPTER 18:18-30 Luke presented us with the story of the rich ruler who could not bring himself to part company with his riches and follow Christ. Now, in a story found only in this Gospel, Luke introduces us to a tax collector who freely offers to give half his riches to the poor, and restore fourfold the amounts he has unjustly extracted from others. Again in Luke's Gospel, Jesus leads the outcast from the kingdom of the lost to the kingdom of the found, where salvation is given as the gift of God. And it is the outcast rather than the outraged who accepts the opportunity of salvation.

At the opening of the story, Luke tells us that Jesus intended to pass through Jericho on his way to Jerusalem. But something happens in Jericho which makes Jesus change his plan and stay for dinner. Jericho was a wealthy city, an important customs centre, and on a trade route between Jerusalem and the East. It was an ideal spot for an ambitious tax collector who had a head for convenient arithmetic. Zacchaeus as chief tax collector would seem to have more than distinguished himself in exploiting others for his own purposes. Although his occupation made him very rich, it would also have made him an obvious target for the hatred of his fellow Jews. Tax collectors were put in the same company as thieves, murderers and prostitutes; but, unlike that particular group of outcasts, they were regarded as traitors who had sought employment from the enemy, and whose employment was an open betrayal of their own people.

Confined to his own small circle of friends, Zacchaeus would have led a life of loneliness and isolation; his riches gave him a loveless privilege, which, in human terms, must have taxed his own contentment and will. But Zacchaeus has heard of the prophet from Nazareth and his reputation in dealing with sinners and outcasts. Perhaps Zacchaeus had heard that Jesus had a former tax collector in his own company, Levi, who had begun his new calling by organising a feast for his new master (5:27-32). Little Zacchaeus wants to see Jesus very much, so he risks mixing with a crowd whose undisguised hostility would drive anyone up a tree. Zacchaeus climbs a tree so that he can see this unusual prophet. Tree-climbing might not appear a particularly dignified activity for an adult; but then, perhaps if tax collectors were sensitive about their dignity they would hardly be tax collectors.

Jesus does not pass by the sycamore tree; he notices the little man up a tree and directs his attention to him. Jesus initiates the contact and calls Zacchaeus by name. He does not shout condemnation at Zacchaeus which might have served to drive him further up the tree; Jesus invites him to make haste and come down from his lonely perch. Jesus does not address a vague wish to see Zacchaeus sometime, but says that he *must* stay at his house *today*. There is an urgency to see this man, and for Jesus the time of salvation is always now. And as he has shown throughout his public ministry, Jesus has a good instinct for when a dinner is needed as the occasion for the event.

So, the professional outsider plays host to Jesus of Nazareth. But the crowd do not share the joy of Zacchaeus; they are in a different mood about what is happening, and they indulge in the deadly whisper and the murmured complaint. They have not learned yet that Jesus is not embarrassed in the company of sinners, that he does not treat them as untouchable, but is happy to share a dinner with them. Unlike the crowd, Jesus does not write off Zacchaeus as a hopeless case beyond the boundary of salvation. Jesus does not believe that traitor or tax collector is a final description of any man. The crowd is limited in their outlook because they have but a view of Zacchaeus, while Jesus has a vision of who he could be; and as Yeats wrote: "The vision's always finer than the view". Jesus' vision offers Zacchaeus release, and it tells him what he hopes is true—that his life is not summed up by his wrongdoing, that he has within him the possibility of goodness.

Jesus' vision of Zacchaeus affects Zacchaeus' own view of himself; Jesus' vision is catching. Zacchaeus is moved to make public amends for what he has done; he wants to rectify his vicious arithmetic. As Jesus called Zacchaeus publicly, Zacchaeus now returns the gesture and makes his own promises in the presence of the public. The Jewish law required that when an individual defrauded others, he had to repay them plus one-fifth of the original total (Num 5:7). Zacchaeus now errs on the side of generosity and promises to repay four times over.

In response, Jesus proclaims that salvation has come to the house of Zacchaeus. It is not an individual event, but is extended to the whole household (Cf. Acts 11:14). Jesus says unambiguously that Zacchaeus is a son of Abraham— not because Zacchaeus is a Jew: God can raise sons of Abraham from the very stones; the tax collector is a faithful son of Abraham because of his generous response to Jesus. Luke concludes the episode with the Son of Man saying: he is the one who has come to save the lost. Jesus has shown himself to be the seeker after the lost. He did not leave Zacchaeus as one of the discarded and forgotten: Zacchaeus was misplaced until he was reclaimed by the one who took notice.

One wonders whether the crowd treated Zacchaeus any differently when Jesus left the dinner party and continued on his way to Jerusalem. Perhaps they still regarded him as a traitor. Is it possible to be a *former* traitor? Is God the only one who forgives traitors?

Luke 19: 11-27   *The Parable of the Pounds*

[11]As they have heard these things, he proceeded to tell a parable, because he was near to Jerusalem, and because they supposed that the kingdom of God was to appear immediately. [12]He said therefore, "A nobleman went into a far country to receive kingly power and then return. [13]Calling ten of his servants, he gave them ten pounds, and said to them, 'Trade with these till I come.' [14]But his citizens hated him and sent an embassy after him, saying, 'We do not want this man to reign over us.' [15]When he returned, having received the kingly power, he commanded these servants, to whom he had given the money, to be called to him, that he might know what they had gained by trading. [16]The first came before him, saying, 'Lord, your pound has made ten pounds more.' [17]And he said to him, 'Well done, good servant! Because you have been faithful in a very little, you shall have authority over ten cities.' [18]And the second came, saying, 'Lord, your pound has made five pounds.' [19]And he said to him, 'And you are to be over five cities.' [20]Then another came, saying, 'Lord, here is your pound, which I kept laid away in a napkin; [21]for I was afraid of you, because you are a severe man; you take up what you did not lay down, and reap what you did not sow.' [22]He said to him, 'I will condemn you out of your own mouth, you wicked servant! You knew that I was a severe man, taking up what I did not lay down and reaping what I did not sow? [23]Why then did you not put my money into the bank, and at my coming I should have collected it with in-

terest?' ²⁴And he said to those who stood by, 'Take the pound from him, and give it to him who has the ten pounds.' ²⁵(And they said to him, 'Lord, he has ten pounds!') ²⁶'I tell you, that to every one who has will more be given; but from him who has not, even what he has will be taken away. ²⁷But as for these enemies of mine, who did not want me to reign over them, bring them here and slay them before me.''

In the previous episode, Jesus proclaimed salvation as a present reality, one which had come to the house of Zacchaeus "today" because of the faithful response of the chief tax collector. Now, addressing the same audience, Jesus tells the parable of the pounds in which he develops two thoughts. Firstly, Jesus speaks of a kingdom which will not appear in the near future, but which will appear only when the man of noble birth travels to a far country to receive confirmation of his kingship and then returns to judge those who have rejected him. Secondly, his servants will be entrusted during his absence to capitalise on what they have received; those who have been productive will be rewarded, while those who have not attempted to use and develop what they have received will be rejected.

In his editorial introduction to the parable, Luke explains that Jesus chose to tell his parable because he was near Jerusalem, and because his hearers supposed that the kingdom of God was to appear immediately. According to the popular expectation, the consummation of the kingdom would take place in Jerusalem in the near future; however, Luke argues that Jesus uses the parable to confound the expectations of an imminent parousia by pointing to a delay. Jesus is going away, not coming; and the crisis which will take place in the near future will be Jesus' own death.

The parable is complicated in that it appears to be the conflation of two parables, or the mixture of allegory and parable, or possibly one parable developed for different purposes. Verses 12, 14, 15a, and 27 speak of the near departure of Jesus who will not be finally recognized as king until his return. While he is gone, his own people will seek to frustrate his mission by rejecting him, but they will face judgement on his return. The other verses make up a complete parable similar to the parable of the talents in Matthew, in which the emphasis is on how the servants handle the trust they have received while their master is away. In Luke's parable, the two strands are closely inter-woven into one piece which has a double application.

The parable opens with a nobleman travelling to a far country to receive kingly power. This event had striking parallels in contemporary history.[1] Herod the Great had to travel to Rome before his own kingship was ratified by the emperor. When Herod died in 4 B.C. his kingdom was divided among his family in accordance with his will, but that division was not recognized until Caesar Augustus ratified it. Archelaus travelled to Rome to submit his own claims for kingship over Judea, but a deputation of fifty Jews also travelled to Rome with the purpose of per-suading Caesar Augustus to withhold the appointment. The delegation was partly successful: Archelaus was granted half the kingdom without the title of king; the remaining half was divided between two other brothers, Philip and Antipas.

In Matthew's parable (25:14-30), the master entrusts all his possessions to three servants, who receive considerable sums of money, which vary with the ability of each ser-vant. In Luke's parable, the nobleman calls ten servants and entrusts each with the *same* small amount, a *mina,* which was the equivalent of three months' wages for a labourer. He instructs them to use the money for trade, and trusts in their flair and imagination to do it in their own way. The focus switches from his servants to the peo-ple, who send a delegation to stop his accession to the throne. The nobleman eventually returns as king; the em-bassy has been unsuccessful in its mission.

The new king calls his servants to see how they have managed the trust he placed in them. Three servants ap-pear. The first two have caught the mood of their master who is used to taking risks in making his money grow; they have made a profit of 1,000% and 500% respectively, and they are rewarded accordingly with further responsibility. The attention is shifted to the third servant. In Matthew's parable, the third servant plays undertaker to his talent and organizes a funeral service; in Luke's account, he does not even take the precaution of burial, but simply keeps the money in a napkin. The servant tries to justify what he has done by focusing on the king's meanness rather than on his own. He places the problem with his master, not with himself. The king condemns the servant according to his own outlook: if he saw his master in those terms, why did he not at least gain interest on the money he had received?

The king's question goes unanswered, and he orders those who stand by to take the servant's pound and give it to the servant who made the most out of what he had been given. The identity of the speakers of verses 25 and 26 is unclear, but the point is clear. People protest at the rich servant being given the small amount which will leave the third servant with nothing, but there is a teaching in the move. The third servant still fails to see that he was trusted by the master in the first place, that the whole risky enterprise was one of mutual trust. The servant did not travel on the trust; he stayed with his own fear. Those who have travelled on the trust they have received will be rewarded with more; those whose meanness of spirit is such that they bury that trust do not deserve it. Finally, the king turns his attention to his enemies who opposed his appointment and orders that they be slain.

Jesus' imagery and language are heavy with seriousness. He has not much time left to impress his hearers with the gravity of their situation; he needs no persuasion about the gravity of his own. His departure is imminent, after which there will be an indefinite period before the final judgement of history. Jesus has risked sharing his own goods, his life, his trust, his values, with his own people. What purpose is all that if they are unwilling to make all that grow and work? So, Jesus takes another risk in portraying the situation in terms of extreme crisis. And he trusts—yet again—that people will take it and benefit from it.

Luke 19: 28-40   *Jesus Approaches Jerusalem*

²⁸And when he had said this, he went on ahead, going up to Jerusalem. ²⁹When he drew near to Bethphage and Bethany, at the mount that is called Olivet, he sent two of the disciples, ³⁰saying, "Go into the village opposite, where on entering you will find a colt tied, on which no one has ever yet sat; untie it and bring it here. ³¹If any one asks you, 'Why are you untying it?' you shall say this, 'The Lord has need of it.'" ³²So those who were sent went away and found it as he had told them. ³³And as they were untying the colt, its owners said to them, "Why are you untying the colt?" ³⁴And they said, "The Lord has need of it." ³⁵And they brought it to Jesus, and throwing their garments on the colt they set Jesus upon it. ³⁶And as he rode along, they spread their garments on the road. ³⁷As he was now drawing near, at the descent of the Mount of Olives, the whole multitude of the disciples began to rejoice and praise God with a loud voice for all the mighty works that they had seen, ³⁸saying, "Blessed is the King who comes in the name of the Lord! Peace in heaven and glory in the highest!" ³⁹And some of the Pharisees in the multitude said to him, "Teacher, rebuke your disciples." ⁴⁰He answered, "I tell you, if these were silent, the very stones would cry out."

Jesus is coming to the end of a long journey and to the completion of his own mission as he approaches the city of Jerusalem. Luke mentions the beginning of the journey at 9:51: "When the days drew near for him to be received up, he set his face to go to Jerusalem." At that time, as Jesus was about to enter a Samaritan village he sent messengers on ahead of him to make ready, but "the people would not receive him, because his face was set towards Jerusalem" (v. 53). Now, Jesus sends two of his disciples ahead to another village to prepare for his approach to Jerusalem by borrowing a colt. Jesus' face is still set towards Jerusalem. As Helmut Flender writes: "Jerusalem is the scene where redemptive history is fulfilled. The divine salvation is planted firmly in a definite place in history, which prevents it from evaporating into a timeless idea and preserves the humanity of the divine revelation. For to be man means to be tied to a particular place in history."[2] Certainly, Jesus is tied to Jerusalem—as he has already admitted: "it cannot be that a prophet should perish away from Jerusalem" (13:33). That prophecy will be fulfilled, for the death of Jesus and the fate of Jerusalem are inextricably linked.

But before the prophecy is fulfilled, a parade is organized. Jesus deliberately stages his own procession, and although Luke does not actually mention Jesus' *entry* into Jerusalem, the procession leads Jesus closer to the city. Jesus sends two of his own disciples ahead to bring the colt: whether the disciples had already made a prior arrangement with the owner for the loan of the colt, or whether Luke is pointing to Jesus' prescience as a prophet is unclear. Certainly, it was a custom of the time for animals to be hired to travellers, rather like an early version of car hire. Jesus specifies that it must be an unridden colt, and this requirement underlines the importance Jesus attaches to the procession: as J. M. Derrett points out, animals for sacred use or those to be ridden by royalty were not used for any other purpose.[3] Everything goes as planned, and the disciples bring back the colt and throw garments on its back to make a saddle. They set Jesus on the colt. And so the unusual parade begins.

The setting recalls the words of Zechariah, 9:9:

> Rejoice greatly, O daughter of Zion!
> Shout aloud, O daughter of Jerusalem!
> Lo, your king comes to you;
>   triumphant and victorious is he,
>   humble and riding on an ass
>   on the colt the foal of an ass.

If anyone remembered the prophecy of Zechariah, no one shows that he remembers the point of it. Christ consciously presents himself as the merchant of peace riding on an ass, not as the warrior-king riding a charger in a bid for power. The disciples begin their chants of praise, hailing Christ as the king. According to Luke, the kingdom has not yet come, though the king is in the midst of his people (19:11). But he is a king who is rejected by his own people. The disciples proclaim "Peace in heaven and glory in the highest", recalling the chant of the angels at a more innocent time (2:14).

Luke mentions a multitude, but he does not say that they join the disciples in their chants of rejoicing. It is the disciples rather than the crowd that the Pharisees complain about, and it is likely that they felt threatened by a demonstration which had such messianic overtones. Not everyone loves a parade, and the clamour of this one leads the Pharisees to ask Jesus to control his disciples. But Jesus is in no mood for controlled enthusiasm; he supports his disciples, for he wants his parade to continue. Jesus does not want his disciples to be petrified; if they were, the very stones would take their place and give Jesus song for his parade.

There is a profoundly ambiguous quality about the whole parade. If it is the coronation procession of a king, does anyone anticipate the kind of crown Jesus will receive in the city? Is Jesus deliberately staging the procession of a Messiah? If so, for whose benefit is it? Is there a peculiar irony about the supportive acclamation of the disciples which is underlined all the more by their silence when the passion gets under way? If the multitude is silent now, they will find voice soon enough when they follow the tune of the priests. Is Jesus dramatizing the predicament of the previous parable—receiving support from his "servants" and being rejected by his own people? The mood of rejoicing is soon to change when Jesus draws near the city: the sight of the place provokes weeping. But, meantime, the parade is still on.

Luke 19: 41-48
Lament over Jerusalem and Cleansing the Temple

⁴¹And when he drew near and saw the city he wept over it, ⁴²saying, "Would that even today you knew the things that make for peace! But now they are hid from your eyes. ⁴³For the days shall come upon you, when your enemies will cast up a bank about you and surround you, and hem you in on every side, ⁴⁴and dash you to the ground, you and your children within you, and they will not leave one stone upon another in you; because you did not know the time of your visitation."

⁴⁵And he entered the temple and began to drive out those who sold, ⁴⁶saying to them, "It is written, 'My house shall be a house of prayer'; but you have made it a den of robbers."

⁴⁷And he was teaching daily in the temple. The chief priests and the scribes and the principal men of the people sought to destroy him; ⁴⁸but they did not find anything they could do, for all the people hung upon his words.

Jesus is near journey's end, and the sight of Jerusalem moves him to tears. The manufactured enthusiasm of the disciples is not enough to sustain Jesus when he is confronted with the fate of the city he loves; it is not enough of a distraction to dull the pain Jesus is experiencing at the price the city will pay for its lost opportunity. Jesus is caught between the fate of Jerusalem and his own regard for the holy city, and the only thing he can do is weep. In a scene which is peculiar to Luke, and which is all the more surprising coming from a writer who rarely reveals Jesus showing his own emotions, there is no mention of the disciples' reaction to the tears of their master. But, as Saint-Exupery wrote: "It is such a secret place, the land of tears." Jesus' own knowledge isolates him: he is the only one who knows why the fate of Jerusalem and his own fate are so closely linked.

In his lament, Jesus hopes for the impossible—that "even today you knew the things that make for peace." But Jesus' own sense of reality tells him that it is too late, that his final appeal is addressed to a blind and deaf tribunal whose members no longer see or hear the one who stands before them, the one who witnesses to peace between God and man. In his prophecy of the destruction of Jerusalem, an event which took place in A.D. 70 under Titus, Jesus foretells the terrible destruction which will befall the city and its people. Some commentators argue that Luke wrote this after the event took place, but Jesus' prophecy is in the tradition of the ancient prophecies of destruction, and he uses imagery and language which were true of any military siege. There is nothing in Luke's writing which suggests a particular knowledge of the atrocities which did take place and which are recorded by Josephus. Jesus gives a reason for the collapse of Jerusalem, one which has nothing to do with military warfare. At the beginning of the Gospel, Zechariah proclaimed that God's time had come "for he has visited and redeemed his people" (1:68). Jerusalem has ignored the visitation, for rather than welcoming salvation, it has brought judgement on itself. *Hinc illae lacrimae.*[4]

Luke does not tell us of Jesus' entry into the city, only of his entering the temple. Luke begins and ends his Gospel in the temple, and now the final chapter of Jesus' life opens in the temple. Jesus moves from weeping over Jerusalem to demonstrating how unprepared Jerusalem is for the moment of God's visit by driving out those who have turned a house of prayer into a house of exchange. The sacrificial animals had to be bought for sacrifice, and money had to be exchanged into the coinage acceptable to the temple authorities, but there was no need to conduct this business, with all its profiteering, within the temple precincts. The merchants did their business in the Court of the Gentiles, the part of the temple reserved for non-Jews; in so doing, they were making it impossible for Gentiles to pray in peace. In that quotation from Isaiah which Luke uses, it seems strange that Luke does not complete the saying which speaks of "a house of prayer for all the people" (Is 56:7). It might be that Luke omits the last phrase because, as Marshall writes, "he is aware that in fact the temple did not become such, and he did not want to make Jesus the author of a false prophecy."[5]

The Court of the Gentiles is now cleared of traders, and the temple is prepared for the teacher, the one who is "the light to enlighten the Gentiles" (2:32). Jesus now teaches in the temple daily, in spite of the fact that he is wanted by the authorities. Luke underlines the contrast between the powers of the establishment who oppose Jesus and the people who support him. Jesus' provocative action in the temple was an affront to the authority of the chief priests under whose title the merchants did their business. Apart from anything else, Jesus was depriving the chief priests of their economic stake in the temple transactions. But the chief priests are not alone in their opposition to Jesus. The scribes and the principal men of the people join the opposition and become Jesus' principal adversaries, while the Pharisees now move into the background. But Jesus has the support of the people—not least because they were the ones who were being exploited by the money changers and traders. Jesus makes good their support while he can. There will be no more healings; the short time left will be treasured for teaching. And time is something which Jesus does not have on his side.

Notes

[1]Cf. Josephus, *Antiquities*, 17, 9, 3

[2]H. Flender, *St. Luke: Theologian of Redemptive History*, op cit., p. 107

[3]Cf. J. M. Derrett, "Law in the New Testament: the Palm Sunday Colt", *Novum Testamentum* 13, 1971, p. 248

[4]Terence, *Andria*, 126

[5]H. Marshall, *The Gospel of Luke: a Commentary on the Greek Text*, op cit., p. 721

Chapter Twenty

Luke 20: 1-8   The Authority of Jesus

20 One day, as he was teaching the people in the temple and preaching the gospel, the chief priests and the scribes with the elders came up ²and said to him, "Tell us by what authority you do these things, or who it is that gave you this authority." ³He answered them, "I also will ask you a question; now tell me, ⁴Was the baptism of John from heaven or from men?" ⁵And they discussed it with one another, saying, "If we say, 'From heaven,' he will say, 'Why did you not believe him?' ⁶But if we say, 'From men,' all the people will stone us; for they are convinced that John was a prophet." ⁷So they answered that they did not know whence it was. ⁸And Jesus said to them, "Neither will I tell you by what authority I do these things."

HAVING DISPLACED THE TRADERS, Jesus is now in possession of the temple, where he is teaching every day. His dominating presence and his preaching the Gospel cannot go ignored or unchecked, and it is not long before he is interrupted and asked for his credentials. The question comes from a deputation composed of the three groups which make up the Sanhedrin, the supreme governing body of the Jews. The officials can no longer contain their hostility towards Jesus, and they now confront him with their charge. Jesus has not been delegated by officialdom to do the things he does: from where does he receive his authority? Who gave it to him? Since Jesus commands such popular support, the Sanhedrin cannot remove him without apparent cause, so they try to steal his authority by incriminating him with the occupying power or discrediting him in the face of the people.

Jesus answers them with a counter-question, a practice

which was common in rabbinic exchanges. He asks his accusers to identify the origin of John's baptism: was it from
heaven or from men? In effect, Jesus gives them the opportunity of answering their own question by answering
his, but they are more concerned about their personal sur-
vival than about truthfulness. The members of the
Sanhedrin were expected to make judgements on such
questions, but they are now afflicted with a convenient
shyness in making theological pronouncements. If they say
that John's baptism was from heaven, then they will have
to answer the further question: why then did you not submit to it? If they say the John's baptism was from men, the
people will pronounce judgement on them and stone them.
Telling the truth will cost them embarrassment; telling a lie
could cost them their lives: either way, they have to lose.
They decline Jesus' challenge and plead ignorance. Aspiring
to destroy Jesus' authority in the presence of the people,
they succeed only in diminishing their own—an authority
whose only ally is ignorance.

Jesus in his turn declines to answer the original question.
If the officials admit that they cannot pronounce on the
question of John's baptism, *a fortiori,* they cannot pronounce on the promised one for whom John prepared. If
the members of the Sanhedrin are unwilling to declare their
teachings on such a basic matter as John's baptism, why
should Jesus who teaches openly in the temple submit
himself to their scrutiny? In his own question, Jesus gives
his support to the Baptist, whose own authority did not
derive from officialdom, but from God. Jesus is in the
same tradition; he is subject to a higher authority than the
Sanhedrin. And unlike his critics, Jesus is prepared to pay
the price for the truth which he teaches. The price will be
himself, and that will be exacted soon enough.

Luke 20: 9-19   *The Parable of the Vine Dressers*

⁹And he began to tell the people this parable: "A man
planted a vineyard, and let it out to tenants, and went into

another country for a long while. ¹⁰When the time came, he sent a servant to the tenants, that they should give him some of the fruit of the vineyard; but the tenants beat him, and sent him away empty-handed. ¹¹And he sent another servant; him also they beat and treated shamefully, and sent him away empty-handed. ¹²And he sent yet a third; this one they wounded and cast out. ¹³Then the owner of the vineyard said, 'What shall I do? I will send my beloved son; it may be they will respect him.' ¹⁴But when the tenants saw him, they said to themselves, 'This is the heir; let us kill him, that the inheritance may be ours.' ¹⁵And they cast him out of the vineyard and killed him. What then will the owner of the vineyard do to them? ¹⁶He will come and destroy those tenants, and give the vineyard to others.'' When they heard this, they said, "God forbid!'' ¹⁷But he looked at them and said, "What then is this that is written:

'The very stone which the builders rejected has become the head of the corner'? ¹⁸Every one who falls on that stone will be broken into pieces; but when it falls on any one it will crush him.''

¹⁹The scribes and the chief priests tried to lay hands on him at that very hour, but they feared the people; for they perceived that he had told this parable against them.

Still teaching in the temple, Jesus tells his listeners the parable of the vine dressers, a parable which Luke understands to be directed against the scribes and the chief priests. The background to the story which Jesus tells has historical basis, as it was common in Palestine for land to be owned by absentee landlords who would collect their rent in kind from the tenant farmers, usually at harvest time. The lengthy absence of the landlords alongside the harsh economic climate of Palestine often led to difficulties between owners and tenants, sometimes leading to a revolutionary take-over by the tenants. If the owner died without an heir, the tenants were regarded as the first claimants to legal right of possession and ownership.[1]

It is disputed whether the original parable was intended as an allegory; certainly, the story seems to lend itself to that interpretation, with the vineyard as Israel (Is 5:1-7), the tenants as the leaders of Israel, the landlord as God, the messengers as the prophets, the landlord's son as Christ, the new owners as the Gentiles. Some critics argue that if the story is an allegory, the allegorical features were developed only by the early Church; but this position is difficult to maintain. As Ellis points out: "Very likely, no allegory originating after the resurrection would have stopped short at the murder. Nor would it have put the murder *in* the vineyard. The resurrection was too central and the excommunication of Jesus too vividly remembered for that (cf. Heb 13:12)."[2] However, Luke, unlike Mark (12:8), does situate the murder outside the vineyard; although it is unclear whether this relocation has strict allegorical significance if the vineyard represents Israel, not Jerusalem.

In the parable, the landlord plants a vineyard, leases it to tenants, and in his absence entrusts them with the responsibility of caring for his estate and paying their dues. The fact that the vineyard is just planted means that it will be some time before there is a yield—usually four years. In due course, the landlord sends one of his servants to collect the proportion of the annual produce, but the servant is beaten and sent away empty-handed—which could mean that he was also robbed. The master sends a second servant who receives similar treatment. The third servant is wounded and cast out. In the wake of such violent opposition, the landlord asks himself what to do. The tenants have taken liberties with his trust; his servants have been maltreated; he has received no rent. The landlord comes to the conclusion that things might change if he sends his "beloved son"—although he is not totally persuaded that the measure will work.

When the son arrives to collect the rent, the tenants recognize him as the heir and decide to kill him in the hope that they will inherit the land. It is unclear whether the tenants thought that the original owner was dead and that in killing the sole heir they would become the rightful inheritors, or whether they thought that the landlord would leave the estate to them by default in the face of such repeated opposition and violence. The tenants cast the son out of the vineyard and then kill him. The son's fateful story ends with his murder.

Jesus asks his listeners what they think the owner will now do in the face of his son's murder. In answering his own question, Jesus says the owner will come—not to plead with the tenants, but to destroy them and hand over the vineyard to others. So, the tenants will forfeit their livelihood and lose their lives. The people express their horror—whether at the reaction of the owner, or at the desperate violence of the tenants is unclear. Luke reintroduces Jesus as the speaker with two sayings that do not seem to be immediately related to the parable. Jesus reminds his hearers of an old text which speaks of the rejected stone, the one which people thought they could dispense with, becoming the one that held the structure together (Ps 118:22). In the next saying, the stone imagery is maintained, and Jesus speaks of the judgement which will befall those who reject the stone.

The scribes and the chief priests react with hostility, but they cannot yet lay hands on Jesus without endangering their own position. At the same time, they cannot allow Jesus to continue when his teaching is so clearly directed against their own authority. At the moment, Jesus is in possession of the temple, the place over which the Jewish authorities are supposed to exercise control. Ironically, Jesus is using their arena of power to criticize their performance, and they are helpless to reclaim the focus of authority. In wanting to lay hands on him, they underline the truth of the parable; and it will only be a matter of time before they create the opportunity to enact the conclusion of the parable.

Luke 20: 20-26   Tribute to Caesar?

²⁰So they watched him, and sent spies, who pretended to be sincere, that they might take hold of what he said, so as to

deliver him up to the authority and jurisdiction of the governor. [21]They asked him, "Teacher, we know that you speak
and teach rightly, and show no partiality, but truly teach the
way of God. [22]Is it lawful for us to give tribute to Caesar, or
not?" [23]But he perceived their craftiness, and said to them,
[24]"Show me a coin. Whose likeness and inscription has it?"
They said, "Caesar's." [25]He said to them, "Then render to
Caesar the things that are Caesar's, and to God the things
that are God's." [26]And they were not able in the presence of
the people to catch him by what he said; but marveling at his
answer they were silent.

The religious authorities are committed to bringing
about the downfall of Jesus, and they are not overly
scrupulous in the methods they choose. Fearing for their
own reputation, which has already suffered in open debate
with Jesus, they now send spies to entrap him. Jesus has
already shown that he is not intimidated by the religious
authorities into agreeing with their practices; they now test
him to see whether Caesar's imposed rule has intimidated
him into agreeing to pay the yearly tax. The spies try to lay
the ground for the charge of treason: if Jesus denies the
need to pay tax to Caesar, he could be charged with treason
before the governor, Pontius Pilate. Failing that, if Jesus
answers affirmatively, he will alienate the people who are
supporting him. Either way, it appears that Jesus has to
lose in the exchange.

As a preface to their question, the spies flatter Jesus by
addressing him as teacher and professing their admiration
for his impartial teaching of the ways of God. Only then
do they ask the question—whether it is lawful for God's
people to pay tribute to Caesar—a question which they
have already loaded in favour of a negative reply. The
tribute they refer to is the yearly tax of one denarius which
had to be paid to the emperor. When the poll tax was first
introduced, it was the cause of riots and bloodshed: as an
annual reminder of Israel's political subjugation to Rome,
it was still cause for grievance among the people. Should
the people of God pay tribute to a foreign ruler?

Before Jesus' reply, Luke mentions that Jesus is aware of the questioners' cunning; but he turns a potentially dangerous situation into a teaching. Jesus asks them for a coin. In Matthew's Gospel, Jesus explicitly asks to be shown the money for the tax; in Luke's account, the coin is unspecified. As Kennard pointed out, there were three principal coinages: the Attic drachma, the Tyrian shekel, and the Roman denarius.[3] The denarius was a silver coin which bore the image and inscription of the emperor; many pious Jews refused to use this because it violated the Mosaic prohibition against images: the coin which they used to pay tribute to Caesar was the Attic drachma. The fact that Jesus' listeners can produce a Roman coin might suggest that they implicitly recognize the rule of Caesar, in which case they have answered their own question.

In his reply, Jesus does not answer the original question, but makes a pronouncement which seems engagingly vague. Most commentators interpret the reply as a teaching on temporal and religious obligations and argue that Jesus is acknowledging the need to pay taxes to Caesar, while stressing one's primary duty to God: one must pay tribute to Caesar and to God. But Jesus does not specify the things which belong to Caesar, for Caesar does not possess anything independently of God; he does not need to specify the things which belong to God, since everything does. Jesus is hardly arguing to two independent spheres of power and obligation, that of Caesar and that of God, with parallel sets of obligations. Since God has dominion over the whole of creation, Caesar's relative power is subservient to the ultimate power of God.

Richard Cassidy, after evaluating the assumptions present in the interpretations which seem to imply that Jesus was designating two sets of obligations, writes: "Our interpretation is that, instead of positing the existence of two realms, Caesar's and God's, Jesus really taught and acted in terms of only one realm: *God's.* Far from having any kind of independent existence of its own, Caesar's realm, the social order of the Roman empire, was in Jesus' view a part of the larger order of creation, whose only author was God. Therefore the Romans' social patterns were to be evaluated against the standard of the social patterns desired by God, and supported or not on that basis. . . . Thus, the only areas in which Caesar can expect allegiance are those in which his patterns are in conformity with God's desired patterns."⁴

This interpretation does not make Jesus a political revolutionary: it simply avoids making Jesus into an un-critical supporter of a military power because it happens to be in possession at the moment—a stance which seems unlikely for one who has already made it clear that the religious authorities cannot command his support simply because they are the authority. All authority and power have to be evaluated in the light of God's plan. The spies would hardly have marvelled at Jesus' reply if the only thing he did was to avoid a question by a debating trick. In his reply, Jesus gives a teaching: it is for the people to evaluate whether in demanding tribute, Caesar is reflecting the things of God. So, the evaluation continues.

Luke 20: 27-40   *God of the Living*

²⁷There came to him some Sadducees, those who say that there is no resurrection, ²⁸and they asked him a question, saying, "Teacher, Moses wrote for us that if a man's brother dies, having a wife but no children, the man must take the wife and raise up children for his brother. ²⁹Now there were seven brothers; the first took a wife, and died without children; ³⁰and the second ³¹and the third took her, and like-wise all seven left no children and died. ³²Afterward the woman also died. ³³In the resurrection, therefore, whose wife will the woman be? For the seven had her as wife."

³⁴And Jesus said to them, "The sons of this age marry and are given in marriage; ³⁵but those who are accounted worthy to attain to that age and to the resurrection from the dead neither marry nor are given in marriage, ³⁶for they cannot die any more, because they are equal to angels and are sons of God, being sons of the resurrection. ³⁷But that the dead are raised, even Moses showed, in the passage about the

bush, where he calls the Lord the God of Abraham and the God of Isaac and the God of Jacob. ³⁸Now he is not God of the dead, but of the living; for all live to him." ³⁹And some of the scribes answered, "Teacher, you have spoken well." ⁴⁰For they no longer dared to ask him any question.

The spies having failed in their mission to entrap Jesus, the Sadducees now appear on the scene to continue the questioning. The Sadducees were a select party within Judaism; conservative and aristocratic, most of them held positions of power in church and state. They originated as a party in the second century B.C. during the time of the Maccabean priest-kings when the nation was divided over its attitude to foreign culture and influence. The Sadducees proclaimed their tolerance of Greek culture and ideas, and, at the time of Christ, they were regarded as collaborators because of their willingness to accept Roman rule and customs in exchange for retaining their own power and influence over the temple and the Sanhedrin. Adept at political compromise, the Sadducees were theologically conservative; unlike the Pharisees, they accepted only the Torah as authoritative, and rejected oral tradition along with belief in the resurrection, angels and spirits. When the temple was destroyed in A.D. 70, the Sadducees ceased to exist as a party since the base of their influence no longer existed.

As fundamentalists in the interpretation of the law, the Sadducees now pit the law against what they regard as an unorthodox innovation, the belief in the resurrection. They put a question to Jesus which attempts to ridicule belief in the resurrection by recalling the law on levirate marriage (from the Latin, *levir,* brother-in-law) and citing an absurd example. The law stated that if a man dies and has no son, and, therefore, no legal heir, his brother must marry the widow and the "first son whom she bears shall succeed to the name of his brother who is dead" (Deut 25:5); thus the continuity of the family line is guaranteed. The Sadducees then develop an example to the point of absurdity by instancing seven brothers each of whom marries the same woman, but each of whom dies childless. None of the brothers has proved husband in terms of producing an heir: in that case, whose wife would the woman be in the resurrection?

In their questions, the Sadducees suppose that Jesus' idea of the resurrection is the one commonly held—that the human condition will persist in the next world with some agreeable extras; in his reply, Jesus makes it clear that there is no comparison between human life shared by all, and the resurrection, shared by those who are the sons of God. Jesus makes the distinction between two ages and two peoples: the men of this age who live a life peculiar to this age, and the just who are resurrected from the dead into a new age. Jesus does not speak of the resurrection of all people, but resurrection from the dead of those people who "are accounted worthy" to share the new age. As sons of God, they cannot die again; therefore, marriage does not apply to them. There will be no need to propagate the human race or to ensure legal succession; therefore, the question of the Sadducees is irrelevant. The prevailing relationship in heaven will be Fatherhood and sonship; and since the resurrected are all sons together, relationships are therefore as members of the same family. And it does not make heavenly sense to talk about marrying one's sister.

Jesus continues to give a teaching on the resurrection, using as his source a familiar text from the Torah. In his argument, Jesus appeals to the scripture which the Sadducees especially revere, and tells them that in it there is foundation for belief in the resurrection (Ex 3:1-6). In Mark's account, it is God who calls himself "the God of Abraham. . ." (12:26); in contrast, Luke appeals directly to the authority of Moses by saying that he calls God "the God of Abraham. . .". The title, "God of Abraham, Isaac and Jacob," was used when all three patriarchs were long dead; so, if God is God of the living and not of the dead, it means either that the patriarchs are still alive or they await resurrection. It can hardly be that they are still alive since that argues to immortality, whereas Jesus speaks of "resurrection *from the dead*"; rather, it is an assertion that God will keep his promise with his faithful ones even when they die, since their covenant relationship does not conclude with death.

As he often does, Jesus turns an insincere inquiry into an occasion for genuine teaching—a characteristic which confounds his already confused opponents. Some of the scribes, who believed in some form of resurrection, commend Jesus for his teaching; but there is no encouraging word from his questioners who no longer dare to question him: they cannot afford to, when such teaching arises from it. In his teaching, Jesus assures his hearers that God cannot be the God of the dead: that is not a relationship, but the absence of one. A relationship requires life and continued promise, and God is the author of life and promise. God makes a forever of his promise, one which no graveyard can destroy. Jesus himself will have to depend on that soon enough.

Luke 20: 41-44   Son of David

> ⁴¹But he said to them, "How can they say that the Christ is David's son? ⁴²For David himself says in the Book of Psalms,
> 'The Lord said to my Lord,
> Sit at my right hand,
> ⁴³till I make thy enemies a stool for
>   thy feet.'
> ⁴⁴David thus calls him Lord; so how is he his son?"

After answering a series of questions from his opponents, Jesus now takes the initiative and asks the questions himself. The questions which he poses here are about the characteristics of the Messiah, the Coming One. The most popular title which the people used of the Messiah was 'Son of David': that was the title Bartimaeus used to stop Jesus' party in its tracks (18:38). With the title, which had its origins in God's promise to David, went an understanding of the Messiah which underlined his military power and national importance: one who would lead the people to dominion and to the final defeat of their foes. Thus in one of the psalms of Solomon:

> Behold, O Lord, and raise up for them their king,
> the Son of David,
> At the time which you, O God, decree for his reign
> to begin over your servant, Israel;
> And gird him with strength to crush unjust rulers,
> And to purge Jerusalem from Gentiles that trample
> her down to destruction. (17:23-25)

In his teaching, Jesus focuses on the inadequacy of this view of the Messiah, and says that the Messiah is much more than this: in the Old Testament, he is not just the one who will occupy the throne of his ancestor David, but will share the throne of God.

In common with his contemporaries, Jesus attributes authorship of the psalms to King David, and quotes David as saying that he heard God speak to his Anointed One and tell him to sit at his right hand (Ps 110:1). How then can the Messiah be both David's son and David's lord?

In this passage, Luke is hardly questioning whether the Messiah really is the Son of David: he has given ample evidence of his belief (1:27, 32, 63; 3:23, 31; 18:38). Luke has placed this passage after a teaching on the resurrection, one which had a foundation in the Old Testament—that might be a hint to the answer. Jesus now returns to the Old Testament to suggest that the Messiah is not adequately summarised in the understanding of the title, Son of David. David himself addressed him as 'my lord'. But how can the Son of David also be his lord—especially given the understanding that in the patriarchal tradition the younger is never set above the elder?

Given the previous teaching on the resurrection, the question could be answered by way of the resurrection: the one who is David's son becomes David's lord in the new age of the resurrection. But, as Burger points out,[5] this changes the question from "If the Messiah is David's lord, how can he be his son?" to "If the Messiah is David's son how can he be his lord?". But Luke's understanding is that the Son of David and the Lord are brought together in the person of Jesus; therefore, it is in him that they find their full sense and meaning, not in the political expectations of the people. The Son of David is not an adequate summary of the Messiah. He is much more, because he is Lord. And he stands before them now.

Luke 20: 45-47   The Scribes

⁴⁵And in the hearing of all the people he said to his disciples, ⁴⁶"Beware of the scribes, who like to go about in long robes, and love salutations in the market places and the best seats in the synagogues and the places of honor at feasts, ⁴⁷who devour widows' houses and for a pretense make long prayers. They will receive the greater condemnation."

In the presence of the people, Jesus now addresses his disciples and warns them against the scribes. The scribes, originally the copyists of the ancient Biblical texts, were regarded as the leading scholars of Judaism because of their specialist knowledge of the law. The Gospel sometimes refers to them as lawyers because they are often called upon to interpret the law and issue pronouncements on matters of observance. The scribes had the title of Rabbi, but they were legally forbidden to accept money in return for their teaching; instead, they were supposed to support themselves by a trade. Most of the scribes belonged to the party of the Pharisees, but a number of them were Sadducees. In his own prediction of the passion, Jesus has already enumerated the scribes among those who will reject him (9:22). He now criticizes the scribes for playing pretenders in a drama of hypocrisy to further their own prestige and material gain.

If the scribes expect people to gasp in admiration at their stylised performance, they are disappointed in Jesus who publicly catalogues their faults. He begins by criticizing the way they dress up: Jesus is probably referring to the *tallith,* a resplendent robe worn by those renowned for piety or scholarship, which advertised the supposed virtue of the wearer. Jesus goes on to criticize the scribes for their love of public acclamation, and for ensuring their prominence in the public eye by taking the best seats in the synagogues and the place of honour at banquets. They also exploit defenceless widows: Derrett argues that this reference refers to the practice whereby lawyers were appointed as guardians of widows' estates; instead of taking their rightful remuneration, they often helped themselves freely to the proceeds from the property.[6] Finally, Jesus criticizes their prayers—lengthy speeches addressed to the audience rather than to God, in the hope that the hearers will judge prayer by its length rather than its depth. Jesus argues that all this make-believe adds up to their own condemnation. The scribes have abused their position of responsibility and they will be held accountable for that abuse.

Notes

[1]Cf. C. H. Dodd, *The Parables of the Kingdom* (London, 1961) pp. 93-98

[2]E. Ellis, *The Gospel of Luke,* op cit., p. 232

[3]Cf. S. Kennard, "Judaism and Images" in *Crozer Quarterly* 23, 1946, pp. 259-266

[4]R. Cassidy, *Jesus, Politics and Society: a Study of Luke's Gospel,* (New York, Orbis, 1978) p. 58

[5]Cf. C. Burger, *Jesus als Davidssohn* (Gottingen, 1970), p.115

[6]J. D. Derrett, "'Eating up the houses of widows': Jesus' comments on lawyers?", *Novum Testamentum* 14, 1972, pp. 1-9

Chapter Twenty One

Luke 21: 1-4   The Widow's Offering

> 21 He looked up and saw the rich putting their gifts into the treasury; ²and he saw a poor widow put in two copper coins. ³And he said, "Truly I tell you, this poor widow has put in more than all of them; ⁴for they all contributed out of their abundance, but she out of her poverty put in all the living that she had."

IN CONTRAST TO THE SCRIBES in their drama of conceit interested only in their own advancement and prestige, Luke introduces a poor widow as an example of authenticity. Jesus is sitting in the temple teaching; he looks up and notices the difference between the gifts of the rich and the offering of a poor widow. The contrast is between riches and poverty, arrogance and simplicity, self-importance and self-forgetfulness, parsimony and generosity. Again, Jesus hallows the wisdom of the contrary: the one who can least afford to give is the one who gives everything. And her gift is more precious in the eyes of Jesus than all the others.

The treasury formed part of the Court of Women: in it there were thirteen collection boxes—all shaped like trumpets—for offerings of various kinds. As Marshall points out: "Evidence is also adduced. . .that gifts were offered for various purposes, especially in relation to vows, and the offerer declared the amount and purpose of the gift to the officiating priest. In these circumstances it is not surprising that Jesus knew how much the various people were offering."[1] But Jesus is not so much concerned with assessing the value of the gifts as in elevating the generosity of the givers: he measures generosity by what is left over, rather than what is actually given. The rich have

an abundance left over, the poor widow has nothing—
therefore, she is the model of true generosity.

For Jesus, little is never belittled. The poor widow is
herself a summary of all that is little—the least important,
the poorest of the poor, the people who have no status or
influence, the ones who have to depend on the kindness of
others. She is among the quiet of the land who await the
consolation of Israel. Jesus' support for the poor widow
recalls the lines of the *Magnificat:*

he has scattered the proud in the imagination of
    their hearts,
he has put down the mighty from their thrones,
and exalted those of low degree.

(1:51, 52)

The poor widow sacrificed everything she had, and it
will not be long before Jesus himself will sacrifice
everything.

Luke 21: 5-24   *Troubled Times and Judgement*

⁵And as some of the temple, how it was adorned with noble stones and offerings, he said, ⁶"As for these things which
you see, the days will come when there shall not be left here
one stone upon another that will not be thrown down."
⁷And they asked him, "Teacher, when will this be, and what
will be the sign when this is about to take place?" ⁸And he
said, "Take heed that you are not led astray; for many will
come in my name, saying, 'I am he!' and, 'The time is at
hand!' Do not go after them. ⁹And when you hear of wars
and tumults, do not be terrified; for this must first take
place, but the end will not be at once."
¹⁰Then he said to them, "Nation will rise against nation,
and kingdom against kingdom; ¹¹there will be great earthquakes, and in various places famines and pestilences; and
there will be terrors and great signs from heaven. ¹²But
before all this they will lay their hands on you and persecute
you, delivering you up to the synagogues and prisons, and
you will be brought before kings and governors for my

name's sake. ¹³This will be a time for you to bear testimony. ¹⁴Settle it therefore in your minds, not to meditate beforehand how to answer; ¹⁵for I will give you a mouth and wisdom, which none of your adversaries will be able to withstand or contradict. ¹⁶You will be delivered up even by parents and brothers and kinsmen and friends, and some of you they will put to death; ¹⁷you will be hated by all for my name's sake. ¹⁸But not a hair of your head will perish. ¹⁹By your endurance you will gain your lives.

²⁰"But when you see Jerusalem surrounded by armies, then know that its desolation has come near. ²¹Then let those who are in Judea flee to the mountains, and let those who are inside the city depart, and let not those who are out in the country enter it; ²²for these are days of vengeance, to fulfil all that is written. ²³Alas for those who are with child and for those who give suck in those days! For great distress shall be upon the earth and wrath upon this people; ²⁴they will fall by the edge of the sword, and be led captive among all nations; and Jerusalem will be trodden down by the Gentiles, until the times of the Gentiles are fulfilled.

In a series of collected sayings, Luke now gives us Jesus' eschatological discourse, the final address of his ministry. The complete discourse (6-36) is a complex interweaving of two strands of thought which speak of the destruction of Jerusalem and the end of world history, although Luke makes it clear that between the two events there will be an indefinite period of time. Throughout the discourse, Jesus is not so much concerned about apocalyptic signs as preparing his hearers for the events which are to come, particularly his disciples for the persecution and the temptations to give up their faith. Most scholars would agree that Luke's account is related to the parallel discourse in Mark 13, but there is disagreement over whether that relationship is one of sole dependency or not. Some scholars, supposing Luke to be writing after the events of A.D. 70, argue that Mark formed Luke's only source, which Luke edited in the light of the destruction of Jerusalem; others argue that along with rewriting Mark, Luke also used an independent source, possibly pre-Marcan. The dispute still continues.

Luke sets the climax of Jesus' ministry in the temple, where Jesus gives his last public teaching in the presence of the people and the disciples. Some of the people draw his attention to the splendid furnishings of the temple, but Jesus replies by predicting its destruction. Jesus points to the folly of trusting in the temple which will surely collapse: its decorative beauty will be no safeguard against destruction. The people ask him when this will happen and what sign will herald the event, but Jesus does not answer this until vv. 20-24.

Instead, Jesus turns to warning his hearers against messianic pretenders who will come announcing that the time is at hand; but both they and their proclamations are false. Jesus counsels his hearers not to be terrified by war and tumult: they do not signal the end of time, but they are a mocking witness to the fact that the old age has to pass, and with much suffering and pain. Jesus goes on to widen the horizon of affliction to include universal strife in world war and natural disaster; famines (*limoi*) and pestilences (*loimoi*) will take place, as well as unnamed terrors and enigmatic omens. In a comprehensive catalogue of disaster which borrows heavily from traditional prophetic apocalyptic literature, Jesus does not camouflage what appears to be nothing less than cosmic catastrophe against which human efforts at control must surely be hopelessly ineffective.

Before such universal calamities take place, the disciples will have to face particular difficulties in their own stories. The time of discipleship will always be a time of trial, and Jesus uncovers a whole list of painful experiences which no disciple in the early Church will be able to ignore. They will be manhandled and persecuted; they will be accused of crimes against the state in the Gentile courts—all because they preach the Gospel. Jesus emphasizes that the time of persecution will be a time for testimony, and he assures the disciples that they need not prepare their speeches and gestures with the calculated care of the actor, for a greater power will take care of their words which will be so compelling that their accusers will be unable to gainsay them.

Since hate respects no ties, opposition to the disciples will know no bounds: even blood ties will not save them from betrayal by their own family and possible death. After all this talk of persecution, to assure the disciples that not a hair of their head will be harmed seems a somewhat misplaced sentiment; but it may be that Jesus is simply recalling his own paradox: that the disciples' spiritual safety will never be in doubt because their enduring fidelity will gain them their lives—lives which will appear lost to the eyes of the world.

Jesus now returns to the question of v. 7 and tells of the event which will signal the destruction of Jerusalem: when the city is surrounded by troops, its desolation is close at hand. Jesus enjoins his hearers to flee the city and take refuge in the hills; even those living in Judea are advised to find safety in remoter climes, probably in Transjordan. Eusebius, writing in the fourth century, does mention that Christians fled to Pella before the destruction of Jerusalem because they were warned in the oracle of an unnamed Christian prophet; but that oracle is hardly this passage, since Eusebius would have mentioned it.[2] Jesus gives as reason for the flight that these will be days of vengeance, and God's judgement against the apostasy of Jerusalem will be executed. Distress will be evident everywhere, and the first casualties of war will be those least able to protect themselves, especially pregnant women and those caring for small children. Josephus records that 97,000 were taken prisoner and just over a million killed in the siege:[3] even given room for exaggeration, the account of Josephus is staggering. The city will be dominated by the Gentiles until their allotted time is fulfilled.

Througout these complex sayings Jesus has displayed a marked unwiliingness to camouflage the grimness of certain issues which preoccupy him or to diminish the terror which he sees ahead. Set against the casual remark on the beauties of the temple, Jesus' discourse might appear a thundering over-reaction; but he is hardly going to spend his last public discourse exchanging views on ornamental furnishings, when he senses what lies ahead. Jesus has run out of time, and he matches his last address to what lies ahead. And what lies ahead for him holds little comfort and much pain.

Luke 21: 25-38   End Age

[25]"And there will be signs in sun and moon and stars, and upon the earth distress of nations in perplexity at the roaring of the sea and the waves, [26]men fainting with fear and with foreboding of what is coming on the world; for the powers of the heavens will be shaken. [27]And then they will see the Son of man coming in a cloud with power and great glory. [28]Now when these things begin to take place, look up and raise your heads, because your redemption is drawing near."

[29]And he told them a parable: "Look at the fig tree, and all the trees; [30]as soon as they come out in leaf, you see for yourselves and know that the summer is already near. [31]So also, when you see these things taking place, you know that the kingdom of God is near. [32]Truly, I say to you, this generation will not pass away till all has taken place. [33]Heaven and earth will pass away, but my words will not pass away.

[34]"But take heed to yourselves lest your hearts be weighed down with dissipation and drunkenness and cares of this life, and that day come upon you suddenly like a snare; [35]for it will come upon all who dwell upon the face of the whole earth. [36]But watch at all times, praying that you may have strength to escape all these things that will take place, and to stand before the Son of man."

[37]And every day he was teaching in the temple, but at night he went out and lodged on the mount called Olivet. [38]And early in the morning all the people came to him in the temple to hear him.

Luke continues with his complex grouping of prophetic sayings which make up the last public discourse of Jesus. The catalogue of disaster broken off in v. 11 is now resumed: Jesus tells his hearers that the time will come when the whole structure of the universe will show signs of collapse which will lead to profound anxiety and confusion among all peoples. Confusion will lead to fear at what is going to happen to a world which is visibly coming apart and which shows no hopeful signs of repair. Leaney, in the company of a number of scholars, believes that Luke is referring to the fall of Jerusalem rather than to the parousia, since it "is his desire to invest the fall of Jerusalem, not the end of the world (as Mark), with catastrophic solemnity."[4] But since Luke speaks about these events taking place after "the time of the Gentiles"(24b) and since he is aware of the time difference between cosmic catastrophe and the persecution of the early Church (12a), it would seem that he is in fact referring to the parousia, the end age.

In the imagery of Daniel 7:13, the Son of Man will appear at the final consummation in a cloud—one which signifies the glory of God. The singular use of cloud recalls the cloud of the Transfiguration in which Jesus was seen as glorified by those who beheld him (9:34). The coming of the Son of Man in power and glory will be something which all men will be able to see, and it is a sign of hope for the true disciples, because it announces the moment of deliverance and liberation. The old age will have collapsed to give way to the new age: in the end is the beginning.

Jesus now illustrates his teaching in a parable and asks his hearers to take a lesson of comfort from the cycle of nature which they see every year. By winter time, the trees have lost their leaves and appear dead—especially the fig-tree; but then the trees spring to life again by growing leaves which herald the coming of summer. Winter does not have the final say, for the spring has its revenge on the winter, and out of apparent lifelessness there comes the promise of new life. The same story of life will be told when the terrible events happen: they will signal the dawn of a new age in the future coming of the kingdom of God. Jesus reinforces his point by saying that all this will take place before "this generation" will pass away. Luke can hardly be referring to the generation of Jesus which at the time of writing has already passed; among possible interpretations, the most probable seems to be the generation of the end age itself. Jesus stresses the enduring validity of his words: even if heaven and earth should pass away, his words still stand true.

In the final admonition, Jesus appeals for vigilance at all times because the end day will come suddenly. He exhorts the people not to dull their sense of awareness by wordly cares and drunkenness: hangovers are no help to alacrity of spirit. He enjoins his hearers to watch at all times and to pray that their faith will endure through the coming trials so that they can stand unashamed before the Son of Man.

Thus, Luke brings to a close the public ministry of Jesus. Jesus spends the day teaching in the temple and the night across the valley of the Kidron on the Mount of Olives. Luke concludes by noting the continued support of the people in coming to hear Jesus, as if to highlight the time of horror which is to come. Jesus continues to possess the temple, which seems innocent of threat and conspiracy; but enemies are closing in, and betrayal has a date in the calendar. It will soon be time for Jesus to go and face his own time of trial with faith and endurance.

Notes

[1]H. Marshall, *The Gospel of Luke: a Commentary on the Greek Text*, op cit., p. 751

[2]Eusebius, *Historia Ecclesiastica*, 3, 5, 3

[3]Josephus, *War*, 6, 420

[4]A. R. C. Leaney, *The Gospel According to Luke*, op cit., p. 262

Chapter Twenty Two

Luke 22: 1-6   Conspiracy

22 Now the feast of Unleavened Bread drew near, which is called the Passover. [2]And the chief priests and the scribes were seeking how to put him to death; for they feared the people.

[3]Then Satan entered into Judas called Iscariot, who was of the number of the twelve; [4]he went away and conferred with the chief priests and captains how he might betray him to them. [5]And they were glad, and engaged to give him money. [6]So he agreed, and sought an opportunity to betray him to them in an absence of the multitude.

LUKE OPENS THE LAST SECTION OF HIS GOSPEL, the narrative of the passion and resurrection of Jesus, by noting how the conspiracy against Jesus is gaining momentum as Passover approaches. Luke mentions the feast of Unleavened Bread and the feast of Passover as one, but strictly speaking they were different. The Passover Lamb was to be eaten at sunset on 14 Nisan and the unleavened bread was to be eaten from the evening of 15 to 21 (Ex 12); but since the feast of Mazzoth followed immediately on the feast of Passover, they were sometimes referred to as the one feast.

Luke has already drawn attention to the desire of the Jewish leaders to destroy Jesus (19:47); now they give shape to their desire in the form of plotting, but they are still afraid of the power of the people who show their support for Jesus by listening to him daily in the temple. In attributing the conspiracy to the chief priests and the scribes, Luke dissociates the people from the plot to kill Jesus: at the moment, they are a fragile barrier between Jesus and unwarranted arrest, but that barrier is only active during the day.

However, the barrier has been breached from the inside and the Jewish leaders find an unexpected ally within Jesus' own company in the person of Judas Iscariot. It is not the conspirators who discover Judas, it is Judas who offers himself as a co-conspirator in the plot against Jesus. Luke describes Judas as "of the number of the twelve", as if to emphasize that he was among them but not of them. There have been guesses at the significance of the name, Iscariot: "man (*ish*) of Kerioth", which would make Judas the only disciple not from Galilee; an Aramaic version of the Latin, *sicarius,* dagger-bearing, referring to the Zealots who were committed to liberating the nation from the oppression of the Romans. John, however, refers to Judas as "son of Simon Iscariot" (6:71), which suggests that it is simply a family name.

What motivated Judas to betray the one who trusted him? In consonance with John's view of Judas as a thief (12:6), some argue that Judas betrayed Jesus for the money, in which case he struck the most terrible bargain in history. Others argue that if Judas was a Zealot he would have been disappointed in Jesus' timidity in the face of the occupying forces and his betrayal was no more than a contrived plan to force Jesus' hand in establishing the earthly supremacy of his kingdom. Whatever the reason, Luke is clear that it was because "Satan entered into Judas". Satan tempted Jesus in the desert at the beginning of Jesus' public ministry, and Luke stated that Satan had left "until an opportune time" (4:13). It is significant that Luke mentions Satan here at the beginning of the passion narrative: the opportune time is now, when Jesus' life and friends are beginning to fold around him.

It is unclear what Judas actually betrayed to the chief priests. Certainly, he informed them when and where they could apprehend Jesus without risking the opposition of the people; but it does not seem beyond the capability of the chief priests' intelligence network, the "spies" previously commissioned to entrap Jesus (20:20), to discover that. Did Judas betray something which Jesus' accusers were able to use later in their charges against him, or was his betrayal confined to the business of time and place?

Judas confers with the chief priests and the commanders of the temple guard. There is gladness in the air—no doubt at the prospect of the whole affair being over soon without too much risk to its organisers. Judas agrees to the offer of money for the services which he will perform. The scene is set: all the conspirators have to do is wait for the opportune moment which will be decided by Judas. The multitude could be a problem, but even multitudes have to go to sleep sometime. The darkness in which they leave Jesus unattended will cover the right time. Jesus' own choice of a place for quiet will serve as his betrayer's choice of a place for arrest. So, it is only a matter of time.

Luke 22: 7-13   Preparations for the Passover Meal

[7]Then came the day of Unleavened Bread, on which the passover lamb had to be sacrificed. [8]So Jesus sent Peter and John, saying, "Go and prepare the passover for us, that we may eat it." [9]They said to him, "Where will you have us prepare it?" [10]He said to them, "Behold, when you have entered the city, a man carrying a jar of water will meet you; follow him into the house which he enters, [11]and tell the householder, 'The Teacher says to you, Where is the guest room, where I am to eat the passover with my disciples?' [12]And he will show you a large upper room furnished; there make ready." [13]And they went, and found it as he had told them; and they prepared the passover.

The conspirators have put their plot in motion and they now wait for the opportune time to move in for the kill; meanwhile, Jesus makes preparations for the last meal which he will have with his apostles. Luke states clearly that the preparation for the Last Supper is a preparation for the Passover feast, and, along with the other synoptists, sees the Last Supper as a paschal meal. There has been a long debate among scholars about the question of whether the Last Supper was a paschal meal or not, and the question has not been satisfactorily resolved. John's chronology dates the crucifixion before the Passover—at the time when the paschal lambs are being slaughtered—but Jeremias argues to a theological understanding of John's dating: "While there were hundreds and thousands of paschal lambs being killed in the Temple, the true Paschal Lamb. . .died unrecognized outside the gates of the city."[1]

With the discovery of the Qumran manuscripts there was the important finding that the legal Jewish calendar was not universally accepted among the Jews of Jesus' time. Following on that point, Jaubert has presented the hypothesis that Jesus was following a sectarian calendar based on solar readings, and that the Last Supper was held on Tuesday: this arrangement comes close to reconciling the dating of the meal in the synoptics with the chronology of John.[2] However, the debate continues. It is agreed that the Last Supper has paschal characteristics, but one cannot argue from the *form* of a meal with paschal characteristics to the *fact* of the paschal meal. Also, it has to be recognized that primitive liturgical practice distinguished between the pasch and the Supper, and that the symbolism of the lamb has left no trace on the tradition of the Last Supper; however, as Jeremias points out: "if the Synoptists nevertheless describe the Last Supper as a Passover, with no attempt at concealment, the reason is obviously that the recollection of the fact was so firmly established that it could not be removed by the established ritual."[3]

In Luke's account of the preparations, Jesus sends Peter and John to make ready for the Passover meal. This would involve buying the lamb and roasting it, purchasing the unleavened bread, wine, and bitter herbs, and preparing the room for the meal. As Galileans, they naturally ask where the meal is going to be held within the city. Although the people of Jerusalem were obliged to provide hospitality free to the pilgrims, with so many pilgrims coming into the city to celebrate the Passover meal it was difficult to find a room. Jesus tells them that they will notice a man carrying a water-jar—a distinctive sign in a land where only women carried water-jars. Rather than speaking to him in public, the apostles are instructed to follow him to his house, and only when they are inside tell him the purpose of their call. On hearing that they have come from the "Teacher" and the nature of their request, he will show them a large upper room. The apostles are to prepare it. The two apostles go off on their mission, and everything goes as planned.

The instructions which Jesus gives for the preparation of the Passover meal are similar to those which he gives before the entry into Jerusalem. In both instances, it would appear that Jesus made prior arrangements with the two men: the householder, like the owner of the colt, was probably a follower of Jesus who recognized him as "Teacher". Instead of giving cryptic instructions to Peter and John, why does Jesus not give them the address of the house? Some scholars argue that Jesus is showing his prophetic foreknowledge in his instructions, but this does not address the caution with which the instructions are given. It seems more likely that Jesus is concerned to avoid detection by the group intent on his elimination, especially as the group has an ally in his own hearing. So, Jesus does not risk telling the address in the hearing of Judas or allowing others to overhear what he plans to do and where. At the moment, Jesus is in possession of the situation. The last free act which he does is to have a meal with his own apostles, one which he has "earnestly desired" to share with them.

Luke 22: 14-23   The Last Supper

[14]And when the hour came, he sat at table, and the apostles with him. [15]And he said to them, "I have earnestly desired to eat this passover with you before I suffer; [16]for I tell you I shall not eat it until it is fulfilled in the kingdom of God." [17]And he took a cup, and when he had given thanks he said, "Take this, and divide it among yourselves; [18]for I tell

you that from now on I shall not drink of the fruit of the vine until the kingdom of God comes." [19]And he took bread, and when he had given thanks he broke it and gave it to them, saying, "This is my body which is given for you. Do this in remembrance of me." [20]And likewise the cup after supper, saying, "This cup which is poured out for you is the new covenant in my blood." [21]But behold the hand of him who betrays me is with me on the table. [22]For the Son of man goes as it has been determined; but woe to that man by whom he is betrayed!" [23]And they began to question one another, which of them it was that would do this.

Throughout his ministry, Jesus has hallowed the meal as an occasion of fellowship and forgiveness and as an image which caught something of the unseen reality of the kingdom of God. In offering table fellowship to outcasts and sinners, Jesus incurred the anger of his opponents whose complaints reflected the belief that only the righteous could dine with the righteous; but Jesus used the meal as a way of coming to righteousness. In the context of the meal, Jesus brought sinners to an understanding of their worth before God, and offered them salvation through the forgiveness of God. In that sense the meal was a real education (*ex-ducare*) and an opportunity for commitment: it was a time of discovery and a time of change, both of which took place in the social setting of the human community.

Now, the time has come for Jesus to have the last meal of his lifetime and he assembles his twelve apostles to share with them this last occasion of fellowship and teaching. This is a meal which has special significance: in the context of the paschal meal, Jesus establishes a new meal for a new age in the Last Supper. Jesus is conscious that this is a farewell meal: his own awareness of his approaching death is clear, and he knows that this is the last time in a calendar of times. As Schillebeeckx writes: "As Jesus was no fanatic. . .then from a particular moment in his career he must have rationally come to terms with the possibility, in the longer term probability and in the end actual certainty of a fatal outcome."[4] Luke presents Jesus as one who is clear about the fatal outcome of his story and who uses the Last Supper to tell his disciples of it and to interpret its significance to them.

The structure of Luke's account of the Last Supper would seem to be: Jesus' vow of abstention from future passovers until the new age of the kingdom of God, vv. 15-18; the words of interpretation of the bread and wine, vv. 19-20; the prophecy of the betrayal, vv. 21-23. There is a widely debated textual problem concerning the shorter text which excludes vv. 19b-20 and the longer text which includes these verses. The majority of scholars would agree that vv. 19b-20 originate in a non-Lucan source, but the debate centres on whether these verses should be omitted because they come from the hand of an interpolator, or whether they should be accounted as original because Luke included them in his account, using an earlier liturgical usage as his source. The longer text is attested by the majority of N. T. manuscripts, and this weight of evidence in its favour, alongside the arguments of Schurmann and Jeremias,[5] is overwhelmingly persuasive.

Luke opens his account by noting Jesus' express desire to share this Passover with his chosen few, which he knows will be a preface to a time of terror. It is not clear whether Jesus actually "eats" this Passover meal—whether his vow of abstention includes the present meal, leaving unfulfilled his desire to share it with his apostles until his fulfilment in the kingdom of God. Jesus says that he will not eat the Passover meal until the new age which will be inaugurated by his own death. He takes the cup and makes the prayer of thanksgiving before offering the wine to his apostles. He repeats his eschatological saying, vowing that he will not partake of the fruit of the vine until the kingdom of God comes. In sharing the cup, the apostles share in the fellowship which Jesus offers them; but how much they are aware of what that fellowship involves will be shown soon enough.

In the context of the Passover meal, the paterfamilias recalled the meaning of the feast and pointed out the symbolism of the various dishes which were used; but nothing in the ritual required him to interpret the bread and the wine in the way Jesus does. Jesus points to the significance of the bread and the wine and interprets them in the light of his approaching death. It might seem unusual for a host to concentrate the attention of his guests on the food, but in focusing on the bread and the wine Jesus is focusing on himself: it is his way of speaking about what is going to happen to him. He takes the familiar realities of the bread and the wine and gives them an unparalleled significance by identifying himself with them. Jeremias points out that in focusing on the bread and wine separately, speaking of them as *den bisri* (this my flesh) and *den 'idhmi* (this my blood), "Jesus made the broken bread a parable of the fate of His body, the blood of the grapes a parable of His outpoured blood. 'I must die a victim's death', is the meaning of the last parable of Jesus."[6]

There is a sacrificial sense to Jesus' sayings which suppose the separation of flesh and blood in death. Jesus sees his coming death in terms of the prophet-martyr's sacrifice, the one whose body and blood are "given for you" and "poured out for you". Jesus' death is not seen as a lonely act which is characterized by its absurdity: it has purpose in that it goes beyond itself as a gift to others. Thus, in offering table fellowship to his apostles, Jesus is not asking them to share in an absurd mission which has collapsed in death—there would be little point in offering anyone fellowship in failure; if Jesus can proffer fellowship at a time when his death is imminent, it is because that offer is also an offer of salvation. Jesus sees a purpose in his mission which his death does not negate but somehow confirms. His life's work does not collapse because of his death, but is vindicated by it.

This is not to isolate Jesus' death as if it had significance apart from the life which led to it. Luke sees Jesus' death in the context of the whole of Jesus' prophetic life, one which is given for others and which is summed up in the final act of consummation on the cross. Jesus did not die a natural death: he was put to death precisely because of his mission, his message, his priorities, his values, his claims. Jesus' death is the price he has to pay for the kind of life which he led: in being willing to accept his death, Jesus accepts as worthwhile the life which led to it. So, when Jesus enjoins his disciples to "Do this in remembrance of me", he is asking them to remember his complete story, not by celebrating the Passover, but by recalling his interpretation of these events in this kind of meal.

The question for the apostles, therefore, is whether they are willing to accept the kind of fellowship which communion with Jesus signifies. Immediately after offering them the cup, Jesus prophesies the betrayal of one of their number: presence at the table is no guarantee of fidelity to its purpose. Jesus is aware that one of his chosen few is not willing to commit himself to what table fellowship involves. And this is all the more hurting because Jesus is conscious that the hand which can signal a person's friendship or hostility is "with me on the table." The hand of hostility is on the table of fellowship, a sad mockery of friendship. But Jesus reminds his table companions of the divine purpose of his appointed destiny and grieves for the man who has such a hand in it. The apostles then question each other about the identity of the traitor, but none of them discovers what the betrayer and the betrayed know. It will not be long before they know the identity of the traitor and realize that he has no monopoly of betrayal.

Luke 22: 24-38   Farewell Discourse

[24]A dispute also arose among them, which of them was to be regarded as the greatest. [25]And he said to them, "The kings of the Gentiles exercise lordship over them; and those in authority over them are called benefactors. [26]But not so with you; rather let the greatest among you become as the youngest, and the leader as one who serves. [27]For which is the greater, one who sits at table, or one who serves? Is it not the one who sits at table? But I am among you as one who serves.

[28] "You are those who have continued with me in my trials; [29] as my Father appointed a kingdom for me, so do I appoint for you [30] that you may eat and drink at my table in my kingdom, and sit on thrones judging the twelve tribes of Israel.

[31] "Simon, Simon, behold, Satan demanded to have you, that he might sift you like wheat, [32] but I have prayed for you that your faith may not fail; and when you have turned again, strengthen your brethren." [33] And he said to him, "Lord, I am ready to go with you to prison and to death." [34] He said, "I tell you, Peter, the cock will not crow this day, until you three times deny that you know me."

[35] And he said to them, "When I sent you out with no purse or bag or sandals, did you lack anything?" They said, "Nothing." [36] He said to them, "But now, let him who has a purse take it, and likewise a bag. And let him who has no sword sell his mantle and buy one. [37] For I tell you that this scripture must be fulfilled in me, 'And he was reckoned with transgressors'; for what is written about me has its fulfilment." [38] And they said, "Look, Lord, here are two swords." And he said to them, "It is enough."

If the apostles understand the significance of the Last Supper and Jesus' interpretation of his impending death, they show no signs of it now. In Luke's arrangement of events, the apostles move from questioning each other which of them is the traitor to bickering among themselves over which of them is the greatest. It is as if Jesus is not in the room. There is a peculiar human logic in their attempts to identify the villain of the drama and then the hero: they want to keep the record straight. Jesus, however, is about to upset their tidy logic by saying that betrayal and greatness can be shown by the same person, and that the real question is which of these will have the upper hand. Luke does not present the upper room as a place of light and clarity: there is a helpless honesty in his account which moves from apostasy, through self-seeking and denial, to total misunderstanding. There is confusion and ambition and hurt in the room: Jesus and his apostles are at cross purposes, and all this seems to underline Jesus' failure to get himself across to his chosen few. Yet in the midst of all this misunderstanding and hurt bewilderment, Jesus speaks words of encouragement to those who will survive him.

Jesus interrupts the apostles to rebuke them for attending to ambition, which reflects the way of the world not the way of the kingdom of God. Jesus reflects how the Gentile kings exercise authority through power and domination, some managing to be recognized as *Euergetes,* an honorific title which was used by the kings of Egypt and Syria. The apostles are not to take their cue from pagan quarters, but from the example of Jesus. Jesus does not dispute that there is a greatest, but focuses on how the greatest should behave. The greatest should become as the youngest, the one who traditionally had the least going for him; the leaders should become as the ones who serve. Jesus sums up the point in a parabolic saying in which he offers service as the model of true discipleship. Jesus admits that the wisdom of the world recognizes the one seated at table to be greater than the one who serves; but he asks the apostles to notice the reversal of that in his own life. He is the greatest of their company, yet he comes among them as the one who serves. In their wisdom, they should do no less.

As he approaches death, Jesus looks back over the period of his own ministry, and, although he sees it in terms of "my trials", his memory is a grateful one: he recalls the faithful support of the apostles and praises them for it. And as they have shared in his past trials, they will share in his future glory, for as God has assigned the kingdom to Jesus, he in his turn will share it with them. That share will include feasting at the Messianic banquet and ruling over the new Israel. Luke does not specify "twelve" thrones to judge the twelve tribes: given his plac-ing of the saying here, he can only suppose that Jesus is aware that one of the prospective occupants has recently withdrawn as candidate.

It was after he offered the cup of fellowship that Jesus prophesied the betrayal of Judas; now after mentioning the feasting at the Messianic banquet, Jesus prophesies the denial by Peter. He tells Peter that Satan wanted to put all the apostles to the test (the first 'you' in Greek is plural), and that the accuser wants to try Peter in particular. They will all fail Jesus in the trials to come which gives Satan a claim on their fidelity. But if Satan is the Accuser, Jesus is the supporter, and he assures Peter of his prayerful support. Jesus' prayer has not been in vain because he tells Peter that when he does retrace his steps to the land of fidelity, he must support the community of believers. Out of Peter's folly and dark experience, something great can come. Peter, however, confidently asserts his readiness to go to prison and to die; but if he wants specificity he gets it in Jesus' reply. The coming events will tell their own tale.

Jesus reflects with them on their earlier ministry when they lacked nothing and came back joyful from the experience. Then they could depend on the kindness and goodwill of strangers, but these times are no more for hostility will replace hospitality, and good news will be received as bad news. Now they will have to arm themselves for the time of trial by taking a purse and bag with them, and they should sacrifice a cloak for a sword, for they will need all the protection they can get. However, there is a purpose in all this, for the mysterious will of God is being unfolded. Referring to the Suffering Servant of Isaiah 53:12, Jesus tells them that he will be regarded as one of the ungodly, one of the outsiders, the kind of people he lived for and died for. The apostles do not respond to this thought, but pick up Jesus' ironic reference to a sword and take it literally. Sword-talk they can understand—except that Jesus is not talking about violent resistance. The R.S.V. translates *hikanon estin* as "It is enough"; but Jesus is not saying that two swords will be sufficient. The phrase would be better translated, "Enough of this!" In an expression of weariness, Jesus terminates the discussion. No amount of explaining will bring the apostles to an understanding of his meaning now; and when they produce a sword at the time of arrest, Jesus will tell them what to do with it.

So, the Last Supper ends. Although Jesus and the apostles are in the same room, it appears that they are worlds apart. But, as McCauley writes: "notwithstanding the confusion and even the tension, Jesus thinks it is worthwhile celebrating with his followers. Their perfect assimilation of his mentality never becomes a precondition of their celebrating with him or with each other. The Last Supper is itself a point in a developing relation between Jesus and his followers and among his followers themselves."[7] It will not be until later that the apostles will understand the significance of what has happened in the upper room; and when they do, they will celebrate in remembrance of the one who makes it possible.

Luke 22: 39-46   The Agony

[39]And he came out, and went, as was his custom, to the Mount of Olives; and the disciples followed him. [40]And when he came to the place he said to them, "Pray that you may not enter into temptation." [41]And he withdrew from them about a stone's throw, and knelt down and prayed, [42]"Father, if thou art willing, remove this cup from me; nevertheless not my will, but thine, be done." [45]And when he rose from prayer, he came to the disciples and found them sleeping for sorrow, [46]and he said to them, "Why do you sleep? Rise and pray that you may not enter into temptation."

Jesus leaves the city of Jerusalem and crosses the Kidron Valley to the Mount of Olives. The disciples follow him to the accustomed place which has served as their nightly retreat for some time, their secret place of quiet and rest. Peter, James and John do not receive special mention; Gethsemane is not named as the place—perhaps because Luke thought that the name would be of no interest to his Gentile readers. Unlike Mark's account, there is no report of conversation on the way: Luke's sparse presentation simply states that they moved from one place to the other. The time for words appears to be over; what is left to be said must be spoken in prayer. When they arrive at their destination, Jesus enjoins his disciples to pray that they will not be lost in the coming trials which they will have to face; then he withdraws alone to pray to his Father.

Jesus kneels down. The normal posture for prayer was standing, but perhaps the weight of the present time and the urgency of the occasion drive Jesus to his knees. Jesus' whole ministry, the growing opposition, the friends who are getting scarcer by the hour, his own unnamed doubts and fears, the coming terror which has to be faced alone— all mix together to make a cup of grief which Jesus is asked to drink willingly. Does Jesus have the stomach for it? After offering a cup of fellowship to his own disciples, can Jesus take the cup which his Father offers him?

Jesus has just implored his own disciples to pray, and now he implores his own Father for permission to bow out from a drama which is tilting so heavily in the direction of tragedy, and which awaits his acceptance if it is to continue. If Jesus can make his exit now, he can slip quietly into obscurity. Perhaps it might not be the will of God after all that he has to go through with the last act and leave the cause of the kingdom which now appears perilously shaky to a group of men who are so clearly unready for the task. Perhaps the last act could be rewritten. In this perhaps is the last temptation of Jesus.

Jesus' request, however, is conditional on the will of his Father. Jesus has a passion to do his Father's will. Luke states that an angel comes to strengthen Jesus, after which he prays more earnestly until his sweat becomes like drops of blood. A considerable number of manuscripts omit vv. 43-44, and the reason is not difficult to understand. As Solle writes: "According to Epiphanius, the bishop of Salamis (about 375), later manuscripts deleted the references to Jesus' weeping here and in his announcement that Jerusalem would be destroyed (Luke 22:43 ff., 19:41), 'out of fear that Jesus' dignity would be diminished.' From the modern perspective, however, Jesus' dignity lies precisely in his fear of death. A person without fear is deformed, despising himself too much to be able to have fear for himself."[8]

Jesus is going through a profoundly human agony, and he gives voice to it in his earnest prayer. Jesus sweats prayer. If the experience of suffering has isolated him from his disciples, Jesus does not want it to isolate him from God. So, he prays, and in that prayer comes to accept that it is the will of his Father for him to drink the cup. In drinking the cup, Jesus accepts what has been and what is to follow. And in his assent, his strength is renewed.

In the accounts of Matthew and Mark, the three trips to and from the disciples give an indication of the length of time of Jesus' lonely agony: Jesus makes repeated attempts to get his disciples to help him through the terrors of the night. In Luke's account, Jesus prays and waits alone. The experience of waiting, the mind's rehearsal of the tragedy, can be worse than the reality. But by the time Jesus has come to the end of his prayer there is a profound change: in staying on, Jesus signals his willingness to drink the cup. He rises from prayer. The man who rises from prayer is different from the man who knelt in prayer: between the kneeling and the rising, there is the resolution to accept the future as the will of God. He goes over to his disciples who have gone to sleep on his suffering. He asks them why, and Luke offers a kind reason that they are exhausted by grief; but whether sorrow induces sleep is a question which the disciples do not answer. Jesus tells them again to pray that they may not enter into temptation. He tells them that they should not be mute, but that they should give their fear and sorrow voice in prayer, just as he has done, rather than bury it in silence and in sleep. Jesus' own prayer has helped him face the reality which is to come. He is ready for the night and the morrow.

Luke 22: 47-62   *Arrest and Denial*

⁴⁷While he was still speaking, there came a crowd, and the man called Judas, one of the twelve, was leading them. He drew near to Jesus to kiss him; ⁴⁸but Jesus said to him,

"Judas, would you betray the Son of man with a kiss?" ⁴⁹And when those who were about him saw what would follow, they said, "Lord, shall we strike with the sword?" ⁵⁰And one of them struck the slave of the high priest and cut off his right ear. ⁵¹But Jesus said, "No more of this!" And he touched his ear and healed him. ⁵²Then Jesus said to the chief priests and officers of the temple and elders, who had come out against him, "Have you come out as against a robber, with swords and clubs? ⁵³When I was with you day after day in the temple, you did not lay hands on me. But this is your hour, and the power of darkness."

⁵⁴Then they seized him and led him away, bringing him into the high priest's house. Peter followed at a distance; ⁵⁵and when they had kindled a fire in the middle of the courtyard and sat down together, Peter sat among them. ⁵⁶Then a maid, seeing him as he sat in the light and gazing at him, said, "This man also was with him." ⁵⁷But he denied it, saying, "Woman, I do not know him." ⁵⁸And a little later some one else saw him and said, "You also are one of them." But Peter said, "Man, I am not." ⁵⁹And after an interval of about an hour still another insisted, saying, "Certainly this man also was with him; for he is a Galilean." ⁶⁰But Peter said, "Man, I do not know what you are saying." And immediately, while he was still speaking, the cock crowed. ⁶¹And the Lord turned and looked at Peter. And Peter remembered the word of the Lord, and how he had said to him, "Before the cock crows today, you will deny me three times." ⁶²And he went out and wept bitterly.

Jesus is still speaking to his disciples when he is interrupted by the arrival of the group intent on his arrest. The group is led by one of the twelve, Judas, who now approaches Jesus to kiss him. Luke does not actually state that Judas kissed Jesus, but focuses on Jesus' last words to Judas. Jesus asks Judas if he is really intending to go through with his plan of using a sign of friendship as a signal of betrayal. It appears that even at the eleventh hour, Jesus is still hoping that Judas will realize the enormity of his betrayal and repent; but events are now irreversibly under way.

Luke moves to the reaction of the disciples who now come to understand what is going on. They ask Jesus whether they should go the way of violence, and, without waiting for an answer, one of them, whom John identifies as Peter, cuts off the ear of the high priest's servant. Jesus commands a stop to the violence, and Luke shows him to go further by healing the afflicted servant who has come as his enemy. This is the only example in the Gospels where Jesus heals by replacing a severed part of the body: the act is an emphatic statement of Jesus' position on violence. Jesus meets violence not with counterviolence but with compassion and healing; he puts together what has been torn apart.

Jesus turns to address those who have come to arrest him. In Mark's account, the arresting party is composed of thugs employed by the authorities; Luke mentions the chief priests, the captains of the temple guard, and the lay members of the Sanhedrin—a heavy grouping which points to the importance of this arrest. Still on the matter of violence, Jesus reproaches them for coming to arrest him as if he were a robber. Did they anticipate armed resistance? Jesus reminds them that he taught openly in the temple: why, if they wanted to arrest him, did they not do so in the light of day? Why elect to arrest him under cover of darkness? They reveal their true intentions only in the dark, which time belongs to the power of darkness, Satan. The trial ahead, therefore, is not a local one between the authorities and Jesus; it is the eternal one between the power of darkness and the power of light.

Until this moment, Luke shows Jesus to be in command of the situation, and it is only after Jesus has finished his address that the arresting party move in and seize him. Jesus is now in the hands of his enemies who lead him to the house of the high priest where he spends a night of waiting. Luke does not have the interrogation of Jesus until the morning: Jesus stays in the background, while Luke brings the story of Peter's denial to the fore. Before Jesus' trial, Peter will be tried.

Peter follows the arresting party "at a distance"; the violent protest in the face of the enemy has given way to a cautious pace in their wake. When a fire is kindled in the centre of the courtyard, Peter joins the circle, but it proves a place of no comfort. In the light of the fire, a servant girl stares at Peter and gives voice to her thought: he was with Jesus. Peter denies knowing Jesus. Time passes, and a man recognizes Peter as one of Jesus' company, but Peter denies it. After another interval, another man insists that Peter was with Jesus, and presses his case by pointing to Peter's origin. After having denied knowing Jesus and being a member of his company, Peter now denies having any knowledge of Jesus: he claims not to know what his accuser is talking about. Unlike Mark, Luke does not present Peter as cursing to protest his innocence.

Earlier, while Jesus was speaking to his disciples he was interrupted by the arrival of the arresting party; now, while Peter is "still speaking", he is interrupted by the cock crow. But it is the look of the Lord which arrests Peter: Jesus turns and looks into the eyes of Peter, and in the exchange, there is the remembrance. Peter leaves the lit courtyard and goes out into the darkness where, with tears of regret, he repents of what he has done.

Luke 22: 63-71   Before the Guards and the Sanhedrin

⁶³Now the men who were holding Jesus mocked him and beat him; ⁶⁴they also blindfolded him and asked him, "Prophesy! Who is it that struck you?" ⁶⁵And they spoke many other words against him, reviling him.

⁶⁶When day came, the assembly of the elders of the people gathered together, both chief priests and scribes; and they led him away to their council, and they said, ⁶⁷"If you are the Christ, tell us." But he said to them, "If I tell you, you will not believe; ⁶⁸and if I ask you, you will not answer. ⁶⁹But from now on the Son of man shall be seated at the right hand of the power of God." ⁷⁰And they all said, "Are you the Son of God, then?" And he said to them, "You say that I am." ⁷¹And they said, "What further testimony do we need? We have heard it ourselves from his own lips."

Before the formal assembly of the Sanhedrin in the morning, Jesus is left in the charge of the temple guards who use him for their own entertainment. The guards mock and beat Jesus, and then blindfold him in a game of blind man's bluff. Jesus is the blindfolded, rejected prophet; the guards strike their prisoner and then challenge him to prove himself a prophet by identifying his assailant. Luke does not mention that they spat on Jesus or slapped him, but makes a general statement that they added insult to injury by speaking against him.

From the mockery, Luke's account moves into the morning trial before the Sanhedrin—although in the absence of witnesses and a verdict, the purpose of the gathering seems more as interrogation than trial. The difficulties of reconciling the conflicting Gospel accounts of the interrogations and trial of Jesus in an attempt to establish an historical sequence are well known, and attempts have been made to harmonize the accounts.[9] Both Matthew and Mark have a night sitting of the Sanhedrin, but this seems unlikely since the Sanhedrin by their own rules were not permitted to try a capital case at night. However, the historical accuracy of the claim that only the Romans had the right to execute a Jewish capital offence has been questioned.[10]

John has an informal inquiry by Annas during the night, and Luke's setting in the house of the high priest would seem to be in accord with this possibility. There is no record of the Sanhedrin meeting in the high priest's house: Luke mentions that they assembled in their own quarters, away from the high priest's house where Jesus was being held (v. 66). Why, then, did the arresting party take Jesus to the house of the high priest? While a night trial appears unlikely, a night interrogation following immediately on the arrest would have been an acceptable practice as a preliminary to the trial to gain information for the morning session. Particularly as the high priest was the chairman of the Sanhedrin.

The supreme court of the Jews assembled, the members dispense with charges and witnesses and move immediately to question Jesus on how he understands his own role.

They first ask Jesus if he is the Messiah, but Jesus' reply questions the court's ability and willingness to engage in a discussion which would enlighten them on Jesus' understanding of Messiahship. Jesus knows that he cannot give an unqualified yes to their question, and asking them about their own thinking is an escape route to nowhere. Jesus has already tried in vain to engage them on their understanding of the Messiah (20:41 ff.), and there is no reason to suppose that they will be forthcoming this time. Jesus moves on to speak of the Son of Man: Luke's phrase, from now on (*apo tou nun*), speaks of Jesus' hour which is beginning, the hour of his exaltation. In referring to the completion of the ministry in the image of the Son of Man sitting in power in the heavenly court, Jesus reverses the roles in the present scenario: the Son of Man is not to be finally judged by this court, but this court will be finally judged by the Son of Man.

Jesus' reflections arouse the Sanhedrin: Luke states that they "all" ask the next question. The atmosphere is heightened as they move in for the kill: is Jesus *the* Son of God? This is a different question to that of his claim to be the Messiah: claiming to be the Messiah does not bring with it the charge of blasphemy; claiming such a unique relationship with God does. Jesus does not deny the truth in the question, but simply focuses on their affirmation. In the absence of denial, the Sanhedrin find what they are looking for, and they construe his reply as consent and find that they have no need of further testimony.

Although Jesus responds to the questions of the Sanhedrin, he does not answer them: in effect, he is silent (Cf. Mark 14:60-61). Schillebeeckx argues that it is Jesus' silence in the face of the Jews' highest authority, *contemptus auctoritatis,* that gives the Sanhedrin grounds valid in Jewish law for condemning Jesus.[11] Jesus does not submit to the authority of the court by giving them an account of himself, but elects to speak of the heavenly court which will call everyone to account. The sufficiency of the "testimony" the Sanhedrin claim to have against Jesus is

not any claim Jesus has made before the assembly. In his
refusal to either affirm or deny the titles contained in their
questions, Jesus has refused to respond to the supreme
authority of Judaism. Even apart from blasphemy, that is
ground enough for condemnation.

Notes

[1] J. Jeremias, *The Eucharistic Words of Jesus,* (Oxford, 1955),
p. 56

[2] A. Jaubert, *La Date de la Cene,* (Paris, 1957) pp. 81-82 Cf. also
A. Jaubert, *"Jesus et le Caledrier de Qumran" New Testament Studies*
7, 1960, 1, pp. 1-30

[3] J. Jeremias, *The Eucharistic Words of Jesus,* op cit., p. 37

[4] E. Schillebeeckx, *Jesus: an Experiment in Christology,* (London:
Collins, 1979) p. 301

[5] Cf. H. Schurmann's discussion of the question in *Biblica* 32, 1951,
pp. 364-392, 522-541 and J. Jeremias, *The Eucharistic Words of Jesus,*
op cit., pp. 87-106

[6] J. Jeremias, ibid., pp. 145, 146

[7] G. McCauley, *Sacraments for Secular Man,* (New York, 1969)
p. 101

[8] D. Solle, *Suffering,* op cit., p. 80

[9] Cf. P. Benoit, "Le proces de Jesus" in *Exegese et Theologie*
(Paris: Cerf, 1961) 1, pp. 265-289

[10] Cf. E. Bammel (ed.), *The Trial of Jesus* (London, 1970)

[11] Cf. E. Schillebeeckx, *Jesus: an Experiment in Christology,* op
cit., pp. 312-318

Chapter Twenty Three

Luke 23: 1-12   The Trials before Pilate and Herod

23 Then the whole company of them arose, and brought him before Pilate. ²And they began to accuse him, saying, "We found this man perverting our nation, and forbidding us to give tribute to Caesar, and saying that he himself is Christ a king." ³And Pilate asked him, "Are you the King of the Jews?" And he answered him, "You have said so." ⁴And Pilate said to the chief priests and the multitudes, "I find no crime in this man." ⁵But they were urgent, saying, "He stirs up the people, teaching throughout all Judea, from Galilee even to this place."

⁶When Pilate heard this, he asked whether the man was a Galilean. ⁷And when he learned that he belonged to Herod's jurisdiction, he sent him over to Herod, who was himself in Jerusalem at that time. ⁸When Herod saw Jesus, he was very glad, for he had long desired to see him, because he had heard about him, and he was hoping to see some sign done by him. ⁹So he questioned him at some length; but he made no answer. ¹⁰The chief priests and the scribes stood by, vehemently accusing him. ¹¹And Herod with his soldiers treated him with contempt and mocked him; then, arraying him in gorgeous apparel, he sent him back to Pilate. ¹²And Herod and Pilate became friends with each other that very day, for before this they had been at enmity with each other.

THE WHOLE ASSEMBLY OF THE SANHEDRIN are united in their opposition to Jesus, and they now take him to Pilate, who, like Herod, is in Jerusalem for the Passover. The members of the Sanhedrin were fully aware that no charge of a theological nature would warrant the judgement of the Roman authority, so they translate their charge into political language in the hope that the governor will support their case for execution. They make three charges against Jesus: unspecified political agitation, subversion by inciting the people to withhold tribute to Caesar, and claiming royal status. To the three charges brought by the Jewish leaders, Pilate makes a triple declaration of Jesus' innocence (vv. 4, 14, 22), as well as expressing his desire to release Jesus (v. 20).

In Luke's account of the trial, Pilate asks Jesus only one question: "Are you the King of the Jews?", and receives Jesus' enigmatic reply which neither affirms nor denies the charge. Clearly, Pilate sees no revolutionary figure before him who constitutes a threat to the political stability of the land, so he makes a public statement declaring that there is no substance to the charges brought against the prisoner. Pilate's judgement should have been sufficient to end the affair, but, whereas the accusers persist in their charges, Pilate does not insist on his judgement. They give a summary of Jesus' ministry in terms of subversion, specifying Galilee as the beginning of Jesus' activities. Pilate seizes on the mention of Galilee, and when he discovers that Jesus is a Galilean, tells them that Jesus is in Herod's jurisdiction. Pilate is relieved to take what appears to be a promising escape route from his present difficulty: Jesus is Herod's responsibility. So, the legal runaround begins.

Jesus' trial before Herod, tetrarch of Galilee, is peculiar to Luke's Gospel and some scholars have questioned its historical authenticity. Tinsley writes: "Luke has certainly included the incident as part of his attempt to remove responsibility for the death of Jesus from the Roman authorities."[1] Luke's purpose, however, does not prove that his account is fabricated: Luke had his own sources in Herod's court (8:3) which would have given him access to information denied others.

Herod has wanted to see Jesus for some time (9:9) and he is delighted now that the prophet is brought before him. The tetrarch is not remotely interested in Jesus' teachings; he is attracted by Jesus' reputed power to perform the spectacular. He interrogates Jesus, but is confronted with a silent prisoner: Herod is the only person in Luke's Gospel to whom Jesus says nothing at all. The chief priests and the scribes ensure that the silence is interpreted by their own accusations. Herod, however, does not take the prisoner or his accusers seriously; and when Jesus does not perform on demand, Herod makes sure that he is not deprived of entertainment. So, he and his soldiers mock Jesus and dress him up in fancy apparel and then return him to sender. Jesus is sent back to Pilate, and, ironically, proves the means of a new friendship between the governor and the tetrach.

Luke 23: 13-25   *Jesus Is Sentenced by Pilate*

[13]Pilate then called together the chief priests and the rulers and the people, [14]and said to them, "You brought me this man as one who was perverting the people; and after examining him before you, behold, I did not find this man guilty of any of your charges against him; [15]neither did Herod, for he sent him back to us. Behold, nothing deserving death has been done by him; [16]I will therefore chastise him and release him."

[18]But they all cried out together, "Away with this man, and release to us Barabbas" — [19]a man who had been thrown into prison for an insurrection started in the city, and for murder. [20]Pilate addressed them once more, desiring to release Jesus; [21]but they shouted out, "Crucify, crucify him!" [22]A third time he said to them, "Why, what evil has he done? I have found in him no crime deserving death; I will therefore chastise him and release him." [23]But they were urgent, demanding with loud cries that he should be crucified. And their voices prevailed. [24]So Pilate gave sentence that their demand should be granted. [25]He released the man who had been thrown into prison for insurrection and murder, whom they asked for; but Jesus he delivered up to their will.

In the light of Herod's verdict, Pilate calls together "the chief priests and the rulers and the people" to make a public statement about the outcome of the recent trial. After repeating the charge against Jesus, Pilate recalls his own unambiguous finding which exonerated Jesus from all the charges brought by his accusers. Further, Herod, whom Pilate regards as qualified to make a judgement on these matters, confirms the judgement of Pilate in his release of Jesus. Thus, Luke makes it clear that the governor and the tetrarch are in considered agreement on the innocence of Jesus and the unfounded accusations made against him, while the chief priests and their supporters are primarily responsible for Jesus' approaching death.

Pilate proposes to release Jesus while at the same time appeasing the crowd by chastising him beforehand. The chastisement was a light beating which was intended in Roman judicial practice to serve as a lesson to the prisoner. Luke does not mention the scourging (Mark 15:15) which was a normal preliminary to crucifixion, and Sherwin-White argues that the disciplinary action proposed by Pilate was in fact an alternative to crucifixion.[2] The crowd express what they think of Pilate's scheme, and demand the release of Barabbas. In order to bridge the gap in the narrative between v. 16 and v. 18, some manuscripts include v. 17—which explains the Roman practice of releasing a prisoner at Passover time; but most scholars agree that this inclusion is a scribal clarification. There is a supreme irony in the crowd's plea to release Barabbas who has been found guilty of the charge Jesus stands acquitted of—sedition against Rome. The reversal is complete: the innocent is condemned while the guilty is set free.

Pilate does not respond to the crowd's demand, but again repeats his intention to release Jesus. At this, there is an uproar, and the crowd makes the first cry for Jesus' crucifixion. Pilate tries the art of the impossible by attempting to engage a mob in a debate as to why Jesus should be crucified if he has done no wrong; but the mob is in no mind for such judicial niceties. The governor seems to have run out of lines, and again protests Jesus' innocence and reverts to his idea of beating Jesus and releasing him; but the longer Pilate spends repeating what he is going to do, the less likely he seems capable of actually doing it. The crowd is becoming more impatient and threatening—

according to John's account (19:12), they come close to accusing Pilate of sedition by association. The climate is too uncomfortable for Pilate, and he finally gives in. His insistence on justice has not added up to justice, and he reverses his own finding by acceding to the demand of the crowd. Barabbas is released; Jesus is "delivered up to their will".

Throughout his account of the trials, Luke has emphasized the contrast between the authorities in Pilate and Herod who hold that Jesus is innocent, and the chief priests and their supporters who are clearly intent on Jesus' execution. Luke is clear about who was responsible for the death of Jesus: his account does not actually specify that the Romans carried out the execution, but simply "they led him away" (v. 26). In specifying the chief priests and their supporters as the organisers of Jesus' death, Luke is not promoting anti-Semitism. As Morris writes: "He (Luke) is dealing with a specific group of people and maintaining that they brought about Jesus' death. . . .But this means no more than that one group of men was guilty. Luke is not indicting a race and neither should his readers."[3]

Luke 23: 26-31   The Way of the Cross

[26]And as they led him away, they seized one Simon of Cyrene, who was coming in from the country, and laid on him the cross, to carry it behind Jesus. [27]And there followed him a great multitude of the people, and of women who bewailed and lamented him. [28]But Jesus turning to them said, "Daughters of Jerusalem, do not weep for me, but weep for yourselves and for your children. [29]For behold, the days are coming when they will say, 'Blessed are the barren, and the wombs that never bore, and the breasts that never gave suck!' [30]Then they will begin to say to the mountains, 'Fall on us'; and to the hills, 'Cover us.' [31]For if they do this when the wood is green, what will happen when it is dry?"

Luke's account moves straight from the sentence to the way of the cross without mention of a scourging or mockery by Pilate's soldiers. The procession which moves from the praetorium to the place of crucifixion outside the city is in sharp contrast to the triumphant process which approached the city: Jesus is still the focus of attention, but the climate is now one of doom and personal destruction. Jesus has been sentenced to a punishment of the utmost cruelty, crucifixion, which the Romans imposed on slaves and violent criminals. Cicero refers to crucifixion as *summum supplicium*,[4] the extreme penalty of the Roman legal tradition which was intended more as a public deterrent than a personal punishment.

The cross was in the form of a T and the prisoner was usually required to carry the crossbeam, *patibulum,* which was attached to his shoulders. Luke does not present Jesus as the superman who can carry the cross effortlessly: Jesus needs help, and the Romans press Simon into service to bear the weight of the cross. Simon was from Cyrene, on the coast of North Africa, where there was a large Jewish colony. He was probably either coming to Jerusalem for the Passover or else he was a repatriated exile. It appears that his sons, Alexander and Rufus, became Christians as they were known to Mark's readers (Mk 15:21). So, Simon is charged to carry the cross behind Jesus—an image which Jesus himself gave of the true disciple (9:23).

The legion of the curious follows the grim procession, as well as those who are sympathetic to Jesus, including some women. The crowd does not mock Jesus: clearly, not all the people are intent on his death. The daughters of Jerusalem anticipate Jesus' approaching death in their mournful cries and weeping; but Jesus in turn anticipates their fate in the coming destruction of Jerusalem. He tells them that if they realized the nature of the forthcoming events, they would weep for themselves rather than for him. And Jesus gives them permission to pity themselves. They are the daughters of a doomed city, and Jesus reaches out to them in compassion; but he is not so much interested in their sympathy for him as he is in their preparation for the horrors ahead. As throughout the passion story, Jesus, in the midst of his own time of trial, reaches out to others.

In his last beatitude, Jesus reverses an old understanding which saw pregnancy as a blessing and barrenness as an affliction. Because of the violence of the coming times, women will be glad that their wombs are untenanted, and their breasts are untended by babes; they will account it a blessing. The times will be so cruel that they will pray for the hills to cover them, which will be a kinder death than Jerusalem's fall. In the last proverbial saying, Jesus reflects that if he in his innocence has to suffer so harshly, what will be the fate of the guilty Jerusalem? So, the women of the fateful city have reason to weep for themselves.

Luke 23: 32-38   The Crucifixion

[32]Two others also, who were criminals, were led away to be put to death with him. [33]And when they came to the place which is callled The Skull, there they crucified him, and the criminals, one on the right and one on the left. [34]And Jesus said, "Father, forgive them; for they know not what they do." And they cast lots to divide his garments. [35]And the people stood by, watching; but the rulers scoffed at him, saying, "He saved others; let him save himself, if he is the Christ of God, his Chosen One!" [36]The soldiers also mocked him, coming up and offering him vinegar, [37]and saying, "If you are the King of the Jews, save yourself!" [38]There was also an inscription over him, "This is the King of the Jews."

None of the evangelists dwells on the cruelty and personal agony of Jesus' crucifixion; the saving event is recalled in accounts which are noted for their brevity and austerity. Luke recounts the reaction of the crowd, the rulers, the soldiers, the two criminals, and the centurion—all of whom make their own comment on what is happening before their eyes. In the midst of all this reaction, there is the solitary figure of Jesus who speaks words of forgiveness to his enemies, words of promise to the penitent thief, and words of acceptance to his Father. Luke presents the dying

Jesus as he presented Jesus in his public ministry: the one who reaches out to others, and who prayerfully accepts the mission given by his Father.

The unspeakable punishment which crucifixion inflicted on the individual can only be guessed at, but the social and religious effects are better known. As Hengel writes:

> By the public display of a naked victim at a prominent place—at a crossroads, in the theatre, on high ground, at the place of his crime—crucifixion also represented his uttermost humiliation, which had a numinous dimension to it. With Deuteronomy 21:23 in the background, the Jew in particular was very aware of this. This form of execution, more than any other, had associations with the idea of human sacrifice, which was never completely suppressed in antiquity. . . . In Roman times, crucifixion was practised above all on dangerous criminals and members of the lowest classes. . . . Because large strata of the population welcomed the security and the world-wide peace which the empire brought with it, the crucified victim was defamed both socially and ethically in popular awareness, and this impression was heightened still further by the religious elements involved.[5]

Paul in his preaching had to reckon with this scandal of the cross, "a stumbling block to Jews and folly to Gentiles" (1 Cor 1:23).

Jesus is not to be crucified alone: Luke introduces the two criminals who have to make their own way of the cross to the place appointed for the public execution. Luke does not use the Semitic name, Golgotha, but designates the place for crucifixion as "The Skull"—in Latin, *calvaria;* in English, Calvary. Jesus is crucified between the two criminals: thus he is "reckoned among transgressors" (22:37). Jesus spends his last hours in the company of the lost people he has spent so much time and energy seeking out, and whom he now ministers to in a supreme act of compassion.

In a prayer of forgiveness addressed to his Father, Jesus

asks that his executioners and all those involved in his death be forgiven because they fail to understand the enormity of what they are doing. Jesus prays that their ignorance will not be held against them—an ignorance which would have been seen in New Testament times as morally culpable. There is a dispute about the originality of v. 34a. An impressive number of early manuscripts do not include it, which leads some scholars to argue that it is a later interpolation. However, it can be argued that in the light of the events of 65-70 A.D. the verse was omitted because of a possible reading that Jesus' prayer was unanswered. Also, it is conceivable that some scribes would have regarded Jesus' prayer of forgiveness as unthinkable. Certainly, when Luke writes of Stephen's martyrdom in Acts 7:60, it appears that Stephen's forgiveness of his executioners is modelled on the example of Jesus.

Luke relates the reactions of those who are witnessing the crucifixion. The executioners busy themselves dividing Jesus' garments among themselves, a traditional custom which was regarded as one of the few perquisites of the job (Cf. Ps 22:18). The crowd is described in neutral terms as those who watch. The rulers engage in mockery and taunt Jesus with the challenge to save himself "*if* he is the Christ of God"—which seems an echo of an older voice in another wilderness (4:3, 9). The soldiers join in and offer Jesus cheap wine, which Luke interprets not as an act of compassion but as an act which mocks the man who understands himself as a king. Taking their cue from the inscription above Jesus' head, the soldiers challenge Jesus to save himself—*if* he really is the King of the Jews.

The irony of the whole scene is that the titles which are pronounced in mockery are true: the king does hang on his cross between two unlikely attendants. But the challenge which has led him to this place is not the challenge to save himself in an act of self-preservation; the challenge which has haunted and driven him throughout his life is the one which he now answers fully: if he is who he claims to be, can he save *others*?

Luke 23: 39-43   The Two Criminals

> ³⁹One of the criminals who were hanged railed at him,
> saying, "Are you not the Christ? Save yourself and us!"
> ⁴⁰But the other rebuked him, saying, "Do you not fear God,
> since you are under the same sentence of condemnation?
> ⁴¹And we indeed justly; for we are receiving the due reward
> of our deeds; but this man has done nothing wrong." ⁴²And
> he said, "Jesus, remember me when you come in your kingly
> power." ⁴³And he said to him, "Truly, I say to you, today
> you will be with me in Paradise."

One of the criminals adds his own voice to the chorus of
jeers and goes further by challenging Jesus to save himself
"and us". Rather than associate himself with Jesus who
stands under the same final condemnation, the criminal
joins the company of the mockers. A man from whom
Jesus might have expected a measure of sympathy in their
shared fate turns instead to ridicule: he wants to die believing that there is someone more ridiculous than himself.
Jesus does not answer the criminal, who is rebuked by his
companion for not fearing God—an attitude which seems
particularly foolish since he is soon to stand under God's
judgement.

The criminal admits that he and his companion have
come to this extremity guilty as charged, whereas Jesus is
innocent. If the first criminal joins the rulers and soldiers
in mocking Jesus, the second criminal joins Pilate and
Herod in acknowledging Jesus' innocence. He goes on to
address Jesus by name—the only man to do so in the
Gospels—and asks Jesus to remember him when he comes
into his kingdom, which in Lucan terms will be the time of
Jesus' exaltation.

Jesus replies to the second criminal, and his words are
the last he utters to any man during his life on earth: appropriately, they are addressed to an outcast; appropriately,
they offer salvation as a present reality. Jesus promises the
criminal a share in his own fellowship in Paradise. Today.
Paradise, an old Persian word for a garden or a park, was
used to describe the Garden of Eden, and later the future

home of those who died in faith. Jesus rewards the penitent criminal with the assurance that this day the Messiah
will open the gates of Paradise for those who find fellowship with him.

Luke 23: 44-49   *The Death of Jesus*

⁴⁴It was now about the sixth hour, and there was darkness
over the whole land until the ninth hour, ⁴⁵while the sun's
light failed; and the curtain of the temple was torn in two.
⁴⁶Then Jesus, crying with a loud voice, said, "Father, into
thy hands I commit my spirit!" And having said this he
breathed his last. ⁴⁷Now when the centurion saw what had
taken place, he praised God, and said, "Certainly this man
was innocent!" ⁴⁸And all the multitudes who assembled to
see the sight, when they saw what had taken place, returned
home beating their breasts. ⁴⁹And all his acquaintances and
the women who had followed him from Galilee stood at a
distance and saw these things.

According to Luke, the crucifixion took place about
midday and was accompanied by two portents. At the time
of his arrest, Jesus associated darkness with Satan's realm
and the hour of his enemies (22:53); now that darkness
makes its presence known by covering the land for three
hours. An eclipse of the sun at the Passover season which
was always held at the time of the full moon is an astronom-
ical impossibility; hence it is hardly likely that Luke had this
meaning in mind. Possibly Luke wanted to show that nature
itself was affected by the suffering and death of Jesus.
Along with the sun losing its light, the holiest place in
Judaism loses its special importance: the veil of the Temple
is torn in two. The veil marked the entrance to the Holy of
Holies, the shrine of God's presence, which was entered only by the high priest once a year when he would pray for the
atonement of the sins of the nation. Now the remoteness of
God has been pierced in the saving act of Jesus, and the
Temple, which will soon be destroyed, has been visited by
God's judgement.

Luke, however, seems more interested in recounting

changes of a more personal nature than the two portents. As Hans-Ruedi Weber writes: "For Luke. . .the signs which accompany Jesus' death are not primarily cosmic apocalyptic occurences, but changes that take place in the heart of men".[6] The penitent criminal has already made his peace with Jesus, and after Jesus dies, the Roman centurion and the crowd show a change of heart because of what they have witnessed in the death of Jesus.

Unlike Mark and Matthew, Luke does not include in his crucifixion account the darkest moment of Jesus' suffering in the experience of being forsaken by God. Jesus' awareness of the real absence of God is not mentioned. Rather than Psalm 22, Luke takes his final prayer from Psalm 31:6, which formed part of the night prayer of the pious Jew who entrusted himself to the care of God before his appointment with sleep. Jesus uses this prayer, addressing it to his Father: in a final act of conscious commitment Jesus entrusts his whole life to the care of the Father before his appointment with death. Thus, Jesus finishes his life dying to do the will of the Father, and only when he has prayerfully put himself in the presence of his Father does he breathe his last.

Luke goes on to tell how Jesus' death affected those who witnessed the event. The centurion has the last word at Jesus' crucifixion: he joins the unusual company of Pilate, Herod, and the penitent thief in proclaiming Jesus' innocence. Luke goes further to say that the centurion praises God. The recognition of Jesus' death as the martyrdom of the righteous man is a prayer of praise to God. The crowd, many of whom came for their afternoon's entertainment of violence, now leave the scene saddened by the experience. The beating of breasts is often associated with repentance, but it would seem to be reading too much into Luke's rendering to interpret it so; it seems more likely that the action signifies the people's grief at what has happened. This experience might be the preparation of heart for the later preaching which converted so many (Acts 2:41).

Luke makes no mention of Jesus' relatives, but brings his account of Jesus' crucifixion to a close by calling attention to the associates of Jesus who are there—among whom are the faithful women who followed Jesus from Galilee (8:1). They stand at a distance—whether they do this because they are not permitted to come closer or because they are afraid, Luke does not say. The important thing for Luke is that they have seen for themselves all that has happened and so are witnesses to the event of the death of Jesus (Cf. 1:2).

Luke 23: 50-56   *The Burial of Jesus*

> [50]Now there was a man named Joseph from the Jewish town of Arimathea. He was a member of the council, a good and righteous man, [51]who had not consented to their purpose and deed, and he was looking for the kingdom of God. [52]This man went to Pilate and asked for the body of Jesus. [53]Then he took it down and wrapped it in a linen shroud, and laid him in a rock-hewn tomb, where no one had ever yet been laid. [54]It was the day of Preparation, and the sabbath was beginning. [55]The women who had come with him from Galilee followed, and saw the tomb, and how his body was laid; [56]then they returned, and prepared spices and ointments. On the sabbath they rested according to the commandment.

The Romans often inflicted a last indignity on the bodies of crucified slaves and criminals by leaving their bodies unburied to serve as food for wild beasts and birds of prey. The Mosaic Law, however, regulated against this practice and required that the bodies of criminals be buried before nightfall (Deut 22:23). Joseph of Arimathea now makes his appearance on the scene to fulfill the requirements of the law in performing a work of mercy which clearly dissociates him from the other Jewish leaders. Joseph is a member of the Sanhedrin, and Luke in upholding him as a man of integrity states that he did not consent to the decision to execute Jesus. Since the verdict of the Sanhedrin was unanimous (22:70), it can only be that Joseph was absent from that session. Luke describes him as one of the faithful company, like Simeon and Anna, who await the kingdom (2:25, 38).

Joseph has already secured the permission of Pilate to bury the body of Jesus; he takes the body down from the cross, wraps it in a linen shroud, and then lays it in a tomb. In his account, Matthew tells us that Joseph was a rich man (27:57) who had prepared the rock-hewn tomb for himself (27:60). The borrowed tomb, like the borrowed colt on which Jesus approached Jerusalem, is unused (19:30). So, the body of Jesus rests in a new tomb, courtesy of an old kindness.

It is the day of Preparation, Friday, and the sabbath is dawning. At sundown, when darkness comes, there is the breaking of the holy day. Again, the women from Galilee receive special mention: they come and see the tomb where the body of Jesus is laid—thus Luke avoids the possibility that when they return they will mistake the tomb. The law permitted the anointing of a body on the sabbath, but Luke states that the women returned to the city to prepare perfumes and ointments to wrap with the body of Jesus, work which they would do unhurriedly after the sabbath. Luke shows them fulfilling the commandments by resting on the sabbath. The fidelity of the women from Galilee will be rewarded in the most extraordinary way: as they faithfully witnessed the death and burial of Jesus, they will be the first witnesses of the empty tomb, and the first proclaimers of the good news of the resurrection.

Notes

[1] E. J. Tinsley, *The Gospel according to Luke,* (Cambridge University Press, 1965) p. 198

[2] Cf. A. N. Sherwin-White, *Roman Society and Roman Law in the New Testament* (Oxford, 1963) pp. 27 ff.

[3] L. Morris, *The Gospel according to St. Luke* (Inter-Varsity Press, 1977) p. 324

[4] Cicero, *In Verrem,* 2, 5, 168
[5] M. Hengel, *Crucifixion,* (London, SCM Press Ltd., 1977) pp. 87-88

[6] H. R. Weber, *The Cross: Tradition and Interpretation* (London, SPCK, 1979) p. 124.

Chapter Twenty Four

Luke 24: 1-12   *The Empty Tomb*

24 But on the first day of the week, at early dawn, they went to the tomb, taking the spices which they had prepared. ²And they found the stone rolled away from the tomb, ³but when they went in they did not find the body. ⁴While they were perplexed about this, behold, two men stood by them in dazzling apparel; ⁵and as they were frightened and bowed their faces to the ground, the men said to them, "Why do you seek the living among the dead? Remember how he told you, while he was still in Galilee, ⁷that the Son of man must be delivered into the hands of sinful men, and be crucified, and on the third day rise." ⁸And they remembered his words, ⁹and returning from the tomb they told all this to the eleven and to all the rest. ¹⁰Now it was Mary Magdalene and Joanna and Mary the mother of James and the other women with them who told this to the apostles; ¹¹but these words seemed to them an idle tale, and they did not believe them. ¹²But Peter rose and ran to the tomb; stooping and looking in, he saw the linen cloths by themselves; and he went home wondering at what had happened.

NOT ONE OF THE GOSPEL NARRATIVES recounts the actual raising of Jesus from the dead: no one was there, and the witness to Jesus' radical transformation can be registered only in the human terms which attempt to tell of the event, "He is not here. He is risen." The Gospels testify to the witness of the empty tomb ("he is not here") and the appearance of the risen Lord ("he is risen"). The empty tomb itself does not argue to a resurrection: an empty tomb, like an uninhabited room, simply argues to the absence of occupancy. But the empty tomb is fundamental to the Easter proclamation: it testifies against the gnostic spiritualizing of the resurrection (Cf. 2 Tim 2:18). Jesus does not live because he is proclaimed in the Easter event, but he is proclaimed precisely because he lives.

Luke's account of the resurrection begins with the journey of the women to the empty tomb and moves to Jesus' appearances to the two disciples on the road to Emmaus and to the eleven in Jerusalem. Early on Sunday morning when the sun is up, the women go to the tomb bringing with them the spices they had prepared. Firstly, they discover that the stone has been rolled away and then that there is no body to anoint. The enclosure of death is open, and the dead body of Jesus is no longer present. It is only after the discovery of the empty tomb that Luke mentions the presence of the two men in dazzling apparel, who parallel the two heavenly witnesses at the transfiguration who discussed Jesus' departure which was to take place in Jerusalem (9:29), and the two witnesses in white garments who attend Jesus' final departure in the ascension (Acts 1:10).

The perplexity of the women at the sight of the empty tomb grows to fear at the sight of the two angels. The two messengers bring a question and make an announcement: they ask the women why they seek the living in the place reserved for the dead, and proclaim that Jesus is not in this place because he has risen. The tomb, the house of the dead, becomes the place of God's revelation. The tomb is open now, and the darkness has been dispelled by the morning sun and the dazzling garments of God's messengers. Now, the tomb is the place of light and the place of good news. While the women have focused on the empty tomb, the messengers focus on the prophetic word of Jesus. Rather than Mark's version in which the angel announces that Jesus "is going before you to Galilee", Luke's account emphasizes what Jesus has already said in Galilee, and thus keeps his account of the resurrection within the vicinity of Jerusalem. The women remember the words of Jesus (9:22), and in that remembrance they leave the empty tomb to tell the others what has taken place.

The women are the first proclaimers of the message of

the resurrection of the Lord, and Luke names them as the faithful women from Galilee (Cf. 8:2, 3). The apostles do not find their testimony worthwhile and go further to dismiss the witness to the empty tomb, the presence of the divine messengers, the remembrance of Jesus' own prophetic words as an idle tale. Luke uses the medical term, *leros*, which speaks of the demented ramblings of a sick person. Peter, however, who has recently denied Jesus and has more reason than anyone to attend to the prophetic word of Jesus, is more circumspect than his fellow apostles. He decides to go to the tomb himself and check out the story of the women. Verse 12 is missing from a few important manuscripts, but it is attested by the majority, and v. 24 would seem to refer to Peter's visit. Peter runs to the tomb and sees for himself that it is empty. The empty tomb does not lead him to believe that the Lord has risen, but it does lead him to wonder—a preface to belief. Peter is impressed, and it will not be long before he believes the message of the messengers.

Luke 24: 13-35   *The Journey to Emmaus*

¹³That very day two of them were going to a village named Emmaus, about seven miles from Jerusalem, ¹⁴and talking with each other about all these things that had happened. ¹⁵While they were talking and discussing together, Jesus himself drew near and went with him. ¹⁶But their eyes were kept from recognizing him. ¹⁷And he said to them, "What is this conversation which you are holding with each other as you walk?" And they stood still, looking sad. ¹⁸Then one of them, named Cleopas, answered him, "Are you the only visitor to Jerusalem who does not know the things that have happened there in these days?" ¹⁹And he said to them, "What things?" And they said to him, "Concerning Jesus of Nazareth, who was a prophet mighty in deed and word before God and all the people, ²⁰and how our chief priests and rulers delivered him up to be condemned to death, and crucified him. ²¹But we had hoped that he was the one to redeem Israel. Yes, and besides all this, it is now the third day since this happened. ²²Moreover, some women of our com-

pany amazed us. They were at the tomb early in the morning
²³and did not find his body; and they came back saying that
they had even seen a vision of angels, who said that he was
alive. ²⁴"Some of those who were with us went to the tomb,
and found it just as the women had said; but him they did not
see." ²⁵And he said to them, "O foolish men, and slow of
heart to believe all that the prophets have spoken! ²⁶Was it
not necessary that the Christ should suffer these things and
enter into his glory?" ²⁷And beginning with Moses and all
the prophets, he interpreted to them in all the scriptures the
things concerning himself.

²⁸So they drew near to the village to which they were going.
He appeared to be going further, ²⁹but they constrained him,
saying, "Stay with us, for it is toward evening and the day is
now far spent." So he went in to stay with them. ³⁰When he
was at table with them, he took the bread and blessed, and
broke it, and gave it to them. ³¹And their eyes were opened
and they recognized him; and he vanished out of their sight.
³²They said to each other, "Did not our hearts burn within us
while he talked to us on the road, while he opened to us the
scriptures? ³³And they rose that same hour and returned to
Jerusalem; and they found the eleven gathered together and
those who were with them, ³⁴who said, "The Lord has risen
indeed, and has appeared to Simon!" ³⁵Then they told what
had happened on the road, and how he was known to them in
the breaking of the bread.

In one of the most beautiful stories in the pages of world
literature, Luke recounts how Jesus the stranger and
wayfarer disclosed himself to two of his disciples in the unfolding of Scripture and in the breaking of the bread. Luke
uses two of his favourite themes—the journey and the
meal—to share with his readers the central story of his
resurrection account, how two disciples came to recognize
the risen Lord. The recognition scene has been long remembered, while the village has been long forgotten.

The central theme of Luke's Gospel is Jesus' journey to
Jerusalem, the place of his death and triumph. Now, two
disciples are leaving Jerusalem, and putting distance between themselves and the city which they see as the sad
place where the mission of Jesus and their own hopes came
to an unfortunate end. The journey takes place on the day

of the resurrection. They discuss all the things that have happened—all except the event which makes sense of all that has happened. While they are walking along, a traveller joins them on the road. Luke suggests that there is a supernatual restraint which prevents the disciples from recognizing the true identity of their fellow traveller. It is not enough that Jesus is present, he is not yet present to them as Lord, which will come only after a meeting in Scripture and a meeting around the table.

Jesus asks them what they are discussing as they walk along, a question which moves the two disciples to stillness and sadness: it is as the weight of their conversation has burdened them to a halt. Luke identifies one of the disciples as Cleophas: if this is the Clopas mentioned in John 19:25, then probably the other disciple is his wife, Mary, who John says stood at the foot of the cross. Cleophas answers Jesus with a question asking him if he is the only one who has not heard what has been happening in Jerusalem. Ironically, Cleophas asks the man at the centre of the Jerusalem event whether he has not heard of it. In his turn, Jesus replies with another question: before he tells his story, Jesus wants to hear the version which makes the two disciples so forlorn.

The two disciples tell their version of the story of Jesus of Nazareth, speaking of Jesus as a mighty prophet whom the Jewish authorities handed over to be crucified. They speak of Jesus and of their own hopes in the past tense: the one who they had hoped would restore the independence of Israel is now a has-been. They go on to tell Jesus of the testimony of the women and the message of the angels, and how some of their own company verified the empty tomb, "but him they did not see". Nor do the tellers of the tale see him now, for they are so obsessed with what has been that they cannot see what faces them. The disciples' story is told in the language of failure, disappointment and hurt bewilderment. They tell the story from the point of view of its failure, and if people are affected by the significant stories they tell, then the disciples see themselves in terms of their story: they are ex-followers of a prophet, with left-over lives, and nowhere to go but away.

It is not until the two disciples finish their story that Jesus begins his own. He rebukes them for their folly and slowness of heart to believe what is already contained in the words of the prophets. It was long foretold that what happened was not a matter of human absurdity but of divine necessity, so that Christ could "enter his glory". In Jesus' story, a completely different picture emerges from that painted by the disciples: they ended their story with failure, Jesus ends his story with glory. Jesus takes the disciples on a teaching journey back to Moses and goes through the three sections of the Jewish Bible—the law, the prophets, and the writings—to show them the divine purpose in his own story. Jesus points out to them that it is all there in the scriptures, if they had only the eyes to see it. But, it is precisely their eyes which are failing at this moment.

By now, the three travellers are approaching the village and it is time for the parting of ways. Jesus appears to be going on: clearly, he has no intention of imposing himself on the two disciples, but gives them the opportunity of inviting him to stay with them. The disciples have been touched by the story of the stranger and they are unwilling to let him go. The stranger has shared his story with them; they want to share their hospitality with him. So, they press him to stay with them, pointing out that evening is drawing near and the day is almost over. Again, Luke uses the imagery of light and darkness: if Jesus continues on his way alone, the two disciples will indeed dwell in darkness. But the stranger accepts their invitation and goes with them to what probably is their home. The stranger goes to their home, and Jesus comes home to them.

Jesus comes as the guest of the two disciples and becomes their host. After sharing their stories, they gather around the table to share bread: the fellow travellers now share table fellowship. Jesus does not tell the disciples who he is; instead, he reveals himself to them in silence. He takes the bread, says the blessing, breaks the bread and gives it to them. Jesus gives himself away in the breaking of the bread, and the disciples recognize him. And Jesus is a stranger no more.

Scholars disagree about the interpretation of the expression, "breaking of the bread". Some argue that it clearly refers to a eucharist at Emmaus, others hold that the phrase simply refers to the first part of any meal held by Jews in Palestine. Certainly, Jewish meals began with the host giving thanks to God, breaking the bread and sharing it, but, as Dupont points out: "the account which we are reading is not an account written by a Palestinian Jew for other Palestinian Jews. The question to be asked is not what the expression could have meant on the lips of Cleophas, if he used it when telling the story to the apostles; we should ask what Luke, who wrote the story, means by this expression and what he wants us to understand when he uses it."[1]

The expression, "breaking of bread", was never used to describe the Jewish meal *as a whole,* whereas Luke does use it as a shorthand expression to describe the eucharist *as a whole.* Thus when Luke describes the conversion of three thousand people after Pentecost, he writes: "And they devoted themselves to the apostles' teaching and fellowship, to the breaking of bread and the prayers" (Acts 2:42). In a list of religious acts, Luke is clearly referring to the eucharist (Cf. Acts 2:7, 11, 46; 27:35). Luke repeats the expression in the last phrase of the Emmaus account, emphasizing that the recognition took place in "the breaking of the bread."

Although the two disciples were not present at the Last Supper when Jesus clearly identified himself with the bread and the wine, they see that identification now. Jesus gives himself away by giving himself away to them. The disciples now see Jesus as the one who gives himself totally. That was precisely what Jesus had been trying to tell them through the unfolding of the scriptures, but it "came" to them in the act of the breaking of the bread. They recognize the one who made that familiar act of fellowship into a sacred act forever identified with himself. So, Jesus can disappear from their sight for he has left them himself.

The two disciples reflect on their shared experience because they can now explain why they felt the way they did when they listened to the words of Jesus as he opened the scriptures to them. Jesus made sense of the scriptures, and in so doing he gave the disciples a new story to tell. In seeing Jesus, the disciples see themselves differently: where before they were ex-followers of a dead prophet, now they are followers of the risen Lord. Jesus has shown the disciples who they are by showing himself to them, for they can only see themselves as disciples in seeing Christ. Now that they have a new story to tell, they forget their own caution about the dark of night and this time they make their journey *towards* Jerusalem.

They find the eleven and others who are with them. Before the two disciples can catch their breath to tell their story, the others proclaim the good news of the resurrection: "The Lord has risen indeed". They tell the two new arrivals that Jesus has already appeared to Simon. Unfortunately, none of the New Testament writers records the details of the appearance to Peter, but the affirmation serves to focus on his special apostolic position. After this proclamation, the two disciples tell their story, "how he was known to them in the breaking of the bread".

The story of Emmaus gives the Christian community a perfect reminder of coming to know Jesus as Lord in the eucharist:

> the coming together
> the hearing of the story
> the gathering around the table
> the breaking of the bread
> the recognition of Jesus as Lord
> the renewal of personal discipleship
> the departure to share the good news

It is in that fellowship that strangers come to be known,

that the Lord comes to be recognized, and that his message continues to be proclaimed.

Luke 24: 36-53   *The Final Departure*

[36]As they were saying this, Jesus himself stood among them, and said to them, "Peace to you." [37]But they were startled and frightened, and supposed that they saw a spirit. [38]And he said to them, "Why are you troubled, and why do questionings rise in your hearts? [39]See my hands and my feet, that is is I myself; handle me, and see; for a spirit has not flesh and bones as you see that I have." [40]And when he had said this he showed them his hands and his feet. [41]And while they still disbelieved for joy, and wondered, he said to them, "Have you anything here to eat?" [42]They gave him a piece of broiled fish, [43]and he took it and ate before them.

[44]Then he said to them, "These are my words which I spoke to you, while I was still with you, that everything written about me in the law of Moses and the prophets and the psalms must be fulfilled." [45]Then he opened their minds to understand the scriptures, [46]and said to them, "Thus it is written, that the Christ should suffer and on the third day rise from the dead, [47]and that repentance and forgiveness of sins should be preached in his name to all nations, beginning from Jerusalem. [48]You are witnesses of these things. [49]And behold, I send the promise of my Father upon you; but stay in the city, until you are clothed with power from on high."

[50]Then he led them out as far as Bethany, and lifting up his hands he blessed them. [51]While he blessed them, he parted from them and was carried up into heaven. [52]And they worshiped him, and returned to Jerusalem with great joy, [53]and were continually in the temple blessing God.

While the two disciples are giving an account of their experience of the risen Lord, Jesus appears in the midst of the gathering to confirm to all of them the truth of his resurrection. His opening address is the conventional eastern greeting, but now it has a new significance: the first words of the risen Lord to the assembled disciples—who had not exactly distinguished themselves during his time of trial—speak the comforting message of peace. Jesus' presence and assurance, however, have anything but a peaceful effect on the assembly: the disciples react with fear for they imagine that they are being visited by a ghost. They have just been discussing the resurrection of Jesus, but now that Jesus is actually present to them their reaction is one of undisguised panic.

Jesus attends to their fears and doubts and tells the disciples to give voice to them, but Luke does not record any verbal response by the disciples: it is as if they are stunned into silence. Jesus invites them to look at his hands and feet—probably referring to the nail marks which would help them identify him. He goes further and invites them to touch him in the hope that they will calm their fears and answer their doubts—for a spirit does not have flesh and blood. He shows them his hands and his feet, but it does not move the disciples to believe. They remain unconvinced by the marks which distinguish Jesus. Luke states that they disbelieve because they think it too good to be true. They want to believe but cannot bring themselves to do so. Jesus asks for some food; he takes a piece of broiled fish and eats it—a further proof of the physical reality of his presence.

As he did with the two disciples on the road to Emmaus, Jesus now reminds the gathering of the words which he spoke to them during his earthly ministry, and underlines the prophetic significance of those passages in the three sections of the Jewish Bible which referred to him and which are fulfilled in his death and resurrection. Jesus teaches them in such a way that their minds are opened to the truth of what he is saying. He repeats the divine purpose of his suffering and resurrection, and makes the new point that the future mission of the church—preaching repentance and forgiveness of sins—is contained in the scriptures. This preaching will be carried out in the name of the risen Lord, and it will begin in Jerusalem, the place of Jesus' exaltation.

Jesus appoints the disciples as witnesses to the central

event of his death and resurrection: they can now personally testify to its reality and significance. And with the appointment comes the promise; he will send the Holy Spirit, "the promise of my Father", to empower them to make that witness effective. In his last instruction to his disciples, Jesus enjoins them to stay in the city of Jerusalem until they receive the Holy Spirit. It will only be in the power of the Spirit that they will be able to take the Gospel to all nations.

After Jesus commissions the disciples to begin their missionary work in his name and in the power of the Spirit, he leads them as far as Bethany, on the eastern slope of the mount of Olives. His final departure takes place in silence. He gives them a priestly benediction and makes his withdrawal from them to heaven. Luke is the only New Testament writer to present the ascension as a distinct event— although he does refer to it in Acts 2:32 as one with the resurrection. However, in his Gospel account, the resurrection and the ascension are treated separately. The distinction, as Schillebeeckx argues, "is an important one principally because Luke connects the sending of the Spirit not with the risen Jesus but quite expressly with his exaltation alone. . . . Thus according to Luke it is only with the exaltation of Jesus that the Church's proclamation of repentance and salvation can begin (Acts 5:31b); for what is presupposed is the gift of the Spirit, which only the exalted One is able to impart".[2]

Luke's account of the ascension is very brief, but he is probably giving a summary of the story which he later embellishes in Acts 1:1-11, where he says that forty days elapsed between the resurrection and the ascension. The ascension is the climax of Luke's Gospel: Jesus' mission is completed, and he can now take his throne in a unique position of power at the right hand of his Father. The disciples respond to Jesus' departure by worshipping him—the first time they have done this, for it appears that this is the first time that they have recognized the divinity of Jesus. They are not downcast at the departure of Jesus, but they make their return to Jerusalem with great joy, and spend their time in the temple praising God. Thus, Luke brings his Gospel to a close in the same spirit in which he opened it—with the praise of God in the temple.

Notes

[1] J. Dupont, "The Meal at Emmaus" in J. Delorme and others, *The Eucharist in the New Testament* (London, 1965) p. 117

[2] E. Schillebeeckx, *Jesus: an Experiment in Christology,* op cit., p. 534